D0083582

## DATE DUE

| | | |
|---|---|---|
| JAN 3 0 2007 | | |
| | OCT 2 3 2007 | |
| 9/6/09 | | |
| | | |
| | SEP 2 0 2011 | |
| | | |
| | | |
| | | |
| | | |
| | | |
| | | |

GAYLORD     #3523PI     Printed in USA

*of related interest*

**Music Therapy, Sensory Integration and the Autistic Child**
*Dorita S. Berger*
*Foreword by Donna Williams*
ISBN 1 84310 700 7

**Clinical Applications of Music Therapy in Developmental Disability, Paediatrics and Neurology**
*Edited by Tony Wigram and Jos De Backer*
*Foreword by Colwyn Trevarthen*
ISBN 1 85302 734 0

**Clinical Applications of Music Therapy in Psychiatry**
*Edited by Tony Wigram and Jos De Backer*
*Foreword by Jan Peuskens*
ISBN 1 85302 733 2

**Music Therapy and Neurological Rehabilitation**
**Performing Health**
*Edited by David Aldridge*
ISBN 1 84310 302 8

**Roots of Musicality**
**Music Therapy and Personal Development**
*Daniel Perret*
*Foreword by Colwyn Trevarthen*
ISBN 1 84310 336 2

**A Comprehensive Guide to Music Therapy**
**Theory, Clinical Practice, Research and Training**
*Tony Wigram, Inge Nygaard Pedersen and Lars Ole Bonde*
ISBN 1 84310 083 5

**Music Therapy in Context**
**Music, Meaning and Relationship**
*Mercédès Pavlicevic*
*Preface by Colwyn Trevarthen*
ISBN 1 85302 434 1

**Groups in Music**
**Strategies from Music Therapy**
*Mercédès Pavlicevic*
ISBN 1 84310 081 9

DREXEL UNIVERSITY
HEALTH SCIENCES LIBRARIES
HAHNEMANN LIBRARY

# The Music Effect
## Music Physiology and Clinical Applications

*Daniel J. Schneck and Dorita S. Berger*

*Illustrations by Geoffrey Rowland*
*Foreword by George D. Patrick*

Jessica Kingsley Publishers
London and Philadelphia

First published in 2006
by Jessica Kingsley Publishers
116 Pentonville Road
London N1 9JB, UK
and
400 Market Street, Suite 400
Philadelphia, PA 19106, USA

*www.jkp.com*

**WB**
**550**
**S358m**
**2006**

Copyright © Daniel J. Schneck and Dorita S. Berger 2006
Illustrations copyright © Geoffrey Rowland 2006
Foreword copyright © George D. Patrick 2006

The right of Daniel J. Schneck and Dorita S. Berger to be identified as authors of this work has
been asserted by them in accordance with the Copyright, Designs and Patents Act 1988.

All rights reserved. No part of this publication may be reproduced in any material form (including
photocopying or storing it in any medium by electronic means and whether or not transiently or
incidentally to some other use of this publication) without the written permission of the copyright
owner except in accordance with the provisions of the Copyright, Designs and Patents Act 1988 or
under the terms of a licence issued by the Copyright Licensing Agency Ltd, 90 Tottenham Court
Road, London, England W1T 4LP. Applications for the copyright owner's written permission to
reproduce any part of this publication should be addressed to the publisher.

Warning: The doing of an unauthorised act in relation to a copyright work may result in both a
civil claim for damages and criminal prosecution.

**Library of Congress Cataloging in Publication Data**

Schneck, Daniel J.
  The music effect : music physiology and clinical applications / Daniel J. Schneck and Dorita S. Berger ;
illustrated by Geoffrey Rowland ; foreword by George D. Patrick.-- First American paperback ed.
     p. cm.
  Includes bibliographical references and index.
  ISBN-13: 978-1-84310-771-2 (pbk. : alk. paper)
  ISBN-10: 1-84310-771-6 (pbk. : alk. paper) 1. Music therapy. 2. Music--Physiological aspects. I.
Berger, Dorita S. II. Rowland, Geoffrey ill. III. Title.
  ML3920.S358 2006
  615.8'5154--dc22

                                          2005024506


**British Library Cataloguing in Publication Data**
A CIP catalogue record for this book is available from the British Library

ISBN-13: 978 1 84310 771 2
ISBN-10: 1 84310 771 6


Printed and bound in Great Britain by
Athenaeum Press, Gateshead, Tyne and Wear

*We dedicate this book to our families, and to friends, educators, musicians, clinicians, clients, students, and all who seek to understand and appreciate that human behavior and well-being are driven first and foremost by intuition, instinct, and emotions.*

# Contents

# Foreword

This is a book about the use of music as therapy, written for clinicians, scientific investigators, music therapists, and those of us who aspire to be life-long students with a sincere interest in understanding the role of music in human response and expression. The authors have extensive experience in physiology, and the study of music in both human adaptation and clinical application. They have gone a quantum leap beyond the wisdom of leaders in the field of music as an applied science with a wide range of theoretical explanations; however, this book is intended as a first book, a ground-breaking primer for those who would take a studious view of human physiology related to the experience of music. You are forewarned: this book is not an unchallenging read. You may want to read through certain sections carefully and even then to re-read sections.

I suppose that many who will read this book have fully and repeatedly experienced the mood-altering power of music. Mood is not an esoteric, stand-alone phenomenon; it is embedded in physiology. Similarly, many physiological phenomena are linked to music, and the authors present an original thesis on this link. This is a novel idea. Some of you will be made uncomfortable if you try to assimilate this material with your current set of theoretical understandings. This new paradigm requires accommodation, the rearranging of your mental furniture.

The authors will challenge you with the question "What is a music experience?" If you are a bit like me, you will be more than somewhat confused about your own answer. The existing music literature offers a bewildering array of unconnected ideas, thoughts, and theories. This book will directly connect physiology to the music experience by giving examples in the precise use of music in a clinical setting, not so that you must be convinced, but so that you may feel free to test out this hypothesis in a systematic manner. This book is rich in ideas and is complex, offering great rewards for the reader who engages with it head on.

*George D. Patrick*
*Mark O. Hatfield Clinical Research Center, Bethesda, MD*

# Prelude

Whether it is inside the human body or outside, *nature* – as expressed through the laws of physics – works the same way. This book is about one such expression of nature, the music effect, as influenced by *nurture*. *The Music Effect* addresses the role of music in human adaptation, and consequently its effectiveness in clinical applications. This is not a physics book, nor a physiology book, nor a music book, nor a study of music therapy; it is, in fact, all of these! That is to say, the material covered herein addresses a new blending of information, from a variety of disciplines, that collectively explores the symbiotic relationship between music and the human body. The book explores *why* and *how* one (music) affects the other (the human body), and vice versa – why and how the body affects music – all couched within basic principles of physics and physiological function.

The interfacing of basic elements of physiological function with the elements of music, as presented here, conjoins two distinct areas of knowledge: (1) *scientific reality*, as expressed through the laws of physics, basic principles of human physiological function, and (2) sensory information-processing that yields resulting behavior; and the *music aesthetic*, embedded and constrained within the science of the physics of sound and motion, the individual elements of music, and the effect of music on physiological adaptation. The blending of these two areas culminates in a new understanding of the music effect: *music physiology*. Moreover, it provides an understanding that can be exploited quite effectively in *clinical applications* of music in areas such as medicine, psychology, education, and allied therapies, as well as in the home environment.

The use of music as a therapy treatment (clinical intervention for diagnosed populations) is a relative newcomer to the health-care professions. Introduced in the United States just after World War II, primarily as an intervention to help trauma victims of combat, music therapy has grown to be recognized internationally as a medical treatment. Music therapy has the

13

ability to reach beyond many conventional approaches to health and rehabil-itation. As a result, not only has the profession increased in numbers of trained clinicians, but – with ever-expanding applications – the therapy has widened the scope of knowledge required of current practitioners in order to develop targeted, well-focused protocols to address discrete human condi-tions.

The professional collaboration between the two authors of this book evolved gradually over a period of years. Dr. Daniel Schneck is a biomedical engineer with extensive training in physics, physiology, and medicine, and happens also to be a professional violinist. Ms. Dorita Berger is a concert pianist and educator, and is a Board Certified Music Therapist with an extensive clinical practice. The collaboration between us evolved as a result of both Dr. Schneck's extensive research background, experience, and expertise in the study of physiological function, and Ms. Berger's search for the wider scope of knowledge and information required to diagnose and treat her clients properly, and to help her address specific issues related to the clinical practice of music therapy.

Many consultations ensued between us. Each discussed music and human behavior, both from the individual perspective of our professional fields, and from our collective music experiences. From these discussions, there began to be formulated new theories and insights into the subject of music as it relates to fundamental aspects of human behavior. There developed a clearer understanding of why (or why not) specific interventions were, or could be, effective. There also emerged a realization of the enormous potential that music has to be a healing agent, *provided* the princi-ples involved could be clearly identified and explained, and then researched in a truly interdisciplinary sense by both professions (music and science), and the information accumulated by the two disciplines amalgamated and reported in archival journals. Consolidation of basic principles of physiolog-ical function with knowledge of the effect of music on that function could then thrust both the scientific and the music therapy professions to new levels of thinking, in practice and in research.

As we pursued our professional interdisciplinary interactions, there resulted several co-authored articles in just such peer-reviewed archival journals, together with two books previous to this one (Berger 2002; Schneck and Schneck 1997). The publications presented new paradigms that have been well received by investigators in all relevant fields of interest. Our collaboration also led to an international conference on Music in

Human Adaptation (held at Virginia Tech, Blacksburg, Virginia, in 1997), and a series of lectures/short courses/seminars and workshops that have been co-presented at national and international music therapy and biomedical engineering conferences, and in-house at various other facilities.

From issues and questions raised, and responses to the material presented in these various joint endeavors, there emerged an awareness by both of us that the three disciplines – physical science, physiology/medicine, and music/music therapy – were thirsting for more information. A real need was identified to define ways by which to understand how music actually does interact with the science of human physiology (and vice versa), why it does so, and how that information can be efficiently incorporated into the practice of music therapy. The cross-pollination of disciplines had begun.

This book is the product of such cross-pollination. It brings together two authors from entirely different, distinct fields of study and combines their accumulated expertise in an effort to contribute to the other's profession; to help each other understand the precursors of human behavior and how it can go awry – as well as what music is, how music behaves, why music is so powerful in addressing the human system to induce change, and how this knowledge can be instrumental in impacting upon rehabilitative goals.

We believe that the information in this book may provide an opportunity for both scientists and clinicians to immerse themselves in the mechanics of human functionality, coming at it from two distinct perspectives integrated into one document, which is to say: music therapy as viewed from the physiological (scientific) perspective, and science viewed from the music (aesthetic) perspective.

In Chapter 1 the reader is presented with several basic principles and terminologies that recur, and are referred to in depth, throughout the remainder of the book. This chapter also presents the central paradigm upon which the book is based. Subsequent chapters provide interdisciplinary scientific and music information that interfaces knowledge of:

- sensory inputs to the human body, specifically in the form of the elements of music (Chapter 2)
- basic physical principles upon which are based the six primary elements of music – rhythm, melody, harmony, timbre, dynamics, and form (Chapter 3)

- fundamental considerations that relate to anatomy (structure), physiology (function), morphology (form), and acoustics – i.e., the physics of sound (Chapters 4–6)

- the phenomenon of physiological entrainment (Chapter 6)

- the six elements of music and how these interface with physiological function (Chapters 7–11)

- a Coda providing closure to the case studies employed throughout the book (Chapter 12).

The case studies serve as examples of how the information presented can be (or has been) utilized in the clinical environment.

Throughout the book the material is presented and discussed in ways that can aid in increasing understanding of how the human system functions: what principles of physics govern physiological sensory perception and processing; how the body reacts, in particular, to acoustic sensory inputs; and which elements of music need to be understood in order to focus their effective application in treatment interventions. Beyond considering that music *does* or *can* do something, the authors' interests are focused upon exploring *why* and *how* music has the power to effect profound physiological responses, thereby inducing changes in the body's ability to adopt new responses (functional adaptation).

Several illustrations provided along the way help to elucidate some of the more subtle concepts and principles. In addition, threaded throughout many of the chapters are five sample case histories that demonstrate how the information presented has been applied in clinical music therapy settings. These representative cases, selected from several hundred others, are based on actual participants, diagnostic information, and individual responses.

Overall, the content of this book flows in an evolutionary manner, from the basics, to the details, to representative clinical applications. The early chapters lay the foundations, define the terminology, and formulate the theories that are continually referred to in later chapters. This information should become progressively clearer as the reader traverses the scientific landscape, absorbs the information, and reads the case studies.

It is our hope that the fruits of this book will be manifest in further growth and research within both the science and music therapy professions, and that the information herein will inspire more professional relationships among biomedical engineers, physiologists, scientists, music therapists, and other health-care professionals.

Chapter 1

# Introduction

All truth passes through three stages. First, it is ridiculed. Second, it is violently opposed. Third, it is accepted as being self-evident.

Arthur Schopenhauer

## Back to basics

The more researchers learn about the structure and function of the human body – the more its intricate levels of organization are explored, from atoms to molecules to cells to tissues to organs to systems, and the more its input/output characteristics, its hierarchy of sophisticated feedback–feedforward control systems, and the paradigms by which it operates are identified, defined, and quantified – the clearer it becomes that the human body is programmed, first and foremost, to sustain itself for survival. That's as basic as it gets. Underneath all the logic, all the reasoning, all the mathematics and physics and chemistry, the basic instinct for survival is embedded in subcortical, instinctive emotional behavior that pre-dates cognitive behavior by hundreds of millions of years (Damasio 1994; LeDoux 1998; Schneck 2003f). When threatened, or perceived to be threatened, one reacts *emotionally* at first. You might not actually "feel" afraid, even while your body is already in a reaction mode; but you may become consciously aware of such threats, think about them, and intellectualize much later (e.g., see Libet 2002, 2003).

Thus, through its complex ambiensomatic sub-systems (referring to both the environment and the body) the human organism receives, processes, and responds to incoming sensory information (technically called *input signals*) long before cognitive information-processing networks even know about it.

Throughout this book, the reader will come across physiological terminology that formally describes the working mechanisms of the human body and how sensory information is dealt with for the purpose of survival. As one becomes more familiar with the language of physiology, what will also become clearer is its relevance to the physics of sound, as embedded in the elements of music, and how all of this is used in the clinical applications of music therapy.

## Sensory information-processing intended to maintain the internal environment of the body

Physiological sensory information derives from two distinct sources: (1) from within the organism (-somatic, meaning "of or having to do with the body"), through interoceptive pathways, defined further below; and (2) from the external environment (ambien-, a prefix that connotes "having to do with the surroundings"), through exteroception (also defined below), which includes the perception of music. The essence of sensing is *transduction*, which refers to the conversion of one form of energy (e.g., heat, light, sound) into another. We shall have much more to say about this in Chapters 3 and 4.

In the human body, biological transducers – which are various sense organs – are technically known as *ceptors*, from the Latin *capere*, meaning "to take." Hence, *interoception* means "to take information from inside the body"; *exteroception* means "to take information from outside the body." *Proprioception* is the name given to a special type of interoception ("proprietary" referring to "one's own") that provides information specifically about the activity of muscles, muscle tendons, and joints – so that you can tell, for example, where your arms and legs are in space even with your eyes closed.

The ceptors convert (transduce) the various forms of energy to which they are sensitive into electrochemical *bits* of digitized information. The various forms of energy (described further in Chapter 2) are called *adequate stimuli* and include, for example, light which stimulates the eyes, sound to which the ears respond, heat which excites the body's thermal sensors, chemical energy to which taste buds and nasal receptors are particularly sensitive, and mechanical energy which affects the body's tactile receptors. The digitized bits of transduced information are called electrochemical *receptor potentials*, which can be measured as small voltages. These are conveyed as action potentials (sensory nerve signals) to the central nervous system (brain plus spinal cord) for further processing. Such processing, especially as it relates to signals embedded in the elements of music, will be described in some detail in the following chapters.

The central nervous system (CNS) receives, analyzes, and evaluates incoming information. Based on the results of this processing the CNS may choose to ignore the information and do nothing, or it may call for a physiological response through the *motor* (as opposed to *sensory*) portions of the peripheral nervous system, and/or the autonomic nervous system, and/or the system of glands in the body (Schneck 1990, 1997). These, in turn, control *effector organs* that carry out the desired response. This response is in direct proportion to how the information has been perceived, rightly or wrongly, subcortically (i.e., emotionally), in relation to the basic instinct for survival.

Over a period of time, these instinctive responses to perceived reality have been coded into the human body's *operating set-points*, which are reference or baseline physiological quantities. Some of these have values that are commonly called *normal vital signs*, such as optimum blood pressure, pulse rate, breathing rate, body temperature, and so on; others include blood sugar, acidity/alkalinity balance (pH), fluid balance, etc. Thus, equally complex anatomical control systems attempt to maintain the body's actual operating parameters, within very narrow desirable limits based on those baseline operating set-points that have been established as being critical for sustaining life. That is to say, the real-life motor outputs – which include internal metabolic processes, as well as external activities of daily living – in response to sensory inputs are fine-tuned and balanced against optimum performance criteria. This carefully controlled state of affairs, this dynamically equilibrated and delicately balanced milieu, together with the physiological processes by which it is maintained, are collectively referred to as *homeostasis*.

Functional responses and behavioral patterns that are specific to each particular system derive also from each individual system's perception, whether correct or incorrect, of what could be threatening to its survival. This often leads to a phenomenon referred to as the *fear spiral*, which is discussed further in Chapter 5. The following paradigm, developed in the chapters that follow, is a model intended to illustrate how the fear spiral can be truncated through the clinical use of musical intervention, and how the ability of music to work through the body's own adaptive control mechanisms can be exploited to alter behavior in a variety of diagnosed populations.

## The paradigm

Here is the essence of the paradigm developed in the chapters that follow.

1.  The human body acts only upon information received both internally (interoception) and externally (exteroception) through

its various sensory systems (ambiensomatic perception), as developed in Chapters 3 and 4.

2. This information is evaluated first and foremost through instinctive, emotional pathways that are ultimately concerned with maintaining an internal environment that ensures that both the individual and the species will survive – a state of affairs called "homeostasis," as discussed in Chapters 4 and 5.

3. Homeostasis is maintained by finely tuned control mechanisms that keep the body operating as closely as possible to predetermined reference set-points, as explored further in Chapters 3, 4, and 5.

4. Persistent changes and disturbing influences that affect sensory information input, in such a way as to require ceaseless, inordinate control to maintain homeostasis, are known as *continuous disturbances*, or more technically as *environmental driving* or *forcing functions*. Such constant sensory stimulation can result, as necessary, in the body altering its homeostatic operating set-points (including behavior), and/or its responsiveness to those inputs, through a process called *functional adaptation*. The latter refers to the body's ability to "adapt" to whatever it is being asked to do ("function"), provided this new function does not threaten its survival. Functionally adaptive responses are triggered by the body's yielding to continuous forcing functions, a process called *physiological entrainment*, which is discussed at some length in Chapter 6.

5. Thus, by systematically applying forcing functions to the organism, *driving* it through specific types of sensory stimulation (in particular, stimulation such as that embedded in music to which the body attends naturally), and by constantly *repeating* and *reinforcing* such stimulation in ceaseless fashion, one can invoke the processes of physiological entrainment, followed by functional adaptation, to ultimately induce desired changes in systemic operating set-points, including behavioral patterns.

6. Finally, the specific types of sensory stimulation that are addressed here are those embedded in the elements of music (rhythm, melody, harmony, timbre, dynamics, form) and their various combinations, permutations, and configurations.

We shall be presenting plausible hypotheses to explain the nature of the dynamic interactions that take place between the aforementioned elements of music and corresponding elements of physiological function. To the extent that these theories are formulated on a solid foundation of well-established physical principles and anatomical considerations, they are rigorous, reasonable, and reliable predictors of anticipated physiological responses to musical stimulation. They can thus be used as a basis for formulating clinical protocols for the effective use of music in:

- helping the body to heal itself from a wide variety of pathological, emotional, and psychological ailments

- managing patients with special medical needs, including the terminally ill, those dealing with pain, and individuals requiring special geriatric care

- attending to populations with special adaptive needs, including not only clients suffering from formally diagnosed "syndromes," such as autism and Cornelia de Lang syndrome, but also those individuals experiencing phobias, emotional, and anxiety issues which may not be specifically "diagnosed" (such as dealing with stress-provoking situations like public speaking, performing on stage, sitting for examinations, and so on).

They can also be used for developing research protocols that can quantify, in a dose–response sense, the role of music in the human experience.

This book will journey through fundamental principles of physics and physiological function, with particular emphasis on how they relate to the generation and processing of musical inputs. As mentioned earlier, such understanding of how the body functions, and why and how a medical specialty interacts with that function, is crucial to the implementation of effective therapy interventions – which brings us to the main reason for writing this book.

We shall be discussing human physiology from a musical perspective, and music from a biomedical/physiological engineering perspective. Based on this integration, we shall suggest ways in which music can be used effectively as a clinical intervention for any system being treated, whether it be afflicted with autism or Alzheimer's, in need of pain or stress management, undergoing recovery and rehabilitation, or even the most healthy system simply seeking to function more effectively. We also suggest research opportunities: questions still in need of answers, issues worthy of further investigation, problems for which solutions are still being sought, and essential information that is sorely lacking, yet vital to the clinician who is trying to formulate an effective program for patient care.

The authors hope that after reading this book you will have gained an in-depth knowledge of principles that explain not only that music *does* something, but, going one step further, *what, how,* and *why* it does it, and why it is so potent in directly impacting physiological function to produce such profound effects. Aside from the clinical advantages already addressed, using this knowledge as a basis it will also be possible to explain to doctors, educators, administrators, families, and persons in need, the specific applications and effectiveness of focused music intervention.

## Why music?

Why music, indeed! The history of music in the human experience is at least as old as our civilized past, and probably even older. Consider the very origin of the word "music": it derives from the Greek *Muses* (nine of them), who were the goddesses of the fine arts and sciences. The ancient Greeks believed that achievements in the arts and sciences were divinely inspired – in that order (i.e., first through the arts, and second via scientific thought). That is to say, the original two muses, Polyhymnia (literally, "she of many hymns," the muse of music, sacred poetry, and song) and Terpsichore (literally, "the whirler," muse of dance) presided over music, song, and dance long before humans did anything else! Only with the progress of civilization were these original two muses followed historically by the five muses that represented the various functions of poetry in ancient societies, which included:

- the expression of love and passion, presided over by Erato, "the lovely," symbolized by a musical lyre

- lyrical (including musical) expression, presided over by Euterpe, "the giver of pleasure," symbolized by a musical flute

- the recounting of tales of heroic adventures, presided over by Calliope, "the fair-voiced" muse of epic poetry

- the expression of humor in pastoral, idyllic settings, presided over by Thalia, "the flourishing" muse of comedy

- reflections on tragedy, presided over by Melpomene, "the songstress."

Finally, there came along the last two presiding divinities: Clio, "the proclaimer," muse of history; and Urania, "the heavenly," muse of astronomy. And for all? Their ruler was Apollo, the god of music and harmony!

The motivation for ascribing divine inspiration first to artistic achievements was, for the Greeks, directly connected to the particularly moving emotional experience that could be attributed to those achievements. It was inconceivable to the populace of this ancient civilization that anything that could elicit such profound physiological effects could derive from a source other than the sacred daughters of the almighty Zeus (the chief god) and Mnemosyne ("Memory," his Titaness lover). In other words, going back thousands of years, long before scientific advances could provide a rigorous basis to explain it, it was already recognized that certain sensory inputs in the audible range of perception could evoke intense physiological responses, manifesting themselves as *emotional* responses; and since those responses could not be explained in any other way, they had to be of godly origin. This divine association firmly established the importance of music in the human experience, and along with it came the additional abstract realization that this form of sensory stimulation, acting through the body's self-regulating mechanisms, had the profound ability also to allow the organism to express its healing potential. Medicine, too, has a strong Greek heritage.

Going one step further, it is also interesting to note that, through the many years that have elapsed since the days of the muses, only "music," as the word is used today, has maintained its etymological identity with the word from which it is derived. One might thus infer that, of all the arts and sciences, music remains the one most closely associated with the muses, perhaps because it alone shares a unique symbiotic relationship with: (1) the basically emotional organism that it energizes; (2) the gods that presumably originally inspired it as a unique form of expression; and (3) the basic features that characterize fundamental physiological function. But even putting the historical/mythical perspective aside, the overwhelming evidence is perfectly clear that auditory sensory inputs embedded in the organized sounds we call "music" do, indeed, elicit profound physiological responses – responses that capture our attention in ways that can be used clinically to affect desired outcomes, most especially in the patient populations mentioned earlier.

Music provides the means for communicating with the physiological system through a syntax that the system understands, and to which it responds profoundly. The elements of music (Chapters 2 and 3) exactly parallel the functional behavior of the human system, both physiologically (Chapters 4 and 5) and emotionally. Music speaks directly to the body through intuitive channels that are accessed at entirely different levels of consciousness from those associated with cognition. And the body listens attentively, and responds passionately (Chapter 6). Indeed, the two – music and the body – share a unique symbiotic relationship independent of cognition. Music enters one's subconscious mind through pathways that are more indigenous to the organism – emotional ones that require no further explanation, and that are what the system is all about in the first place. Music does not need any form of semantic interpretation; cognition is not essential for processing this input. Thus, music communicates with the body by speaking the language of physiology.

This book is about the power of music to affect and alter physiological function, leading clinicians and scientists toward a better understanding of how and why "the music effect" works. Based on this understanding, we explore (in Chapters 7–12) ways in which music is used clinically to intervene in targeted populations. In its most simplistic sense, one can think of the management of targeted populations as a journey – one that takes the client or patient from a given, undesirable physiological/psychological state, A, characterized by aberrant, even detrimental, operating set-points, to a desirable destination, B, in which new physiological and mental states, derived from reconditioned, favorable operating set-points, have been established, with more optimal values for system performance. Thus:

- The *vehicle* traversing the path of this journey is the human body, transitioning from state A (undesirable) to state B (desirable).

- The components of the *engine* powering this transition include all of the anatomical/physiological mechanisms that participate in the processes of physiological entrainment and accommodation.

- The *road traveled* winds through either collateral neural networks (potential spaces waiting to be activated), or via newly constructed avenues derived from the nervous system's inherent plasticity (i.e., its capability of being molded into new shapes). By *collateral neural networks* is meant side-branches of existing nerve pathways that represent alternative routes for the propagation of nerve action potentials. So long as they are in existence, but not being used, these alternative routes are called "potential spaces," capable of being accessed, but currently dormant. But they can be opened (activated) as needed by mechanisms of entrainment and accommodation. *Plasticity*, by contrast, implies the construction of new neural pathways (new highways) not previously existing.

- The *driver* of this vehicle is music! Music controls the gas pedal (continuous disturbance, as defined earlier), the brakes (through the clinician administering it), and the steering wheel, thus *navigating* the body, through the various elements of music, toward its desired destination.

Keep in mind that physiological entrainment, accommodation or adaptation that is music-driven to alter systemic operating set-points is a process that happens *within* us, not *to* us. To paraphrase the words of Abraham Lincoln in his famous Gettysburg Address: like government, music may be thought of as having been invented by the people, for the people, to satisfy the internal needs of the people – and thus shall never perish from the earth. Logically, the converse of this statement also follows: since music was invented to satisfy the human need for emotional, psychological, and physical well-being, it should obviously be able to fulfill that need in reverse. Thus, as an external stimulus, music has the ability to provide for the emotional, psychological, and physiological well-being of an individual, whether or not such well-being is in jeopardy. It is in the latter sense that music can be thought of as the driver (the persistent, continuous disturbance) of the vehicle, the stimulus that successfully propels the body and mind from state A to state B.

That having been said, the music therapist must therefore appreciate that the path to effective clinical management of targeted populations begins with an understanding of the following:

1. How one's emotional health impacts his or her physical well-being, and vice versa.

2. Where music fits in to this hierarchy of basic physiological functions, to energize and animate mechanisms for entrainment, accommodation, and adaptation.

3. What individual-specific approaches (i.e., what forms of musical intervention, quantified in dose–response relationships) can most effectively "drive the vehicle" to its desired destination.

Exactly *how* the elements of music can be employed clinically is based primarily on those physiological considerations described throughout the book – which considerations, when placed in context, establish the proper perspective for understanding the role of psychology in the hierarchy of human emotion, as it reflects the inherent instinct for survival. The underlying premise throughout the text is that all human behavior, be it typically responsive, or resulting from diagnosed or undiagnosed clinical anomalies, derives from anatomical and physiological considerations: we are, all of us, fundamentally human! As the great nineteenth-century philosopher Arthur Schopenhauer states in *The World as Will and Idea* (1995, p.164), "...the effect of music is so much more powerful and penetrating than that of the other arts, for they (the other arts) speak only of the shadow while music speaks of the essence".

Our treatise discusses what this "essence" – the "me" embedded within the human being – entails, using a paradigm that, for the first time, establishes a theoretical framework that can be quantified, subjected to rigorous research protocols, and thereafter be applied clinically.

One final note: most conventional clinical interventions treat *symptoms*, as opposed to *causes* (Hyman and Liponis 2003). Thus, the "standard operating procedure" involves an effort to keep the patient(s) as "comfortable" as possible while the body essentially heals itself (or, in the case of incurable conditions, while the disease or pathological condition runs its course, positive or negative). When *healing*, in the pathological sense, is not the issue – such as in diagnosed (or undiagnosed) populations with special adaptive needs – the treatment is still symptomatic, which is to say, oriented primarily towards developing "acceptable" modes of behavior, or "tolerable" activities of daily living, as opposed to targeting the actual causes of such aberrant behavioral activity. Music, on the other hand, directly stimulates the body's own self-healing and/or adaptive mechanisms – what Hyman and Liponis (2003, p.71) call "supporting human biology" – rather than interfering with it. The various elements of this form of sensory stimulation work through and with the body, either to enhance its inherent healing powers (i.e., treat actual causes, rather than symptoms) or to help it to adapt to the world in which it has been forced to live. Thus, with these considerations and objectives in mind, let us begin our journey by defining in somewhat more detail what this form of sensory stimulation called *music* is all about.

Chapter 2

# What Is This Thing Called "Music"?

Words seem so indefinable, so inexact, so easy to misunderstand
compared with real music, which fills the soul with a thousand
better feelings. What is expressed to me by music that I love is not
too vague to be put into words, but on the contrary, too precise.

Felix Mendelssohn (letter to Marc-André Souchay, 1842)

## Introduction

Music has power. It can change attitudes, relax or energize the body, animate
the spirit, influence cognitive development, enhance the body's self-healing
mechanisms, amuse, entertain, and foster a general response which can be a
state of comfort, or in some instances even discomfort. The anatomical
systems and physiological processes that comprise the *me* of what is inherently human function are reflected within the content and systems of music.
Why music exists and how it is able to affect such profound physiological
responses are questions that have piqued the interest and imagination of
investigators in fields as diverse as anthropology, biomedical engineering,
education, physiology, psychology, psychiatry, philosophy, neuroscience,
medicine, speech and language research, and of course artists and musicians.

Arthur Schopenhauer (1995), one of the great philosophers of the nine-
teenth century, struggled to explain and define the aesthetic of music,
asserting that music stands alone and apart from all the other artistic forms of
expression, such that "we must attribute to music a far more serious, deeper
significance for the inmost nature of the world and our own self" (p.163). He
observed that although all the arts (poetry, painting, drama, dance, etc.)
generally affect us in the same way as music does, "the effect of music is
stronger, swifter, more compelling and infallible ...its imitative relationship
to the world must be very deep, infinitely true, and really striking, for it is
instantly understood by everyone." (p.164). After deliberating on the repre-

sentational aspects of the arts, he concluded that music is in no way a natural phenomenon of the physical world, but is rather an analogue of it. He extrapolated that "music...is entirely independent...of the phenomenal world ...[it] could to a certain extent exist if there were no world at all; this cannot be said of the other arts" (p.164).

What Schopenhauer is explaining, in essence, is that music, in and of itself, is not something that is naturally "out there" for humans to duplicate, in a physical sense; but rather, quite the other way around. It takes human intervention and *invention* in order for music to exist. *Humans* create music; it is a *metaphor* for the human experience, encompassing the entire spectrum of human emotions – hence, in return, its ability to elicit these emotions. Indeed, the attributes of music (its component parts: pulsations, vibrations, frequencies, form) and its ability to impact upon human emotional, mental, and physiological states stem from this categorical duplication and simulation of human sensory and emotional behavior. Music is the abstraction and transformation of human emotional and physical energies into acoustic energies that reflect, parallel, and resonate in synchrony with the physiological system. Through music a person sees him/herself reflected in the most faithful, intimate, profound, and exposed manner. One cannot hide from it. Music is what human beings are; it behaves as human beings behave, and causes the human system to behave as music behaves. It is the mirror of human physical and emotional energy transformed into sound. It is a temporal, non-static, developmental, evolutionary transcription of life.

## Putting music in proper perspective

A solid, proven theory for why music exists seems as elusive as theories about brain function, consciousness, and human behavior (perhaps for the same reasons). It may be that a scientifically substantiated theory will be determined only by the validity and vitality of the questions driving the theory. And it may be that a thoroughly proven theory for the role of music in the human experience will remain as elusive as, for example, are the theories of relativity, evolution, the "Big Bang," human brain development, and cortical functions, to name just a few.

Whatever the reasons for the nature and purpose of music, the fact remains that music exists everywhere there is humanity on this planet. It therefore follows that it must be a vital tool somehow indispensable to survival, a vehicle that allows human beings to transmit sensations and impulses – human emotions that cannot be otherwise expressed. For example, why is "Happy Birthday" sung? More than likely, it is because words alone do not adequately convey the emotional *energy* behind the thought, for while emotions can be labeled, their energies must be felt.

The voice was perhaps the first instrument through which *Homo sapiens* (or perhaps even earlier species with vocal abilities) could call out to one another, attract animals, convey needs, communicate within groups, establish presence of self and others, and, most of all, to express human conditions such as needs, desires, fears, pain, joy, excitement, etc. (e.g., see Darwin 1998; Deacon 1997; Wallin, Merker, and Brown 2001). To the voice can be added a variety of primitive percussive and blowing implements that were the "original" instruments: hollow bones or plant stalks, sticks and tree limbs, hollowed or skin-covered logs, bells, rattles, and rituals. Thus emerged the earliest evolution of rhythmic, tone-linked, purposefully flowing and systemized incantations expressing human needs and feelings (Brown 2001).

Could it be that this musical form of expression actually *pre-dated* the formalization of language communication? It is interesting to note that, in fact, a number of scientists and anthropologists, including evolutionist Charles Darwin, believe (and believed) this to be more than possible. In *The Expression of the Emotions in Man and Animals*, republished in its third edition in 1998, Darwin states:

> I have been led to infer that the progenitors of man probably uttered musical tones before they had acquired the power of articulate speech, [and] that the pitch of the voice bears some relation to certain states of feelings is tolerably clear! (p.92)

Steven Brown (2001) developed the theory of "musilanguage" which evolved into two distinct expressions of music and language. According to Brown:

> Music and language are seen as reciprocal specializations of a dual-natured referential emotive communicative precursor, whereby music emphasizes sound as emotive meaning and language emphasizes sound as referential meaning. (p.271)

If one accepts the theory that music as a form of expression might actually have preceded the formalization of language communication – and that there was vocal chanting of sorts before communicative utterances were abbreviated and contracted into short rhythmic spurts of vocalized grunts and calls that evolved into speech – then it is not unreasonable to presume further that the human animal requires the expanded musical form of expression for *additional* reasons, not the least of which are those related to basic physiological function.

Does music reach beyond the workings of the cognitive brain? If so, how and why? Since the human species has evolved to such a highly cognitive and verbally developed degree, why does humanity still have or need music? Could it be precisely *because* music is a non-cognitive form of communication? That is to say, one needs to know absolutely nothing about music to instantly respond to and benefit from it. While speech absolutely requires the cognitive brain to provide semantic references for the sound utterances, music circumvents this step, requiring no semantic interpretation of its syntax. It is immediately understood. One does not need to know anything about music in order to become absorbed within, and affected by, its presence. Indeed, music – a human-made event – is the single most abstract form of self-expression, speaking the emotional language of the human "me" within the myriad of atoms, molecules, cells, tissues, organs, and systems that collectively organize and run the "me" machine.

As was mentioned earlier, music does not resemble or remind one of any known or recognizable planetary object. It is *non*-representational, in the concrete sense, as opposed to other physical phenomena that can be held, touched, viewed, tasted, smelled or otherwise described in a rigorous fashion. Music does not issue commands, describe concrete objects, nor is it amenable to empirical methods for measuring and quantifying physical response characteristics – in the same way, for instance, as are forces in time and space. Yet music does exist in time and space, permeating the environment as oxygen permeates the atmosphere, contributing to physiological and psychological states of experience. It is a mind-to-mind, feeling-to-feeling, direct expression of the human condition manifested in feelings, sensations, and energies.

In the process of expressing the human state-of-being, music "cuts to the quick," so to speak, requiring no semantic definition or explanation. Nor does music require any higher forms of cognitive awareness. Music makes immediate sense, reaching directly into the emotional brain to convey or echo moods, sensations, and feelings. In fact, words are inadequate even to describe the musical experience. It can *only* be experienced. We might say that music is the human being's first language, and, in the proverbial sense, the universal language of all humanity. In its presence, human beings are all equals, without deficits, gender, race, color, or special function.

## A definition of music

Because it can only be experienced, and not operationally delineated in words, it is difficult to actually define what one means by the word "music." In Chapter 1, the origin of the word in Greek mythology was explored; but this historical perspective only serves, in a generic sense, to provide some basis for what was thought by the ancient Greeks to be the *source* of this form of human experience. It does not *define* the experience; it only *describes* it. In the modern world, "music" means different things to different people, and what is music to one person might be noise to another. Therefore, the actual definition of music is somewhat arbitrary, although it can be identified as having at least six distinct attributes. As used in this book, then, the term "music" refers to specific combinations of sound attributes, as embedded in what are traditionally considered to be the six elements of music: *rhythm, melody, harmony, timbre, dynamics,* and *form*. But more than that, given that these six elements are inherent within the form of expression defined herein to be "music," and given that there is a direct correlation between these elements and basic aspects of physiological function, our definition goes on to assert that the attributes of music, either individually or in complex combinations, evolve as expressions of its creator's emotions, impulses, intuitions, will (motivation), intentions, and abstract ideas. In other words, in a manner directly paralleling the study of structure and form (morphology) as it relates to function in the human organism (discussed more fully in Chapters 3 and 4), the structure (morphology) of music – its anatomy, consisting of rhythm, melody, harmony, dynamics, timbre, and form – cannot be divorced from its intended *function(s)*, which are emotional expression, subjective experience, and abstract reflection (i.e., "physiology").

The definition of music presented here, then, includes both its structure and function. We are not delving into the aesthetic question of whether or not a rendition is "musical," as dictated by individual aesthetic tastes and preferences; nor are we deliberating the question of what is or is not "music." Our definition of this form of human expression is thus quite rigorous, as it is being used herein. Moreover, we further describe "music" as:

*an artificially contrived, external explication of combined sound events, conjured and organized by human beings, reflecting distinguishing internal and external occurrences, energies, sensations, emotions, and rhythms, derived from corresponding emotional, physiological, psychological, and environmental states and events.*

"Artificial?" you may ask. In fact, literally, this is precisely the case. The word "artificial" derives from the Latin *ars* (from the root *ar*, meaning "to fit" – as in the arm of the body fitting into the shoulder joint), and *facere* (meaning "to make"– as in "manufacture," to make with the hands, and as in "artifact," to make with the arms). Thus, "artificial" connotes made by human skill or labor, as opposed to occurring naturally; and so, we arrive at the derivative of *ars* – *art* – which applies precisely to those drawings, paintings, sculptures, architectural designs, musical compositions, dance routines, literary works (poems, plays, novels, etc.), and other forms of expression that are unique to the corresponding form of human civilization, and that derive from the human imagination, rather than from the existing physical universe.

Music is, in fact, a purely abstract form of human expression, entirely *artificially* conceived, concocted, and fabricated by human beings. Of all the aesthetic forms of expression, music is the only form that is completely non-representational of any concrete, worldly object or event. Rather, music is a metaphor: an abstraction; a fantasy; an analogue; a "virtual reality" of sensations and energies – taking place entirely internally, inside the body, and within the spaces of the mind. It alludes to human sensations, experiences, and possibilities.

Now, at this very moment, the romantics may be shouting: "Not out there? What about the 'music' of the spheres, the 'music' of the wind in the trees, and the 'music' of the birds and whales and animals?" Composer Igor Stravinsky, in his lectures entitled *Poetics of Music* (1942), responded as follows:

> The murmur of the breeze in the trees, the rippling of a brook, the song of a bird…these natural sounds suggest music to us, but are not yet themselves music… they are promises of music; it takes a human being to keep them: a human being who is sensitive to nature's many voices…who feels the need of putting them in order… In his hands all that I have considered as not being music will become music. (p.23)

Thus, in our formulation, music is a "controlled system" (terminology that will be encountered frequently throughout this book) of sound processes, even as the human organism is a controlled system of information processing. In the case of music, its elements are what is controlled and manipulated by its composer to bring an idea to realization. That is to say, music is an acoustic event instigated, structured, and expressed by virtue of human needs and drives (the human condition) at any given moment of a composition's creation. It employs a combination of six well-defined elements that mirror attributes of nature and human behavior; and yet, collectively, they add up to more than merely the sum of its parts, transcending structure in favor of emotional experience. To a great extent, the human body is quite the same, its substance transcending anatomical structure and physiological function to provide a type of energy that is the essence of life itself. Both music and the human body share in common this transcendent attribute of going beyond mere structure and function.

Moreover, because these six basic components correlate directly with corresponding aspects of physics, physiology, sensory perception, and emotion, at both the sub-cognitive and cognitive levels of human function, the elements of music, in various combinations, immediately synchronize with the body, and are promptly recognized by the brain and body at the intuitive, instinctual level. And finally, because music speaks "in physiological tongues," as it were, in a syntactic energy that requires no semantic dictionary in order to be comprehended, a response to it will have already taken place within the body before the awareness of that response ever enters consciousness. The *feeling* label comes after the emotion has occurred (Damasio 2003).

## Levels of organization of the controlled music system

The human body is a controlled system organized in essentially six levels, increasing in size and function, from atoms to molecules, cells, tissues, organs, and systems. Music, too, is a controlled system organized through six basic elements, increasing in size, content, volume, and function – from the smallest structural "atom" (individual pitches, notes) of a sound idea, to molecules (melodic "soundscapes," and harmonic dimensions), functional cells (phrase and rhythmic units), tissues (timbre, sound quality, dynamics, and energized textures), organs (combinations of notes, rhythms, dynamics, phrases, harmonies, timbre, textures, and tonalities that preserve and drive the body of the work), and systems (key-structures, modalities, form, movements, musical styles, variations, etc.).

Note that since music is an analogue of physiological function, it is useful to adopt physiological terms to emphasize parallels between human function and corresponding aspects of the behavior of music, which is viewed as an extension of human behavior. That is to say – in a manner not unlike that employed by scientists when attempting to use the design of the human brain as a prototype for the design of computer central processing units – basic aspects of physiological function, serving, too, as prototypes, are encoded into the elements of music, as composers strive to express human emotions through symbolic emotions (metaphors). Thus, the six basic elements of music can be described in stages from simple to complex, each having a corresponding physiological attribute.

## Periodicity

Defined as *the tendency of an event to recur at regular intervals* (i.e., in well-defined cycles), periodicity is the most rudimentary level of organization in this controlled system, manifesting itself in music as *rhythm*. We discuss in Chapter 3 why rhythm is inherent in, and a necessary attribute of, all of life in the universe (Berger and Schneck 2003; Schneck 2000b). Indeed, all forms of perceptible energy exist within cycles, which are repeating systems in time. All periodic sound energy has an inherent *frequency* (number of cycles repeated per second), which contributes to what one hears as a "tone," identified in music as *pitch*.

## Melody

Melody is the sequential linking of one pitch to another, and another, and so on, in a curvilinear relationship. The pitches are not necessarily following one another in a perfectly straight line, but rather they are bending and arching – unwinding horizontally, to take on a smooth shape, a *contour* (Chapter 8), a soundscape, the tracking of which suggests a *tune* in music – the melodic line.

## Harmony

The architectural superposition and simultaneous compounding of pitches (polyphony = "many sounds"), one on top of the other, sounded at the same time to resonate together, flowing both vertically and horizontally, is known in music as harmony (from the Greek *harmonia* meaning "a fitting together" or "joining"). As will become clearer when this element of music is discussed more thoroughly in Chapter 9, the harmony variables of *dissonant* (disagreeable, irritating) and *consonant* (pleasing, comfortable) intervals (i.e., distances between notes sounded together) are everywhere, even within human physiological function. In music, consonance and dissonance are employed for expression of feelings through compounded sonic dimensions often suggesting certain harmonic centers or "resting" zones.

## Dynamics

The energy inherent in sound, embedded in the amplitude (maximum and minimum spatial excursions) of a sound wave (defined in Chapter 3), is everywhere in physiological and planetary function. Music is no exception. Sound energy levels (more commonly referred to as "volume") in a piece of music define its mood, urgency, and underlying emotion. In music terminology, the volume of sound is referred to as dynamics (Chapter 9). In physiological terms, body dynamics refers to the quality of body movements, such as strong, weak, rigid, and so on.

## Timbre

Timbre provides texture to a sound, and is the phenomenal result of the fact that sound generators do not vibrate the same way throughout their entire substance (Chapter 3). It is the combination of timbre and tone qualities, for instance, that enables one to identify the nature of a sound-producing source (is it a bird, mother's voice, or a tea kettle?), and to differentiate between various instrumental and vocal qualities (male, female, violin, trumpet, etc.) in musical performances.

## Form

All of the above elements are incorporated into an overall, operational, systematic, structural (morphological) configuration known as form – the beginning–middle–end of an idea or impulse (Chapter 10). It is this organization of various elements into form that becomes the final syntactic expression of a human experience, need, and drive.

These six basic elements of music combine to communicate a musical stream of consciousness, flowing across space-time in a non-static, kinetic, evolutionary manner. The understanding of "music" as an impression and expression of human physiological function and emotions underlies the theory formulated herein to explain why and how music has the ability to immediately synchronize with, and in many ways alter, human function.

## Sonic energy and the body

Keep in mind that physical concepts such as gravity, energy, and vibration impact on the behavior and function of the atoms, molecules, cells, etc. that have thus far been, and will continue to be, discussed, throughout this book.

That is to say, sound is *energy* emanating from a source that induces vibrations. The vibrations propagate, like a "domino effect," through any medium that allows that form of energy access and safe passage. In the world of physics, access and safe passage is defined to be the *permeability* of the medium to sound energy. Thus, traveling sound energy can disturb the air, and anything else it encounters along its course that is permeable to its effects. If what it happens to encounter is the human body, it must be presumed that the body's atoms, molecules, cells, organs, tissues, and operational systems will indeed be affected by sonic vibrational energies.

Going one step further, it follows that sound vibrations organized and targeted to arouse certain bodily functions would induce particular physiological responses, some positive, others negative. The developing field of vibroacoustic medicine (Gerber 2001), for example, is an area of study, research, and intervention focused upon the use and influence of sonic vibration in addressing such concerns as pain management, muscular rehabilitation, anxiety and stress, and more. Music is comprised of combinations of sonic vibrational elements. Thus, it contains the vibrational energy stimulus that the body immediately senses, and to which it responds. Precisely how bodily atoms, molecules, cells, tissues, organs, and systems are affected by such targeted energy is a topic in continuous need of research. However, because the aesthetic (sensation) factor of "music" – combined sounds – is more than just a collection of sonic vibrations, it has significant implications for use in medicine. Hence, the emotional component of this art form is *entrained* (captured and assimilated; see Chapters 1 and 6) by the physiological system, allowing it to synchronize and resonate with the musical work to enhance both healing mechanisms and behavior modification.

The six elements of music described above and throughout the book contain within them the emotional "feeling" states of the human being, so that while the molecules and cells are being reorganized in response to such stimulation, the physiological/psychological systems, and the homeostatic set-points (Chapter 1) that command those emotionally driven systems, are also being influenced to yield additional or alternative behavioral responses. In other words, the all-inclusive factor of music as an acoustic clinical intervention can drive a system toward *functional adaptation* (Chapter 1).

At this point it is necessary to reflect on the physics that is embedded in everything we have been talking about so far, and will be in the chapters that follow, using words like energy, pitch, vibrations, tones, rhythm, dynamics, timbre, and so on. After all, in the most basic sense it is this physics that is common to both music and physiology; it is this physics through which music and the body communicate with one another, producing "the music effect." And it is the way music is generated physically, and the way the body responds to it physically, that in the end results in the *physical* manifestation of those responses "the music effect." In order to be an effective clinician, then, the music therapist must endeavor to understand at least some very basic principles of physics germane to the subject at hand – which brings us to the subject matter of Chapter 3.

Chapter 3

# Principles of Physics
# and the Elements of Music

Theories are generally not perfect, and hence, a theory can never be
absolutely verified. Some philosophers therefore emphasize that
testing of a theory can be used only to *falsify* it, not to confirm it.

Douglas C. Giancoli, *Physics for Scientists and Engineers*

## Introduction

A science professor came to class one day and declared, "Chemistry, biology,
geology, art, music, politics, psychology, autism, psychiatry, astronomy,
botany – all of these cannot exist without physics; *there is only physics!*" What
this professor was trying to get his students to understand was that all aspects
of this planet, and the universe within which it exists, ultimately reduce to
the same common denominator, "physics." Indeed, in order to understand
"the music effect" – how the elements of music come into existence to begin
with, what governs physiological function, how the human body is affected
by and responds to the elements of music, what works, why it works, how it
works, and so on – clinicians and researchers must be armed with at least a
rudimentary understanding of the physics in the nature of things, the scientific physics of both objective and subjective "reality."

The human body's ability to react to its environment derives from the
physical stimulation of its sensory receptors. The body interprets what it
perceives to be "real" based on how these sensory inputs are physically
dispensed with through its various information-processing networks. The
human body itself would not thrive were it not for the physics of physiological function. Music would not be possible were it not for the physics of
sound. And certainly, one could not *react* to the elements of music were it not
for the physics of neurological motor function. A music therapy clinician

possessing this fundamental knowledge of how the body works, how it is affected by the physics of sound (as embedded in the elements of music), how the body establishes its own form of "reality" from what its various sensory pathways tell it – and, perhaps most importantly, how its anatomical/physiological/pathological limitations constrain what it is capable of perceiving – is well prepared both to provide effective, individually specific, dose-dependent treatment for his or her clients, and to undertake laboratory investigations based on well-defined research protocols.

In this and subsequent chapters, the reader is introduced to basic physical concepts that underlie all of what humans are capable of perceiving as "real," including the architectural limitations of those perceptions. We begin with the very nature of objective and subjective reality, and continue through:

- how this reality derives objectively from considerations of energy

- how specific attributes of that energy (e.g., frequency, amplitude, wavelength, wave speed) allow it to manifest itself in various forms, some having the capability to stimulate various of the body's anatomical sense organs

- how some of these forms can be translated further to create the six basic elements of music

- how objective sensory inputs to the body, such as the elements of music, are subjectively interpreted, through the organism's information-processing networks, to create a person's individual sense of what is "real" and what is "normal"

- how that personal sense of reality is constrained by anatomical, physiological, experiential, emotional, cognitive, behavioral, and pathological considerations in diagnosed populations.

## Energy and the physics of reality

An old cliché asserts that "perception is reality," because, in the subjective realm of the human experience, that is indeed the case. However, when physicists talk about *objective* reality, they are referring to all of the physical manifestations of various forms of energy. As a concept, "energy" cannot really be rigorously defined (Schneck 2003e); it can only be described, in ways that are discussed below. Historically, such descriptions originated from early observations of the fact that things endowed with a specific (not-yet-named) property had the ability to make things happen, to do "work." This was obvious, given that the physical realization of such efforts could be directly experienced. Thus, to this property the Greeks gave the name "energy" – *en-* meaning "in," and *ergon* meaning "work."

Energy is an inherent property, some unique feature of things endowed with it that is required in order to drive processes that are capable of accomplishing purposeful activities. To the concept of purposeful activities is assigned the word "work," and to the property prerequisite for doing work is assigned the word "energy." Scientists now know, of course, that work derived from energy is but one form of this omnifarious property, because energy can manifest itself in an infinite number of ways, not all of them necessarily discernible to us. Many types of energy can be identified (qualitatively, to this point in our discussion), including sub-nuclear, nuclear, atomic, electromagnetic, infrared, light, ultraviolet, chemical, biochemical (the source of life), thermodynamic, mechanical, infrasonic, sonic (the source of music), ultrasonic, cosmic, super-cosmic, and so on *ad infinitum*. Two realizations of energy that are of particular relevance to the subject matter of this book are: (1) that which manifests itself in the various aspects of human life (see discussion below of energy as a life force, and Chapter 4); and (2) that which humans perceive as sound (which can be organized into the elements of music, as described qualitatively in Chapter 2, and quantitatively in this and subsequent chapters). Still another manifestation of energy is mechanical vibration, of which sound is a sub-form, and which can be perceived through the body's tactile senses. Thus, music can not only be heard, but physically felt as well.

In a form called *potential*, energy is the imperceptible source of all of reality; and in a form called *kinetic*, it is the perceptible realization of all that is possible. Such perception is predicated on *movement*. In other words, energy can only be perceived – which is to say, *capable of being* can only become *being* – when potential energy is converted into kinetic energy.

Going one step further, an important law of physics asserts that, in a global sense, energy is an indestructible attribute. While it can be converted from one form into another (including various different types of kinetic energy, at various levels of perception), more generally it can neither be created, *de novo*, nor destroyed. This is the famous Law of Conservation of Energy (see Schneck 1990 for a fuller discussion). Potential and kinetic energies, then, derive from a finite reservoir that endows the universe with the inherent attribute from which all forms of reality derive.

With the concept of energy in hand, one can move forward to discuss sound, the elements of music, the function of the human body, the symbiotic relationship between the body and music, and how all of these considerations can be effectively applied, clinically. That discussion begins with the realization that conversions between potential and kinetic energies are cyclic – which is to say, manifestations of energy are *vibrational*.

## Energy vibrates

The qualitative concept of energy can be quantified by noting that its various manifestations are characterized by cyclical events, both large scale and small. "Cyclical" implies recurring at regular intervals, called *periods of vibration*. Energy has to vibrate, for reasons that shall soon become clear. These vibrations correspond to alternating periods of energy conversions, from potential to kinetic to potential to kinetic etc., the number of times per second that these conversions take place being called the *frequency of vibration*.

Consider, for example, what happens when an existing equilibrated state of affairs (one that is in a "status quo" configuration) is disturbed. A "disturbance" is more technically referred to as a *driving*, or *forcing function*, which in physiological jargon is known as an *adequate stimulus* – a type of energy to which specific sensory receptors respond. The three terms "disturbance," "adequate stimulus," and "driving/forcing function" tend to be used interchangeably, so it is important to be aware that they all refer to the same type of physical process, one that causes a given status-quo situation to deviate from the existing state of affairs. The adequate stimulus that disturbs such an equilibrated state of affairs can be any specific form of energy to which the "state" is responsive, such as (again, speaking qualitatively):

- light energy, to which the eyes (the responding sensory receptor, or *transducer*, in this case) primarily respond

- sound energy, to which the ears (auditory system) primarily respond

- chemical energy, to which the senses of taste and smell primarily respond

- mechanical and/or thermodynamic (heat) energy, to which the various types of tactile senses (touch receptors), including thermal senses, primarily respond

- gravitational and/or inertial energy, to which the body's kinesthetic receptors (sense of movement) and proprioceptive receptors (sense of "self" – the non-visual perception of internal bodily conditions and limb orientations in space) primarily respond.

Each sense organ is endowed with a stimulus-specific form of potential energy, which allows that particular sense organ (e.g., the ear) to transform an adequate stimulus (e.g., sound) into a perceptible form of kinetic energy. That kinetic energy of movement, in physiological terms, is called a *receptor potential*. In other words, when one disturbs an otherwise equilibrated state of affairs that is capable of responding to that disturbance, there results an energy transformation from potential ("capable of being") to kinetic ("actually being").

In the example presented just now (which is developed and elaborated throughout the remainder of the book), sound energy is produced when molecules of air respond to an impulsive blow from a sound generator. That molecular motion can result from the vibrations set up when one plucks the taut string on a violin, hits the tightly stretched skin of a drum, blows into a wind instrument, or claps the hands together, all of these being sound generators. Sonic vibrations can result also from discharging a bolt of electricity (lightning) through the atmosphere, which is heard as thunder, and so on. But what causes such energy transformations to be cyclic?

To envision what is happening, think of energy transformations as "explosions" that accelerate the affected state from one configuration (previously balanced) to another one (responding to the disturbance). Imagine, for example, that you are holding a rubber ball in your fingers with arm outstretched at shoulder level, and you are maintaining the ball at that level without dropping it (i.e., the ball is in an equilibrated, status-quo physical state). Because of its height above the ground, the ball is capable of dropping; it is endowed with gravitational potential energy that makes it possible for the ball to fall, to be accelerated towards the ground. But the ball doesn't drop, because you are supplying just enough finger muscular effort to prevent that from happening; you are keeping the state of affairs balanced and equilibrated at shoulder level.

Now you let go. The previously equilibrated state of affairs is disturbed by your letting go of the ball. With your muscular effort to counteract gravity now gone, Earth's pull (the adequate stimulus) is allowed to act, uncontested, on the unsupported ball. The gravitational potential energy with which the ball was endowed as a result of its height above the ground allows it to respond to that disturbance. Gravitational potential energy is thus converted into kinetic energy of movement of the ball. When driven by gravity, the ball proceeds to accelerate towards the ground. The transition process is one wherein previously stored (potential) energy – gravitational energy in this case, which is stored in the form of height above the ground – is *transduced*. The energy is converted from one form (gravitational potential) into another (perceivable kinetic energy of movement). The ball falls to the ground, as illustrated in Figure 3.1.

*Figure 3.1 The young man drops a rubber ball and lets it bounce freely on its own. This is an example of free vibrations*

The downward movement of the dropped ball is soon stopped, however, as it hits the ground, so the "explosion" that caused it to drop in the first place is followed by a decelerating, condensing "implosion" as the kinetic energy of downward motion is dissipated. Upon impact between the ball and the ground, much of the kinetic energy of motion is again transduced. Some of it is converted from kinetic into heat energy due to the impact with the ground. Some of the kinetic energy is converted into sound energy, because the impact with the ground also starts surrounding air molecules vibrating, so that the collision can be heard as well. But a good portion of the kinetic energy of downward movement is converted into elastic potential energy that is stored in the rubber material of which the ball is made, when the ground also deforms it on impact. Think of this in the same way that a trampoline yields under the impact of a jumper landing on it.

There follows, then, another "explosion," a new burst of energy. There is an elastic rebound (or recoil) which drives the ball back up almost to where it started – not quite all the way because of the energy lost to heat and noise. It is in that sense that the absolute movement of the ball is referred to as being *irreversible* – it cannot, in and of itself, come all the way back to the original height from which it was dropped. However, at least some of the elastic potential energy is reconverted into upward-moving kinetic energy, which in turn restores some of the gravitational potential energy that the ball started out with. The ball will therefore rise to a new (lower) height at which *all* of the rebound, vertical kinetic energy is used up again, this time being converted (transduced) back into gravitational potential energy.

At this new height the ball will stop momentarily – there will be yet another "implosion." But unless you catch the ball on the rebound, the uncontested action of gravity will once again drive it back to the ground – another "explosion," followed by yet another "implosion." And so the cyclic process continues, the two alternating energy states (potential and kinetic) undulating back and forth like a bouncing rubber ball, or the tides of the sea, or a plucked violin string.

As stated, however, with each cycle some of the energy is lost in irretrievable form, mostly to heat, noise, and aerodynamic drag caused by frictional interactions between the ball and the surrounding air molecules. This is a process called *attenuation*. The cyclic process is said to be *not perfectly elastic*. Thus, eventually, the total energy infused by the original disturbance (like plucking a violin string just once, as opposed to bowing it continuously) is completely dissipated (lost).

If, on the other hand, one continues to add energy in the form of a persistent disturbance (a continuous driving function) – such as when one "dribbles" a basketball, or bows a violin string – the affected state, so long as it is able to, continues to vibrate in response to that disturbance. Alternatively (as will be discussed in Chapter 5) the disturbed state of affairs can adjust its response characteristics to "tolerate" the presence of that disturbance without the need to react to it.

## Recurring events as the essence of all reality

The example of the bouncing rubber ball is intended to illustrate a concept that applies more generally to all manifestations of energy in the universe, from a rotating Ferris wheel to a vibrating reed in a clarinet. That is to say, recognizing the periodicity of energy is the very essence of understanding and quantifying just about anything and everything in this world – most especially as it relates in general to the human experience, and in particular to the relationship between that experience and music. For example, have you ever wondered why we sleep daily, or eat meals several times a day, or have a pulse, or breathe in regular cycles, or eliminate body wastes on a rather regular basis? The answer is really quite obvious. Our bodies are not equipped with the huge resources they would need to carry out the process of living, in one step, from birth to death. Imagine the size of stomach that would be required to accumulate, all at once, at the very instant of birth, all of the food one will ever need throughout a lifetime, to be used as necessary from day one onwards. Not too practical! So, instead, the human body is anatomically endowed with a "gas tank" (called a stomach) that can be regularly filled and emptied several times a day, every day, throughout one's lifetime, to provide for nutritional needs.

Similarly, the heart cannot pump blood throughout the entire body for a lifetime with one single continuous contraction. Because of its limited size, this small organ (having roughly the dimensions of the fist of the individual in whom it resides) must cyclically fill and empty, on average about 60–80 times each minute (at rest) for as long as one is alive. Likewise, one's lungs have to fill with fresh air, and empty the not-so-fresh air about 8–18 times each minute (the resting respiration rate); and, in the absence of a bladder that periodically fills and empties, one would need diapers on a full-time basis.

It is physically impossible for anybody to drink an entire glass of water in a single gulp; or take a long enough stride to get across a room in one single step; or inhale in one breath enough air to last a lifetime. Sensory and motor nerves, like bows and arrows, guns, and other weapons, must load–fire–reload and so on. The essential point is that, given the limited physiological resources and constrained anatomical storage capacity of the human body, it is necessary for it to do whatever it takes to get only part way towards a goal, then repeat the same thing over again to advance a bit further, and so on, going through an iterative process to eventually arrive at its destination.

Inherent to the very way that the body works are *biorhythms*. These are the rhythms of life, the ebb and flow, recurring physiological events that march along at a cadence consistent with the maintenance of both one's own life (survival of the self) and that of the species (which is sometimes affectionately referred to as the human drive for sexual fulfillment).

To be effective, then, any form of clinical intervention that seeks to modulate physiological function, be it through music therapy or otherwise, must be administered with an appreciation for a person's individual-specific biorhythms. The intervention must be individually tailored to be *in phase* (i.e., synchronized) with the regular cycles of physiological function. Otherwise one risks, by ill-timed application of a particular clinical protocol, working against the body, rather than with it to achieve a goal.

## Energy must vibrate

To understand the very essence of music, one must realize further that periodicity is not unique to just the functioning of the human body. As we have seen, energy in all its forms vibrates. It has a *frequency of vibration*, which is the number of cycles per second, determining how that energy is perceived. The unit of measurement for these vibrations is the *cycle per second*, one cycle per second being called a "hertz" in honor of the German physicist Heinrich R. Hertz (1857–1894) and abbreviated to "Hz."

If energy vibrates too fast (beyond ultraviolet light in the electromagnetic spectrum, at around 750–790 million million Hz or higher), humans cannot perceive it at all without technological help in the form of energy-converting transducers. Slow it down into the 400–750 million million Hz (terahertz) range and humans can see the energy, in a *visible spectrum* that ranges from violet at the high end to red at the low end. Slow it down still further, below the color red (i.e., infra-red), into the 1–400 terahertz range, and the energy can be felt as heat through the body's thermal sensors. Infrared radiation from the sun, for example, is the main source of heat on Earth. Below that, at between 100 billion and three million million hertz, one can cook with microwave ovens. FM radios operate in roughly the 80–112 megahertz range (the prefix mega- means one million), and TVs just below that.

Reducing the frequency much further allows one to hear sound energy that vibrates in the 20–20,000 cycle-per-second range (20 Hz to 20 kilohertz, where the prefix kilo- means "thousand"). That is the frequency range within which resides all that is music. The range of the human singing voice is usually from around 80 Hz (a male basso profondo) to 1050 Hz (a female coloratura), and the normal range of speech sounds is between 300 Hz (low-pitched whispers) and 3000 Hz (very high-pitched screams).

In music, the anatomical perception of the frequency at which sound energy vibrates is called the pitch of the sound, with slower vibrations being perceived as lower-pitched sounds, and faster vibrations being perceived as higher-pitched sounds.

The consecutive, step-wise movement from lower pitches (generally not below 30 Hz) to higher pitches (rarely exceeding 8000 Hz) in pre-scribed fashion gives rise to the various musical *scales*. These are specifically designated patterns of sequential step sizes that have a well-defined frequency ratio relative to one another. In fact, the word "scale" derives from the Latin word for "ladder." Together with the *tonal center* upon which the scale is built, known in music as the *key*, this establishes the basis for all musical composition.

Slowing down the frequency of vibration of energy still further allows the body to feel it again, but now as *mechanical* vibrations up to around 2000 Hz, through the sense of touch (the *tactile* sense). Tactile sensations also allow one to touch concentrated, condensed energy that has slowed down so much that it congeals into forms called *mass*.

## Periodicity derived from restoring forces in nature

Periodicity in nature derives also from the further tendency that equilibrated systems have to *maintain their state of equilibrium*. As can easily be demonstrated by examining the physical behavior of a rubber band that is pulled taut and then sharply plucked, *elastic restoring forces* tend to drive systems that have been disturbed back to their previously equilibrated (resting) state. However, *inertia* causes these systems to overshoot their resting position, and like a swinging pendulum again there results cyclical motion. This, too, decays with time if the disturbance is not persistent.

Thus, the combination of the very physics of the way equilibrated states respond to disturbances (i.e., generating restoring forces, complicated by inertia) together with the very nature of how transitions take place from one equilibrated state to another (i.e., alternating between motion-inducing potential and energy-dissipating kinetic states) requires such transitions and responses to *pulsate* with well-defined frequencies. Not all of these pulsations are perceptible to humans. For example, we cannot hear ultrasound frequencies, or see ultraviolet light, or feel X-rays. The human sense of perception is bracketed between frequencies of around zero cycles per second (Hz) and approximately 800 million million Hz.

Cycles are prevalent everywhere in the world of physics. Earth rotates around its axis once every 24 hours. The planets revolve around the sun, each with its own period of revolution (the time it takes to complete one full cycle, as in the monthly female menstrual period). Birds flap their wings; dogs wag their tails; tides come in and out; floating objects bob up and down on the surface of a pond. *Rhythm is everywhere!* So much so, that one can accept as an axiom (a premise accepted without proof) that *all* forms of reality are cyclic in their regular manifestations, such cycles being of large and small scale. Depending on that scale of recurrence, the energy from which all reality derives is perceivable in an entire spectrum of forms; it is, indeed, *omnifarious!*

Given the universality of periodicity, it should not be surprising to note that rhythm is the most fundamental element of music. And rhythms in music coupled with rhythms in physiological function (biorhythms) share a profound symbiotic relationship, so that musical rhythms are capable of eliciting intense physiological effects – as shall be elaborated upon in much greater detail in Chapter 7.

Also of note is the fact that periodicity is an essential ingredient in physiological entrainment (Chapter 6), which, in turn, is perhaps the most basic element of both cognitive learning and sub-cognitive accommodation (Chapter 5). In other words, as every teacher, performer, and athlete knows, the body becomes "convinced" only when sensory stimulation is reinforced through repetition. Practice does, indeed, make perfect!

## Further quantification of energy

It has thus far been established that forms of energy vibrate at frequencies that determine the manner in which they are perceived. The frequencies are from near zero, characteristic of certain concentrated, macroscopic forms of mass, to almost infinite, typical of certain diffuse, microscopic forms of ethereal, virtually imperceptible, sub-nuclear radiation. The frequency of vibration determines how the various realizations of energy are experienced: sub-nuclear, nuclear, atomic, electromagnetic (such as light, X-rays, and radio waves), molecular (e.g., chemical), thermodynamic (e.g., microwave, thermal, heat, infrared), sonic (sound), mechanical, radioactive, gravitational, cosmic, super-cosmic, and so on. Humans are anatomically, technologically, and intellectually endowed with the ability to perceive and interpret energy in but a small window of this infinite range.

## Natural frequencies

In order to extend this reasoning in a way that will ultimately allow one to understand "the music effect," the concepts introduced so far must be developed further. Consider, then, what happens if a tuned violin string is plucked and then allowed to vibrate on its own terms, unobstructed. This string will undergo cyclic vibrations at a very characteristic frequency, perhaps 440 cycles per second (which one hears and is taught to perceive as a concert-pitch "A"). The fact that the string is allowed to vibrate unobstructed (similarly to how the rubber ball shown in Figure 3.1 was allowed to bounce on its own once dropped) classifies this motion as *free vibrations*. They are "free" in the sense of not being under any external control, apart from the string attachments. The frequency at which the string vibrates freely is called its *natural frequency*, which depends on four things: the thickness of the string, its length between fixed supports, the material of which it is made, and the tension to which it is strung.

The first three attributes – thickness, material, and length between supports (which can be varied by putting a finger down on the string to secure it at different points between the finger and the bridge of the instrument) – determine the total mass of string that is actually vibrating. The last attribute – string tension – depends on how tightly the string (mass) is wound, which affects the strength of elastic restoring forces that continuously drive the string back to its unplucked, resting position. All four attributes are unique to the particular A-string that is plucked, hence the term "natural" frequency. For a given length of string, if one increases its mass (making it harder to move, increasing its inertial resistance to changes in movement) and decreases its tension (thereby reducing the restoring forces) the natural frequency of vibration of the string, and hence its pitch, goes down. This is the case, for example, when going from the violin A-string (at 440 Hz) to the D-string (at just under 294 Hz) and down to the G-string (196 Hz). Conversely, if one decreases the mass and increases the tension, the natural frequency of vibration (pitch) goes up – for example, to the thinner, tighter violin E-string at just over 659 Hz.

Like the violin strings, the various organs and tissues of the human body also have associated with them natural frequencies of free vibration, depending on their composition, mass (size), state of muscle tension (analogous to the tautness of the violin string), physical state (including firmness), and body posture relative to the direction of vibration. The natural frequency of the entire human body, taken as a whole, ranges from as little as 4 Hz to as much as 14 Hz. The natural frequency of the brain ranges from around 0.5 Hz to 2 Hz; that of skeletal muscles, 1 Hz to 15 Hz. The trunk vibrates naturally at 3–7 Hz; the abdomen at 4–8 Hz; the heart, passively, at 4–6 Hz (although it "beats" actively at 1–4 Hz); the chest wall at 60 Hz; the entire head at 5–20 Hz; the lower arms at 16–30 Hz; the eyeballs at 1–100 Hz (but especially in the range 20–70 Hz); the jaw of the skull at 100–200 Hz; and individual nerves and neural networks at 2000 Hz down to 5 Hz – to name but a few.

Note that a good number of these natural frequencies of vibration lie in the lower range of human hearing, and within the normal range of the human voice, from 80 to 1050 Hz. Is it any wonder, then, that the human body is so responsive to sound energy in general, and to music in particular?

## Amplitude and attenuation

Before pursuing this thought further, it is necessary to revisit the example of the bouncing rubber ball shown in Figure 3.1, in order to introduce some more physical concepts and technical terminology related to the quantification of vibrations.

If the rubber ball is dropped and then left alone (like plucking the violin string just once), it will bounce up and down freely at its own natural rate. This rate will also depend on the mass of the ball, including the material of which it is made, its size, and the extent to which it is inflated (analogous to the tension in the violin string). But remember that, with each bounce, the ball will rebound a certain vertical distance above the ground before pausing momentarily prior to resuming its downward trajectory. Assuming one does not interfere with this natural motion by catching the ball on the rebound, or "dribbling" it like a basketball, the height to which the ball will rise with each bounce introduces the concept of *amplitude of vibration*, to set alongside the frequency of vibration (the number of times per second that the ball bounces).

Intuitively, one can guess that the height to which the ball will rise with each bounce is, in some sense, related to the energy with which the ball is endowed during its motion, and that is precisely the case. That is to say, the original height from which the ball was dropped (which determines its original gravitational *potential* energy) will determine with what *kinetic* energy of motion it strikes the ground, which in turn will determine how high the rebound will be. That, again, will determine how hard the ball will hit the ground the next time it falls, and so on, until all of that original potential energy is eventually used up, and the ball finally comes to rest on the ground. That the original potential energy *is* eventually totally dissipated (in reality, converted into a pool of non-usable forms) is related to the concept of *attenuation* introduced earlier in this chapter.

Attenuation (literally, energy "thinning") refers to the progressive weakening and eventual dying out of intensity due to the wasting away of energy from usable forms into non-usable ones. As it applies to sound energy, this process includes losses that result from physical phenomena such as:

- reverberation – how echoes deteriorate and eventually die out when sound waves pulsate back and forth from reflecting surfaces

- absorption – how sound waves are intercepted and assimilated by the various media through which they pass

- refraction – the "bending" of a sound wave as it moves *at an angle* from one medium, such as air, into another, such as the human body, where its speed of travel is substantially different

- diffraction – the "bending" of a sound wave around an obstacle in its path, or its spreading out as it passes through an aperture

- dispersion – a term that will be defined and discussed in somewhat greater detail when sound quality, or timbre, is discussed in Chapter 9.

The amplitude of vibration of energy is thus a measure of its intensity.

As it relates to hearing, sound energy is perceived by the human auditory system as the loudness or softness of sound ("volume," in the vernacular), because the energy contained in a sound wave is directly converted into the amplitude of the undulations which the ear drum experiences (discussed in some detail in Chapter 8). In musical terms, the degree of loudness and softness is embedded in the element called dynamics, to which a large portion of Chapter 9 is dedicated. Thus, the frequency of the sound wave becomes the corresponding frequency of vibration of the ear drum (the perceived pitch), and this is paired with the amplitude of the sound wave energy that impinges upon the ear drum, which becomes the corresponding amplitude of vibration of the ear drum (sound dynamics, or "volume"). If the ear drum vibrates too wildly (i.e., is exposed to a very loud sound), it tugs against its anatomical supports with such great pull that the sound energy is experienced as pain.

The ability of the human ear to detect changes in pitch is quite variable between individuals, and depends on many factors, some of which have clinical implications. However, on average, the absolute minimum difference in sound frequency that the human ear can detect is between 2 Hz and 4 Hz (Buser and Imbert 1992, pp.28–32), which in turn determines the minimum step size of any practical musical scale. This ability that a sense organ has to discriminate between two input signals that arrive very close together in space and/or in time is called *physiological resolution* (as distinct from *harmonic resolution* in music, which refers to the progression from one, usually dissonant, sonority to another, usually consonant, one). The concepts of consonance and dissonance relate to how the auditory system perceives two or more pitches that are sounded together, which gives rise to the musical element called *harmony*, addressed more specifically in Chapter 9.

The unit known as a *decibel* (abbreviated dB) quantifies vibration amplitude or loudness. One decibel is defined to be the minimum difference in sound intensity that the human ear can detect, with zero decibels being assigned to the loudness threshold of human hearing. This threshold, the absolutely softest sound that the typical ear can detect, corresponds to a sound intensity of one millionth of one millionth (i.e., one trillionth) of a watt of sound power, per square meter of surface area on which it impacts. On this scale we can identify a few common intensities:

- the average whisper, 10–20 dB

- a quiet radio at home, 40 dB

- normal conversation levels, 50–65 dB

- a person singing fortissimo (very loudly), standing three feet away from you, 70 dB

- chamber music in a small auditorium, 75–85 dB

- the sound of a cello, 82–92 dB

- the sound of a violin, 84–103 dB

- the sound of a flute, 85–111 dB

- a gas-powered lawn mower, 105 dB

- an indoor rock concert, 90–120 dB (which, at an intensity level of one watt per square meter, is the lowest threshold of human ear pain).

In this respect, it is interesting to note that the world's champion "loud-noise-making" animals are blue whales, whose ear-splitting melodies can reach 188 dB underwater (corresponding to 162 dB in air). That is more than 100 times louder than a roaring jet engine!

## "Forcing" the issue

Consider again the case of the bouncing ball, and now suppose that one *does* decide to "dribble" it, as illustrated in Figure 3.2. That is to say, rather than just dropping the ball and letting it bounce free, at its own natural frequency, the number of bounces per minute is now *externally imposed* on the ball, "forcing" it to bounce at a rate that is determined by the person dribbling the ball. That rate is called a *driving* or *forcing* frequency. The result is that the previously defined free vibrations now become *forced vibrations*. The dribbler (technically called the *forcing function*) controls the motion of the ball, not the ball itself. In scientific terminology, the ball has now become a *controlled system*, and the dribbler has taken on the role of a *continuous disturbance* – a persistent, external forcing function that controls the behavior of that system.

In the chapters that follow, in which the role of music in the human experience is examined, the human body becomes the controlled system (the "ball" in the analogue of Figures 3.1 and 3.2), and the various elements of music, as sensory stimuli, become the continuous disturbance (the "dribbler") to that system – the persistent forcing functions that elicit specific physiological responses which have corresponding clinical implications. Chapter 6 introduces the various physiological processes by which the body is endowed with the ability to:

- perceive music (capture it through its auditory architecture, and interpret it through its various information-processing networks)

- allow it to gain access to its various sub-systems ("board the train," so to speak)

- thereby affect a response to that form of sensory stimulation.

*Figure 3.2 The young man is dribbling a basketball, forcing it to bounce at a rate that he determines. Thus, the vibrations are not free, as they were in Figure 3.1, but are forced, being driven at a rate other than the natural frequency of the ball.*

In keeping with the "board the train" analogy, the above considerations are collectively referred to by the very appropriate term, *entrainment* (derived from the French *traîner* meaning literally "to drag"). Chapter 6 is devoted entirely to physiological entrainment, the means by which music gains access to, and hence "dribbles," the human body, thus controlling its physio-logical function.

*Resonance*

One of the most interesting aspects of forced vibrations concerns what happens if one deliberately dribbles the ball at its natural frequency; that is, it is driven at a rate exactly equal to that at which it would bounce on its own if not forced. In physics, this entrainment phenomenon is called *resonance*. You might be familiar with resonance if you have ever experienced a piece of furniture starting to vibrate along with a musical instrument being played in the same or nearby room. In this case, the sound frequencies being generated by the instrument (acting as an external forcing function on the furniture) happen to coincide exactly with the natural frequencies of the material of which the furniture is made. Thus, the material *resonates* with the sound, being driven by it, entraining it, and thereby being set into oscillatory motion through a phenomenon known as *sympathetic vibrations*. Physiological sympathetic vibrations to music are one form of entrainment that elicits profound adaptive responses in humans.

### The frequency spectrum, bandwidth, and harmonic analysis

No material is absolutely perfect. If it is set in motion (like plucking or bowing a violin string to start it vibrating) the material will not generate a pure, single-frequency pitch, which is technically referred to as a *tone*. A string in its entirety *does* vibrate at a predominant number of cycles per second, its fundamental frequency, which depends on its total mass, length between supports, and tension. But, viewing more closely, one observes that within this overall integrated motion, individual parts of the string are actually vibrating at frequencies higher than or lower than the fundamental. This is because neither the material of which the string is made, nor the instrument through which its vibrations are transmitted to an imperfect environment and an imperfect human body, are entirely uniform and perfectly homogeneous (uniform) throughout. None of these sound-generating or sound-transmitting or sound-receiving elements vibrates *exactly* the same way everywhere, nor reacts *exactly* the same way in all directions to being plucked or bowed or otherwise disturbed from an equilibrated state. Quite to the contrary; the imperfections result in the generation not of a *single* frequency of pure vibration (i.e., a tone), but rather a *range* of frequencies centered on the fundamental, this range being known as a *frequency spectrum*.

If one plots, on graph paper, *frequency* along the horizontal axis versus the perceived intensity of that frequency (*dominance*) along the vertical axis, there typically results, for the frequency spectrum of any given sound generator, a bell-shaped curve centered around the fundamental frequency. This is known as *Normal distribution*. The fundamental frequency exhibits the most dominant presence, and the curve falls off "normally" to either side of the fundamental frequency. Thus, what is correspondingly defined is called a *Normally distributed frequency spectrum*.

The generation of a frequency spectrum is, technically, what distinguishes a musical *note* (i.e., a range of frequencies Normally distributed around a fundamental dominant frequency) from a *tone* (i.e., a pure, single-frequency sound). It is this frequency spectrum that gives musical notes a quality (timbre) as well as a pitch. Timbre is addressed in some detail in Chapter 9.

The range of frequencies, from the lowest in the spectrum to the highest, is called the *bandwidth* of the spectrum. A *narrow* bandwidth identifies a more perfect material, since the frequencies are clustered tightly around the fundamental, which indicates that nearly all of the material is vibrating at or near the same fundamental frequency. A *broad* bandwidth identifies a much less perfect material, since the frequencies are spread out widely around the fundamental, indicating that much of the material is vibrating at a wide variety of different frequencies. In physics the quantification of a frequency spectrum is referred to as *harmonic analysis*.

In music the higher harmonics, those generated above the fundamental frequency in integral multiples of that frequency (i.e., 1, 2, 3…times its value), are called the *overtone series* of the note. Although less common, the lower harmonics, those generated below the fundamental frequency in fractional multiples of that frequency (i.e., 0.5, 0.25, 0.125…times its value), are called its *undertone series*.

Life would be rather dull if materials were perfect, because the frequency spectrum generated by imperfect materials is what allows one to experience a characteristic quality to the sound that is generated. In fact, that very quality is what allows somebody to hear a voice and recognize it; to distinguish a violin sound from that of a trumpet, or a trumpet from that of a flute; to "cringe" when scratching his or her fingernails on a chalk-board; to become alert when hearing a siren; to calm down when listening to the gentle ripples of a babbling brook or other sounds of nature. And the broader the bandwidth, the richer the quality of the sound; the narrower the bandwidth, the more "nasal" (computer-like) the sound.

As mentioned, in musical terms the quality of sound associated with its frequency spectrum gives rise to the element known as timbre, which is quantified by a harmonic analysis that defines both the frequency components (in hertz) that comprise the spectrum, and the associated amplitude (in decibels) – which is also a measure of the relative prominence – of each component that contributes to that spectrum. To this point, then, in our developing formulation of the elements of music, *timbre* (Chapter 9) can be added to *rhythm* (the inherent ebb-and-flow attribute of all that is real, considered in Chapter 7), *pitch* (now considered to be associated with the *fundamental frequency* of a *note*, examined in more detail in Chapter 8), and *dynamics* (related to the volume of the integrated sound, as discussed in Chapter 9). Also addressed in much greater detail later in this book are the remaining three elements: *melody* (pitches strung together in specific sequences, considered in Chapter 8), *harmony* (two or more pitches sounded together in specific intervals, considered in Chapter 9), and *form* (the integrated expression of an idea, considered in Chapter 10).

In general, a typical human ear should be able to discriminate among some 400,000 sounds that involve different combinations of pitch, loudness, and timbre, but how does it do this? In other words, how are adequate stimuli received and processed by the body's various senses? Hearing, in particular, will be examined more closely in Chapter 8, but the underlying principles involved, which are common to all forms of physiological sensory perception, are described briefly in the following section.

## Conversion of sensory inputs into digitized information

Earlier, it was pointed out that all of the human body's anatomical sense organs fall into the category of information-processing devices known as transducers. That is to say, they convert an adequate stimulus (a particular form of energy to which each is responsive) from the incident form that excites them into a physiological form that the body can handle. Examples are light which excites the eyes, sound which stimulates the ears, heat to which the body's thermal sensors respond, vibration which energizes tactile sensors, and chemical forms of energy which titillate taste and smell receptors. In each case, the conversion is to an electrochemical, physiological form of energy known as a receptor potential. Should the receptor potential reach a threshold value, it triggers a cascading sequence of events which result in the subsequent transportation of the transduced signal – now in the form of a propagating action potential – through elaborate neural networks, to the central nervous system (spinal cord plus brain) for further processing. These anatomical events are explained further in Chapter 4, and the "further processing" (especially as it relates to the individual elements of music) is addressed more specifically in Chapters 5–11.

Action potentials are the human body's digital syntax, its vocabulary, its "body language" (not to be confused with the more common use of this terminology). Encoded into these Morse-code-like sensory signals is a transduced form of the information that was contained in the original adequate stimulus.

In a way, one can think of the original adequate stimulus as a particular type of foreign language. The sense organ that understands that language then takes on the role of a translator; and the action potentials become the human body's language, into which the foreign language has been translated by the respective sense organ. Viewed in that sense, the elements of music really are a universal language, in that the human body is particularly adept at translating these elements and responding to them quite effectively. Music can "speak" to the body in a way that no other form of communication can, and the body understands, and it responds!

The body's physiological signals are digital. By that it is meant that they have a particular on/off cyclic firing pattern, with a distinct motif or style of presentation, not unlike barcodes on product labels. Moreover, action potentials are of four types, broken down into two groups of two. The two groups are sensory and motor:

- Sensory action potentials are the type that have been addressed thus far, which are transduced signals carrying information from various sense organs to the central nervous system via *afferent* (Latin *afferre*, meaning "to carry to") nerve pathways.

- Motor action potentials carry control signals from the central nervous system out to muscles and glands, exciting them via *efferent* (Latin *efferre*, meaning "to carry away") nerve pathways.

Within each group, the action potentials can be either *excitatory* (*causing* something to happen) or *inhibitory* (*preventing* something from happening).

Action potentials are transported by nerve (communications) networks, the information encoded into them being transmitted from nerve to nerve along these networks at junctions called *synapses* (literally, the plural of "to fasten together"). The transmission mechanism that occurs at neural synapses is not unlike a typical human relay race. It involves the upstream (*pre-synaptic*) nerve, which carries the information being transported, literally squirting (relaying) into the junction a type of biochemical *neurotransmitter*. Depending on the type (opiate-like enkephalins, excitatory norepinephrine, acetylcholine, etc.) and quantity of neurotransmitter involved, it can do one of two things to the downstream (*post-synaptic*) nerve. It can stimulate this nerve, stirring it to become active, in which case it is referred to as an *excitatory impulse* (akin to the receiving runner grabbing the baton and taking off with it). Alternatively the pre-synaptic nerve can enjoin the post-synaptic nerve to remain still, in which case the neurotransmitter involved is said to cause an *inhibitory impulse* (akin to the receiving runner not being able to get the baton out of the previous runner's hand, because the latter is deliberately holding on to it and using it as a way of also restraining the receiving runner from continuing on with the race).

The actual information that is transmitted across a synapse is encoded both spatially (i.e., *which* nerve in the network is "firing" at any given time), and temporally (i.e., the *rate* at which the respective nerve is firing, which in turn determines *how much* neurotransmitter is squirted into the synaptic space). The latter is referred to as *pulse frequency modulation* (better known as FM). To learn much more about the structure and function of human neural networks, see Schneck (1990) and Tortora and Grabowski (1993).

## Energy as a life force

The foregoing elementary discussion of basic principles of energy has used *inanimate* examples of bouncing rubber balls and vibrating strings to illustrate fundamental concepts, but it is necessary to consider how energy manifests itself as a life force, as well. That is to say, inanimate examples can be used effectively to derive the most fundamental physical principles that underlie one's ability to perceive energy, in general, as an adequate stimulus, and sound in particular as the stimulus most closely associated with music. But, after all is said and done, it is the *human being* that responds to such stimulation in ways that are of interest in this book. Furthermore, although the principles of physics introduced in this chapter have allowed for the systematic quantification of one's perception of sound energy, in terms of music elements called rhythm, pitch, dynamics, and timbre (to which are added melody, harmony, and form), they fall short of explaining how and why the body responds the way it does to these elements of music. Why? Because conspicuously missing from the discussion thus far is one very important aspect of the response of physical systems to disturbing forces.

Consider the following. In the examples of this chapter, the response of such physical systems has been tacitly assumed to be totally *passive*. That is to say, except by virtue of its inherent properties, which include the material of which the ball is made, the extent to which it is inflated by the application of internal air pressure, and its physical size, the ball cannot *actively* ("consciously") resist either the effects of gravity, or one's attempts to dribble it! The controlled system (the ball), in this case, reacts only passively to an external forcing function (gravity, dribbler, etc.); and the response (i.e., the *output* of the controlled system) to such a disturbance (i.e., the *input* to the controlled system) is quantified by a fixed parameter known as a system *transfer function*. The controlled system's transfer function is simply the ratio of output to input. It is thus a measure of the effectiveness of the adequate stimulus (input) in causing a passive conversion of potential energy (a system-response attribute) into kinetic energy (output), and so quantifies the passive response characteristics of the system to various adequate stimuli.

But among the most interesting and exciting manifestations of energy are those that result in various forms of *life* on this planet, some of which (like animal forms) can lead to active (controlled, purposeful) responses to adequate stimuli. Thus, as it relates in particular to human life, the obvious questions that arise at this point are: What, exactly, do we mean by "alive"? What makes us different from a bouncing ball? What can the human body do that a bouncing rubber ball cannot? What is meant by an "active" response to an adequate stimulus? And, if the adequate stimulus arrives in the form of the various elements of music, how does the human body receive and respond to these? Finally, how can an understanding of such responses be exploited for clinical purposes? Read on!

Chapter 4

# Principles of Physiology and the Elements of Sensory Information-processing

We know absolutely nothing about physiology, and I can prove it: if we knew anything about physiology, physiology textbooks wouldn't be so thick!

Y. C. Fung, University of California at San Diego

## Introduction

Chapter 3 was devoted to the basic physics of energy and vibration, and although the examples dealt with mechanical vibrations that can be seen, the physical principles involved are exactly the same at *any* scale of perception, including those that cannot easily be visualized. At the level of perception that involves sound energy, the ball dribbler might just as well be the vibrating tongs of a tuning fork, or any other sound generator, such as a musical instrument or one's vocal cords. The "ball" then becomes the various molecules of air that surround the vibrating fork and are thereby struck by it; and one's ear drum takes the place of the "ground" that the ball strikes as a result of its having been driven there by the dribbler (actually, since the ear drum is not rigid, the analogy is closer to a trampoline, rather than a solid surface). So, one now "hears" the vibrating molecules being driven by the tuning fork, rather than "seeing" a bouncing ball being dribbled by an athlete. The *physics* of what's happening is exactly the same in both cases, and the corresponding attributes of this physics (frequency, amplitude, and so on), defined in Chapter 3, carry over verbatim.

In the remainder of this book our attention turns to how the human body, driven by the vibrations inherent in the elements of music (adequate stimuli), responds to such continuous *forcing functions*, and how those responses can be exploited for clinical purposes. In attempting to analyze such responses, however, one cannot avoid dealing with questions like these: When can an assemblage of atoms and molecules be considered to be "living," and thus *actively* and *purposely* responsive to external stimuli? What makes "living" things different from objects that are considered to be "inanimate," and thus only *passively* affected by their environment? As a living creature, what is this thing called "me"? What makes "me" tick? What drives me to respond to external stimulation with a *purpose*, which is to satisfy certain fundamental human needs? What are those needs, and how does music, as an adequate stimulus, relate to all this?

The above are excellent questions, for which, unfortunately, science does not yet have all the answers. Indeed, as was true when the concept of energy was considered in Chapter 3, one encounters the frustration of not really being able to define "life" in a rigorous, precise, unambiguous, satisfying way. And yet, life is what humans are all about – surviving, accomplishing, pro-creating, enjoying, *living* it! Music can and does have a significant influence on all these. This chapter therefore introduces some basic anatomical and physiological concepts that underlie the nature of living systems in general, and how they respond to music in particular (i.e., the music effect), beginning with the specific attributes that distinguish living systems from inanimate ones, and continuing through:

- how the human organism's information-processing networks conform to a standard feedback/feedforward control paradigm

- what it is about this paradigm that allows the human body to be driven by external inputs such as those embedded in the elements of music

- how the body handles sensory information, including the *Gestalt* laws of perception that govern the organization of such information

- the various levels of physiological information-processing, and the hierarchy of priorities that are considered at each level as the body decides if, and how, to respond to sensory stimulation (especially that which is perceived to be a threat to survival)

- how the processing of sensory information is limited by anatomical and physiological constraints.

The material presented below will form the basis for the chapters that follow, in which we will explore where, and how, the clinical uses of music can effectively exploit these physiological principles for the benefit of the patient.

## Attributes of living systems

Life, like energy, can only be described, rather than defined, and to describe life is to list the attributes by which it is characterized. In point of fact, the very essence of life itself was introduced in Chapter 3: its attributes are embedded in the general concept of active (as opposed to passive) physiological *transduction* (the conversion of one form of energy into another). Transduction, as it relates to the processes of life, manifests itself by the ability of living systems to actively:

- metabolize
- move
- respond
- grow and develop
- reproduce
- control.

### Metabolism

Derived from the Greek *metabolē*, which means "change," metabolism is the generic process whereby living organisms actively ingest food and inhale air, and then convert ("change," transduce) that air/fuel mixture into a stored form of potential energy. The transduction process involves converting some of the caloric value of *chemical* energy that is inherent in the ingested air/fuel mixture into stored forms of biochemical potential energy, such as the chemical compound adenosine triphosphate (ATP, the body's "battery"), that later serve to drive all physiological processes. Thus, the term "metabolism" also designates those subsequent conversions or transductions, wherein the *usable* portion of that stored potential energy is drawn upon and converted into kinetic energy to accomplish purposeful activities. The non-usable or non-recyclable portions of the various forms of energy involved in metabolism, as well as the waste products of metabolic conversions, are exhausted to the environment through several excretory systems, such as the large intestine/colon, the lungs, the kidneys, and the skin.

Moreover, all of the various conversions are enhanced by enzymatically catalyzed (i.e., carefully controlled) biochemical reactions. The body leaves *nothing* to chance!

## Movement

As described in the previous chapter, movement (kinetic energy) is the essence of reality in general, and of life in particular. Metabolic processes transduce some of the potential energy stored in the body's "battery" (ATP) into perceptible kinetic energy of motion. Indeed, the biochemical processes themselves rely on movement at the atomic and molecular scales of perception; without such movement, no metabolism would be possible. Similarly, the physical processes by which usable energy derived from metabolism becomes *real* at macroscopic scales of perception, such as those associated with activities of daily living, derive from movement. These activities include maintaining posture, locomotion of all or parts of the body, balance and equilibrium, speaking, hearing, tasting, smelling, touching, hugging, kissing, reproducing, playing musical instruments, and so on. Without movement, no perception is possible. Indeed, without movement, without the transduction of potential energy into kinetic energy, *nothing* is possible! That's why, in feedback/feedforward control terminology, the output of the controlled system that is the human body is some type of movement at varying scales of perception, ranging from microscopic to macroscopic.

## Responsiveness

Responsiveness, in biological terminology, refers to the processes by which living systems are able to perceive (detect) and react to sensory stimulation. Recall from Chapter 3 that perception involves the interoceptive/exteroceptive transduction (in this case, by anatomical sense organs) of adequate stimuli (specific forms of energy), into *afferent action potentials*. The latter are nerve signals that transmit information to the central nervous system (CNS) – the brain and spinal cord. Recall further that reactions to sensory stimulation involve the generation by the central nervous system of *efferent action potentials* (see Figure 4.1) that carry commands *from* the CNS to target organs and tissues, which include peripheral nerve networks, muscles, and glands, either exciting them, or inhibiting them as necessary.

In the language of engineering control theory, afferent action potentials are called *feedback control signals*. These are generated by sensing mechanisms designed to monitor both the environment (exteroceptive special senses,

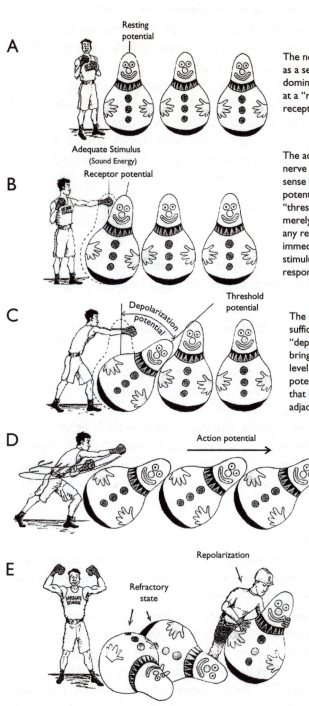

**A** Resting potential

The nerve is depicted schematically as a series of pins (like a line of dominoes) lined up in "readiness," at a "resting potential" that is receptive to an "adequate stimulus."

**B** Adequate Stimulus (Sound Energy)
Receptor potential

The adequate stimulus excites the nerve ending of the corresponding sense organ, generating a "receptor potential" which is below "threshold" – so the head pin merely "teeters" but does not cause any response from the pin to its immediate right. The adequate stimulus is too weak to produce a response ("action potential").

**C** Depolarization potential    Threshold potential

The adequate stimulus is now of sufficient strength to produce a "deplorarization potential," that brings the nerve to the threshold level required to generate an action potential (i.e., a sequence of events that progressively knock down adjacent pins).

**D** Action potential

In domino-like fashion, the action potential causes the nerve to "fire" propagating a signal from its source at the sense organ, to its destination at the central nervous system.

**E** Repolarization
Refractory state

Once the pins are knocked down by the action potential, the nerve is in a "refractory state," unable to respond to a second stimulus until its pins are "reset," a process called "repolarization," back to the resting state (A), so that the nerve is ready to fire again.

*Figure 4.1 Simulation of the generation of action potentials in nerves*

such as vision and audition) and the actual performance or output of the controlled system (interoceptive senses, such as proprioception and those that monitor body temperature and blood pressure).

Information coded into feedback control signals is sent by afferent pathways to a central command station, the anatomical CNS, where the actual state of affairs is compared with a desired one. The latter consists of operating set-points or *homeostatic reference values* that are coded into the CNS's data bank (e.g., its genome). If the actual and desired outputs don't match well enough, a corresponding *error signal* is generated, depending on:

- the *extent* of actual disagreement between existing and desired states of affair, responses to which are known technically as *proportional control*

- the *rate* at which this extent of disagreement is or is not changing, called *differential control* triggered by a varying error signal

- the historical *persistence* of that error signal, responses to which are referred to as *integral control*.

Integral control may eventually trigger *adaptive* responses (see below), which will be discussed further in Chapter 5, and which are the very basis of clinical intervention through the use of music.

In engineering control theory, efferent action potentials generated by the CNS in response to error signals are called simply "control signals" because of their obvious function. Subsequent chapters examine this feature of feedback control systems as it relates specifically to the various elements of music.

### Growth and development

Growth and development is the process by which what started out as a single, viable living cell matures into a fully fledged, totally developed adult organism. Growth of somatic cells proceeds via a process called *mitosis*. Somatic cells are all body cells except red blood cells, which do not reproduce, and reproductive cells, which undergo a different type of cell division, to produce gametes (germ cells). In ripening through mitosis, the parent cell of a plant or animal divides to form two new "daughter" cells, each having the same number of chromosomes as the original cell. The latter then divide again to yield four offspring, which in turn produce eight progeny, and so on, until the number balloons to some one-hundred-trillion cells in the adult human.

The concept of growth, as it applies to more complex living systems, includes two additional considerations, cellular differentiation and regeneration.

### CELLULAR DIFFERENTIATION

The single cell that was originally "me" at conception becomes specialized, so that as I grow from a fertilized egg, to an embryo, to a fetus, to a baby, to a toddler, to a child, to an adolescent, and finally to an adult, the 100-trillion-celled organism that is the new "me" has been differentiated into more than 200 different types of cell that, collectively, can perform all of the functions necessary to keep me and my species alive.

### CELLULAR REGENERATION

A living organism can replenish and renew its various constituents, as necessary, throughout its lifetime. As cells develop, they are actually *programmed* to die, "committing suicide" as it were, through a process called *apoptosis* (derived from a Greek word that describes leaves falling off of trees). The reasons for this are many, including age-related damage to cellular DNA that prevents the cell from reproducing properly.[1] Suffice it to say here that, of the more than 200 different cell varieties in the human body, some (like certain types of brain cells) may survive for virtually the entire life of the individual; others (like certain types of white blood cells) may survive for just a few seconds. In general about 0.003 percent of cells in the body (some three billion) die and are replenished (mostly in the skin and blood) every single minute of every single day!

## Reproduction

One of the key distinctions between living systems and inanimate ones is the ability that the former have to make more like themselves, to beget offspring. In the case of humans, where the reproductive process is sexual (as opposed to asexual, such as is the case in certain plant-like budding mechanisms), reproduction is not just a matter of cloning, but rather of *breeding* as well –

---

1       DNA stands for deoxyribonucleic acid, the natural carbohydrate constituent of cell nuclei. It is a fundamental component of living tissue.

improving the species with each succeeding generation, in the Darwinian sense of "natural selection."

Thus, through the process of *meiosis* (from the Latin for "a lessening"), when the reproductive cells of sexually procreating organisms divide, the number of chromosomes in the "daughter" cells (gametes) is reduced by half, forming *haploid* cells. Haploid gametes from contributing male and female adult parents then combine in a process called *fertilization* to produce a *zygote*, which is the stem cell that will undergo differentiation to ultimately produce an individual who has never existed before, and who will never exist again (Schneck 2001a). The zygote has had the *diploid* number of chromosomes (46 in humans) restored, and if all went well it should grow and mature satisfactorily. Unfortunately, all does not always go well, leading to what are called *congenital* afflications, existing at birth, which may be inherited from either or both parents, or which may result from *in-utero* complications all the way up to the moment of birth.

The drive to procreate is the second strongest human drive (survival of the self being the first). Third is the drive for spiritual fulfillment, and fourth is the need to control one's own destiny. The first two are clearly anatomical/physiological needs common to all living systems. The latter two might be termed "egocentric," or "anthropocentric" needs, in the sense that they are unique to humans. However, at the morphological level, control is much more basic than just a desire to have input into one's own destiny, as alluded to earlier and explained further below.

## Control

In Chapter 1, the concept of *homeostasis* was introduced, which involves all of the processes by which the human body seeks to maintain, within narrow prescribed limits, those variables (such as vital signs) that are critical for the maintenance of life. In living systems, nothing is left to chance because the potential consequences are too great. Thus, as Milsum (1966) aptly points out:

> Living systems are termed goal-seeking or purposive because within limits they clearly choose or adapt their courses of action out of many possible alternatives, so as to sustain their existences under varying environmental disturbances. This statement applies equally to all levels of a hierarchical set of living systems from the cell to the ecology. (p.400)

Note, especially, the facts that (1) the behavior of all living systems is *purpose-ful*, seeking to satisfy both physiological and egocentric needs; and (2) physiological control is *adaptive*, allowing the organism to establish operating set-points that accommodate various environmental threats to both its own survival and that of the species. Thus, the "window for survival" requires that homeostatic variables be coded into the body's various operating set-points.

To summarize, a working definition of human life might go something like this:

> Those energy conversions (processes of transduction) that result in controlled, purposeful activities (output of the controlled system) that are intended to satisfy specific physiological (homeostatic) and egocentric (behavioral) human needs.

Such a working definition, couched in the paradigm developed below, is important, because effective clinical interventions must begin with a fundamental understanding of what motivates human behavior, and how such motivation is coded into physiological operating parameters. In other words, the therapist must work *with* the body, in accordance with *how* the body works!

We will have more to say about operating set-points in subsequent chapters, because it is through its ability to re-set these performance criteria that music can elicit such profound responses that can be used clinically to alter physiological function. In anticipation of that discussion, however, it is of interest to first explore further how sensory information is processed by the body in order to maintain, through purposeful function and adaptive control, the condition of homeostasis that is so critical for survival.

## Feedback control paradigm for the physiological processing of sensory information

Throughout this book so far, and as a result of the research and clinical efforts of the authors (Berger 2002; Berger and Schneck 2003; Schneck 1990, 1997, 2003a, 2003b; Schneck and Berger 1999; Schneck and Schneck 1996), and many other investigators (e.g. Damasio 1994, 1999, 2001, 2003; LeDoux 1998, 2002; Milsum 1966), a feedback control paradigm has evolved to track the flow of information through the human body, from sensory perception to motor response. It is appropriate, before proceeding, to summarize the essential features of this paradigm, introduce some additional details, and customize it, so that it becomes specific to the role of music in the human experience. For this purpose, it is convenient to view the human body as being characterized by: (1) seven basic attributes, that are responsive to (2) the six fundamental elements of music, as interpreted/influenced by (3) five essential laws of perception, subject to (4) four primary constraints, imposed through a hierarchy of (5) three rudimentary levels of information processing and (6) two governing principles, in order to satisfy (7) one "au fond" purpose: a 7-6-5-4-3-2-1 "musical countdown," if you will.

The seven basic attributes of all physiological function fit neatly into the canonical form of a standard engineering feedback/feedforward control model.

## Attribute 1

As has been pointed out several times already, the entire human organism is a controlled system, one that functions in space and time as a basic *engine*. That is, the body takes in air via the respiratory system, and fuel via the gastrointestinal system, converts (transduces) part of this mixture into usable energy to drive its metabolic processes (which further classifies the system as a *living engine*), "does its thing" (i.e., performs all of its various functions), and has a sophisticated excretory system to exhaust the waste products of its various metabolic activities. Fundamental to all physiological function are biorhythms, the "rhythms of life" that maintain a certain cadence to the output of this finely tuned, complex human engine.

Music exactly reflects and parallels these rhythmic aspects of physiological function, and so resonates symbiotically with them, as discussed further in Chapter 6. This symbiosis is one of the reasons why music can be used so effectively as a means of clinical intervention for targeted populations.

## Attribute 2

As also emphasized earlier, the controlled system that is the human body has a mechanical output in the form of kinetic energy. Everything it does, at various levels of organization, involves dynamic activity and motion. Whether it be at the atomic, molecular, cellular, tissue, organic, or systemic level, and whether it be voluntary locomotion of parts or all of the animal body (a specific feature of the animal kingdom), or involuntary mobility, or manifested behavior, if metabolically induced movement ceases then so does life.

For *human* forms of life, however, the output of this animated engine goes beyond being just passively mechanical. Human life forms gain personality through active *emotional expression* – the fifth most fundamental of all human drives, manifesting itself through various literary and art forms, music being one of them. Human beings emote; they have a need to express themselves. Indeed, it needs to be affirmed still again that humans are, first and foremost, creatures of emotion, both in their responses to sensory stimulation, and in their need to express themselves.

Given this fundamental need for emotional expression, it is therefore not any wonder that the same process works in reverse. Music can *drive* the very organism that invented it.

## Attribute 3

All of the controlled system's outputs are *monitored* through interoceptive and exteroceptive sensory transduction, which generates afferent action potentials – feedback control signals. All of the body's operating systems are continuously audited for subsequent verification relative to its homeostatic operating set-points. Such auditing allows for feedback/feedforward control in response to the generation of error signals. The latter are generated when *desired* output (coded into genetically determined reference parameters) is not equal to *actual* output (as sensed by intero- and exteroception). This ability that the human engine has, to sense and react to adequate stimuli (recall that these are various forms of energy), derived from both its internal (corporeal) and external (ambient) environments, is called *ambiensomatic perception.*

In the case of music, two major (although not exclusive) adequate stimuli that are tracked continuously are (1) mechanical vibrations embedded in sound energy, as expressed through vocal/instrumental sound generators and perceived through auditory pathways; and (2) such vibrations as sensed through touch (taction).

## Attribute 4

Verification and, as necessary, responses to transduced, monitored physiological function are accomplished through *sensory integration*, which takes place at a central "command post" that is the human brain and spinal cord, the central nervous system. To understand how this is accomplished, as it relates to effective clinical intervention, requires that one trace the historical development of the human brain, in order to appreciate how and why it manages information the way it does.

### THE TRIUNE BRAIN

The neurologist Paul MacLean (Senior Research Scientist Emeritus in the Department of Neurophysiology at the National Institutes of Mental Health) proposed over a decade ago that modern-day humans actually have three brains, nested within one another in order of evolutionary development. The oldest, dating back some 500 million years or more, is the primitive *archipallium* (literally, "principal cover"), which is also called the *basal*, or *reptilian* brain because it has remained virtually unchanged in the evolutionary progression from reptiles to mammals to humans. This archipallium is also regarded to be the oldest part of the cerebral cortex, and thus also goes by the names *archicortex* ("principal bark") and *allocortex* ("other bark"). The oldest brain, the archipallium, has various areas:

- Moving anatomically head-ward from the upper part of the spinal cord, the brainstem embodies the *medulla oblongata* (literally, "oblong-shaped marrow"), the *pons* ("bridge"), and the reticular ("netlike") formation that is the *mesencephalon* ("midbrain").

- The tri-lobed, bilateral *cerebellum* ("small brain") is attached to the upper rear of the brainstem.

- The *globus pallidus*, or *paleostriatum*, is an ancient mass of gray matter containing the earliest basal nerve cells.

- Since primitive reptiles roamed the planet relying for survival primarily on their sense of smell, there is also the *rhinencephalon* ("smell brain"), or bilateral *olfactory bulbs*.

This reptilian (or R-) complex of tissues is concerned purely with survival functions, which include musculoskeletal balance and equilibrium (posture, locomotion, and coordination of muscular activity), autonomic functions such as breathing and heart rate, levels of alertness (an early-warning system for threatening sensory inputs), and primitive types of survival behavior (often aggressive, mean, and self-serving, which persist even today).

Fast-forwarding about 200 to 300 million years, humans started to evolve the second in this triune brain paradigm, the *limbic system*. This is so called because it comprises a group of interconnected neural structures arranged in border-like fashion (*limbus* is Latin for "a border") surrounding the midline surfaces of the cerebral hemispheres, at the top of the brainstem. Also known as the *paleomammalian* ("ancient mammalian") brain, or the *paleopallium*, or the *limbic cortex* – and, together with the archicortex, forming the *paleocortex* (the "ancient bark," or *paleoencephalon*, which means "ancient brain") – the limbic system connects directly with the brainstem.

This second-oldest brain starts its anatomical journey around the brainstem at the front, ventral surface of the cerebral frontal lobe, under the *septum pellucidum* (literally, the "translucent partition"). It continues rearward, up and over the *corpus callosum*, a bundle of 300 million nerve fibers that connect the left and right sides of the brain. Along this path, it is known as the *cingulate gyrus* (cerebral convolution), which ends as the *parahippocampal gyrus* at the medial (toward the midline of the body) surface of the temporal lobe. The limbic system includes the:

- *hippocampus* ("sea horse," because of its appearance)
- *thalamus* ("inner room") which, as its name implies, receives incoming sensory information
- *amygdala* ("almond," because the amygdaloid body is shaped like one)
- *parolfactory area* associated with the sense of smell
- *mammillary body* ("breast-shaped" structure at the rear of the hypothalamus)
- *fornix* (Latin for "arch")
- *hypothalamus* (literally, "beneath the thalamus"), which, together with the thalamus and sub-thalamus, form the *diencephalon* (the "through-brain," or *thalamencephalon*).

As opposed to raw, reptilian (so-called "paw-to-jaw") survival instincts, the limbic system is concerned with the more sophisticated processes that are associated with the concept of homeostasis. These include the more refined control of body temperature, heart rate, respiration rate, blood pressure, blood sugar levels, acid–base balance, sleep/wake cycles, and "fight-or-flight" survival instincts. This system also moderates behavior related to survival of the individual and the species, such as thirst/hunger reflexes, the drive for sexual fulfillment, and even competition.

Closely allied with the above considerations are emotional instincts, reactions, and memories. This is why the limbic system is also called the *emotional brain*, and why, therefore, music connects so intimately with this second-oldest cerebral structure.

Research by, for example, Ornstein and Thompson (1984) and Damasio (2003) further shows that damage to parts of the limbic system can affect one's ability to react to situations that require making life-and-death decisions (indeed, *any* decisions), confirming yet again that humans are, in fact, creatures of emotion, not reason. The ability to reason comes much later, so it is time to fast-forward again, some 100 to 150 million years.

At this point in time, the animal that was to evolve into modern-day *Homo sapiens* began to develop a *cerebrum*, covered by a one-eighth-inch-thin *neopallium* ("new mantle"), or *neocortex* ("new bark"). The convoluted, four-lobed cerebrum (*telencephalon*, or "endbrain") is also called the *neomammalian brain* because of its development in primate mammals and, eventually, humans.

Many theories, none of them proven, have been offered to explain the systemic increase in brain size that accompanied the evolutionary process. One interesting hypothesis suggests that the neocortex developed as a sort of radiator to cool off blood from the midbrain and hindbrain (the *rhombencephalon*, or "afterbrain," which includes the pons, cerebellum, and medulla oblongata). This is certainly feasible when one considers that, if laid out flat, this convoluted sheet has a surface area approximating that of total skin surface, measuring some 1.5 square meters (about the size of a 5.5 feet by 3 feet office desk top). Another theory suggests that longer prey chases ("flight") along more spread-out landscapes required increased memory, hence the need for more storage space and larger brain size. There are many other theories, all awaiting further evidence.

For whatever reason, the human body of today is endowed with an organ the size of a grapefruit, weighing about as much as a head of cabbage, and wired with more possible internal connections than there are atoms in the universe! Here we list but a few of the many functions of this "new" part of the organ.

- It receives and processes sensory inputs for taste, taction, and proprioception via the *somatosensory cortex*, and responds to them via the *motor cortex* – all functions associated with the *parietal lobe*.

- It helps one to plan, make rational decisions, and consummate them with purposeful behavior – all functions associated with the *frontal lobe*, which is richly and intimately connected to the limbic system.

- It gives the organism the ability to perceive, especially through hearing (*auditory cortex*), and interpret what it experiences in life, and to commit some of those experiences to memory – all functions associated with the *temporal lobe*.

- It allows the body to see (via the *visual cortex*) its world of existence – a sensory modality associated with the *occipital lobe*.

Moreover, because humans are endowed with a neocortex, they can communicate, think, understand, organize, appreciate, create, learn, manipuate symbols (as in reading, writing, math, and musical notation), formulate theories, and deal with cognitive functions of a rather diverse nature. Much of the latter (i.e., cognition) has been the product of the last four to five million years of evolution, and it progressed in well-defined stages. However, that progress seems to have reached a plateau dating back about one million years, which appears to parallel the lateralization of the brain into right-brain and left-brain specialization. That is to say, the popular belief today (though it remains controversial) is that the left brain seems to deal better with temporal, rational, cognitive, linear, and verbal types of information-processing, whereas the right brain appears to be more comfortable with spatial, creative, integrative, abstract, and visual types of activities (Ornstein and Thompson 1984; Springer and Deutsch 1981).

Be that as it may, the current brain (the *encephalon*) with its many inter-connected anatomical regions seems to function as two distinct brains which can be viewed in two ways. On the one hand, this organ can be viewed as consisting of fused left and right cerebral hemispheres, each distinctive in the way that it perceives and processes information. On the other hand, it may be viewed as consisting of an ancient paleoencephalon that acts like the central processing unit (CPU) of an integrated computer system, and a modern neoencephalon that assumes the role of memory and peripheral devices. Note that these two views are not necessarily mutually exclusive, so in fact both might very well be correct. Regardless, the two brains apparently evolved in three stages: from a 500-million-year-old (give or take a few million) *archipallium* inherited from the earliest reptilian ancestors, to a 250-million-or-so-year-old *paleopallium* that came to humans by virtue of their mammalian lineage, and finally to an approximately 125-million-year-old *neopallium* that seems to be uniquely human.

## THE CONTROLLED SYSTEM'S CENTRAL COMMAND CENTER

Bearing the triune-brain model in mind, the human central nervous system may be considered to be the body's command center, where monitored signals are compared against desired operating set-points, and where decisive action, when appropriate, originates. The comparison process proceeds *in series*, which is to say, in a consecutive, step-by-step sequence, through three distinct levels of information-processing. Each level follows, in order, from the immediately preceding one (more on this later in this chapter). The sequential pathways through the CNS correspond anatomically (and very closely) to the evolutionary development of the brain and spinal cord, as described above, which is why it is very important for the clinician to be aware of these information-processing pathways in order to prescribe effective interventions.

It is in the CNS that error signals are generated when actual (monitored, transduced) systemic outputs are not congruent within an acceptable, predetermined *operating window*, with desirable outputs coded into operating set-points. Reference set-points might be a blood pressure of 120 (systolic) over 80 (diastolic), a resting heart rate of 70 beats per minute, a desired mode of behavior, and some optimum way to arrive at a desired goal; indeed, any physiological state that ensures survival, any human drive, any need to be met, and so on.

Recall that error signals result from disturbances to quasi-equilibrated homeostatic states, things that throw the controlled system "off." Also, as mentioned earlier, they are generated as a function of:

- how far away from the reference signal the transduced feedback control signal is (proportional control)

- the rate at which the discrepancy between actual and desired is increasing or decreasing (differential control)

- how persistent this discrepancy is (integral control).

Based on the seriousness of these error signals, then, the CNS makes decisions concerning what to do about them. The "what to do about them" is accomplished through the mobilization of the fifth attribute of this feedback-control paradigm.

## Attribute 5

The human body is endowed with the *autonomic nervous system* (which includes sympathetic and parasympathetic branches), the *endocrine system* (which includes organs of internal secretion), and the *immune system* (which includes antigen/antibody components). These controlling systems respond to commands issued forth as a result of the CNS's reactions to error signals, including, in the case of immune responses, foreign invasion. The autonomic nervous system effects rather instantaneous, short-lived, localized responses to CNS commands. As a general (though not universal) rule of thumb, activity of the sympathetic branch most often results in excitatory responses, while activity of the parasympathetic branch is most often inhibitory. In other words, these two branches of the autonomic nervous system tend to offset one another, so that net reactions are the result of the integrated function of the activity of both systems.

The endocrine system starts mainly in the brain, where the pineal gland and hypothalamus are located, and then works its way down through the pituitary gland (*hypophysis*, or "master gland"), the thyroid and four parathyroids, two adrenal (or suprarenal) glands, the pancreatic islets of Langerhans, thymus gland, paraganglia, and gonads (sex glands). This system effects somewhat delayed, but more persevering and generalized, systemic responses than does the autonomic nervous system.

The body's immune system is trained to recognize and respond to invasion by substances – living or dead – that are not indigenous to the organism into which they gain access. Controlling systems responding to CNS commands issue forth their own control signals that attempt to bring controlled-system outputs back in line with desirable operating set-points, thus completing the feedback control loop.

Typically, electrochemical control signals operating through the autonomic nervous system are digitally coded into corresponding biochemical packets called *synaptic vesicles*. These are embedded in the terminal regions (*boutons*) of motor nerve endings, called *axon terminals*. Each synaptic vesicle carries a quantum amount of biochemical *neurotransmitter*, such as norepinephrine, serotonin, acetylcholine, and dopamine. Every time the nerve "fires," a fixed number of these vesicles is released, so that, over the period of time that the nerve is active, the total amount of neurotransmitter released (squirted) into the synaptic space will depend on the firing frequency of the nerve. As will be discussed further in Chapter 6, neural excitation/inhibition and/or neogenesis can be directly influenced by external stimulation through the various elements of music.

Control signals operating through the endocrine system are similarly digitized in the form of *hormones,* such as corticosteroids, enkephalins, epinephrine, and endorphins (Chapter 5), while those operating through the immune system are coded into antibodies and the nine biochemical ingredients that make up the *complement complex.*

Several of these neurotransmitters, hormones, and antibodies have been shown to be secreted in response to certain types of musical stimulation (to be discussed in subsequent chapters), but much more research is needed in this area if the rapidly growing field of music therapy can effectively exploit these responses in an effort to provide meaningful clinical intervention for a wide variety of medical and social afflictions.

### Attribute 6

Depending on the nature and persistence of disturbances to quasi-equilibrated physiological states, controlled/controlling systems have the ability to *accommodate* (to be discussed in somewhat more detail in Chapter 5). Short-term, temporary disturbances are handled by *reflexive* reactions that do not require changing either the operating set-points or the system's various transfer functions (i.e., its input/output characteristics). More persistent but medium-term disturbances are handled by *functional adaptation* mechanisms that actually do result in changes to the body's operating set-points, but not to its transfer functions (Schneck and Berger 1999). And although it is still somewhat controversial, and definitive evidence to confirm it has thus far failed to materialize, there is a very distinct possibility that long-term, continuous disturbances of a permanent nature, which persist over generations, might be handled by changing *both* the organism's operating set-points *and* systemic transfer functions, through *inscriptive processes* (i.e., genetic natural selection) that are embedded in Attribute 7, described below.

But before leaving Attribute 6, it is interesting to draw a parallel between *physiological* accommodation and *sociological* accommodation, because the musical element of form (Chapter 10) is intimately connected with both of these. For example, in the arts in general and music in particular, as well as in all other aspects of the human experience, history records various styles and periods. These represent a type of acclimatization which is reflective of the then-existing state of social, cultural, political, and economic affairs, the prevailing human needs of the time. The historical styles and periods, if one examines them closely, illustrate once again the human need for emotional expression, being symbolic of the corresponding state of human existence. In those instances where such socio-cultural norms persevered continuously, in a more long-term sense they secured their place in history through the cultural equivalent of biological Attribute 7, which is to say, evolution.

## Attribute 7

As mentioned earlier, two important characteristics of living systems are growth and reproduction, the latter being manifest in the human drive for sexual fulfillment to perpetuate the species. Thus, the human engine has the remarkable ability to make more engines just like it, improving on the design with each succeeding generation. The results of that breeding process are permanently coded into operating set-points embedded in the human *genome* – the recipe for making one complete twenty-first-century *Homo sapiens*.

The functional unit of the genome is the *gene*, which is that part of a chromosome (i.e., an ingredient of the recipe) that determines, or at least has a potential influence on, the inheritance and development of a specific anatomical trait, morphological characteristic, or behavioral pattern. The realization of that characteristic results from the activation of a particular sequence of base-pairs in the long-chain DNA molecule of which most genes are made. Such activation goes by the technical term *gene expression*. The operative word here is "activation," which is where nurture enters the picture to complement nature. In Chapters 6 and 11, the reader will gain a more detailed appreciation for the role of music in nurture, as it relates to gene expression.

## The socio-cultural dimension

Corresponding to the gene in the biological Attribute 7, which connotes growth, procreation, and inscriptive breeding, one has the *meme* in the socio-cultural dimension. The meme, especially in the case of music, connotes creative emergence into novelty, a breaking-away from the status quo. If embraced by enough of a constituency (a cultural following, which is the societal analogue of a continuous driving function), any particular meme can transcend existing norms in favor of a new legacy. This process is the socio-cultural equivalent of natural selection and genetic inscription. Whereas, in biology, scientists talk about evolved *phenotypes*, which are traits defined by their realized appearance, and *genotypes*, which are potential traits defined by the genetic make-up of an organism, musicians and musicologists talk about *styles* (baroque, classical, romantic, modern, country, jazz, folk, rock, etc.), and realized *forms*, the sixth element of music (Chapter 10), such as the suite, sonata, oratorio, opera, fugue, canon, Gregorian chant, cantata, etc. All of these define various stages in the evolution of this medium.

All seven of the attributes discussed above are embedded in, and responsive to, the six fundamental elements of music that were introduced and described briefly in Chapter 2. Rhythm, dynamics, pitch, and timbre were described in somewhat more detail in Chapter 3, and will be addressed also in Chapters 7 (rhythm), 8 (pitch, as an attribute of melody), and 9 (dynamics and timbre). Also examined in Chapter 9 is harmony, followed in Chapter 10 by form, the sixth element. Suffice it to say here, that the elements of music serve as driving functions (continuous disturbances, in the feedback-control sense) in the "countdown" paradigm that is being developed herein.

Acting as continuous forcing functions, these elements have the ability to mobilize physiological processes that act, through entrainment (Chapter 6) and complementary accommodation mechanisms (Chapter 5), to help establish desirable operating set-points for the organism as a whole. It is also important to realize that the human body is not just one huge feedback-control system. Quite to the contrary, it consists of cascading networks of nested sub-systems, wherein output signals from any given sub-system are also *fed forward*, to become inputs (disturbing signals) to downstream controlled sub-systems; hence the technical term *feedback/ feedforward control systems*. In a holistic sense, therefore, there results a living organism that functions as one integrated, coordinated, balanced, and synchronized unit, whose most prioritized need is survival of the self, and which, to satisfy this need, has evolved control mechanisms that are both purposeful and adaptive. The adaptive aspect will be revisited in Chapter 5; its triggering mechanisms (physiological entrainment) in Chapter 6. The purposeful aspect is embedded in five basic *Gestalt* laws governing the perceptual organization of sensory information (Coren and Ward 1989).

## *Gestalt* laws governing the perceptual organization of sensory information

### 1. The law of proximity

This law states that, owing to the *resolution* limitations of sensory transducers, individual elements of adequate stimuli that are received very close to one another in space and/or in time are perceived to be a single unit or figure. That is to say, ambiensomatic monitoring mechanisms cannot discriminate among them or distinguish one from another if incident sensory inputs are closer than the sense organs can deal with.

## 2. The law of directionality

This law asserts that, owing to the *tracking* characteristics of the body's information-processing systems, absent any discontinuities in incoming information, consecutive individual elements of adequate stimuli that are perceived to follow one another in the same direction tend to be grouped as defining that direction. That is to say, the sequential pattern of incident sensory inputs is perceived to be tracing a smooth, unbroken trajectory in the given direction, such that the next incoming stimulus is expected to follow suit, in that direction.

## 3. The law of similarity

This law exploits the fact that the body's information-processing networks are uniquely endowed with the inherent ability to extract essential *common denominators* that may be embedded in adequate stimuli. Thus, those stimuli that share generic features, or are otherwise comparable in the attributes that define them, tend to be perceptually grouped together into the same object category.

## 4. The law of closure

This law derives from the body's basic desire to avoid "loose ends." Thus, if a physical space or region is bounded by a continuous curve that may or may not be closed, it tends nevertheless to be *perceived* as a self-contained figure. That is to say, the body "closes" any existing breaks in information, "filling in the gaps," so to speak. This tends to be the case for any type of sensory input, not just visual; the body will automatically fill in the details that it thinks should be there in order to "connect the dots," to create a continuous flow of information with a logical ending.

## 5. The law of Pragnanz

This law stipulates that, in an effort to evoke the most effective response to specific adequate stimuli (if, indeed, the body decides that a response is even necessary), *sensory differentiation* and *integration* mechanisms embedded in all of the preceding laws attempt to create the most stable, consistent, and meaningful interpretation of those stimuli. That is to say, the body – again, being purposeful – seeks to glean the *essence* of the information contained in the stimuli (the "spirit of the law," so to speak), as opposed to its absolute content (the "letter of the law"). But this is easier said than done, because of at least four anatomical/physiological limitations that constrain the ultimate effectiveness of sensory differentiation/integration processes. Although they are common to information-processing in general, they will be described as they apply to music in particular.

## Limitations to the processing of sensory information
### *The first set of constraints*
Music deals primarily with sound energy, so one set of obvious constraints includes the audible range of hearing, at frequencies (pitches) between 20 and 20,000 Hz. Another constraint is the range of loudness that can usually be tolerated without consequence, which is to say, decibel levels between 0 (the threshold of human hearing) and around 120 (the lowest threshold of ear pain).

More generally, all sensory perception is constrained by the *operating window* specific to the particular adequate stimulus to which the corresponding sense organ responds. Human beings are not anatomically endowed with sensory transducers (organs) capable of perceiving energy in all of its omnifarious forms. In other words, there is an "out there" out there that humans have no way of perceiving, except in some special cases (e.g., X-rays) by technological enhancement.

### *The second set of constraints*
A second set of somewhat more subtle constraints involve harmonic *consonance* (the opposite of "dissonance") and *tempering* of the musical scale. As will be discussed further in Chapter 9, harmonic dissonance derives from interference patterns (*sonic beats*) that originate when two tones close in frequency, but not identical, are sounded together. More often than not, such dissonance, peaking at beat frequencies around 24 Hz (comparable to the "flicker speed" for vision) is unpleasant to the typical listener, consonance being much more agreeable to the auditory system.

As a consequence of this unpleasant phenomenon, tempering of the musical scale has evolved as an optimization process. That is to say, the current twelve-tone chromatic scale (as opposed to the eight-tone diatonic scale) contains the maximum number of equally spaced notes containing the minimum number of dissonant frequency ratios between any two of those notes. In other words, the number of dissonant intervals, expressed as a percentage of the total number of intervals in the scale (D'Attellis 2001), is the least possible. This means that the numerator (which is the total number of dissonant intervals in the scale) of the so-called *optimization fraction* is the smallest it can be; and the denominator of this fraction (which is the total number of possible intervals in the scale) is the largest it can be, for the given numerator. Thus, the optimization fraction itself takes on the smallest (optimal) value.

Going one step further, the actual note-to-note subdivisions of the scale, itself, are further constrained by the resolution capabilities of the auditory system (see the earlier discussion of the first *Gestalt* law), while the equal spacing of the notes is designed to make it convenient to transpose and modulate from one key into another.

More generally, then, all sensory perception is constrained by the ability of the corresponding sensory modality to resolve the adequate stimuli.

## The third set of constraints

But the story does not end here, because now the transduced information needs to be transported to the central nervous system for further processing! Theoretically, a sensory nerve can "fire" at a frequency as high as 2000 action potentials per second (Schneck 1990). Realistically, however, maximum nerve transmission rates beyond 700–800 impulses per second are rarely encountered, and most neurons fire at maximum rates closer to about 400 impulses per second. Now, suppose a single nerve trunk (e.g., the auditory nerve) contains, say, 30,000 total sensory nerve fibers (Coren and Ward 1989). Suppose further that each nerve fiber is firing at the rate of, say, 400 impulses per second, each impulse carrying a "bit" of information (Schneck and Schneck 1996). Then, information flow into the CNS (in this case, the auditory cortex in the upper part of the temporal lobe of the brain), via a single sensory modality (in this case, audition), would be at the maximum rate of 12 million bits per second (30,000 x 400).

However, this line of reasoning assumes that (1) an individual neuron receives an adequate stimulus at a receptor site, and (2) that neuron transmits that stimulus as a transduced afferent action potential directly to the sensory cortex of the brain. Nowhere along the path of transmission is the signal filtered or modulated, and at no point along the way does it interact with any other neurons – which is not quite how this works.

First of all, every single second, of every single day, in excess of well over 100 million adequate stimuli literally bombard the body's sensory transducers. Aside from the fact that the human body is not physically endowed with the capability to process such enormous volumes of information, if it had to undertake such processing the central command post would grind to a complete halt under the burden of a classic case of information overload, with resulting gridlock. Enter the *reticular activating system* (RAS).

The RAS, known more accurately as the *reticular formation*, is a tangled, densely packed cluster of nerve cells containing mostly gray matter interlaced with fibers of white matter. It is an anatomical region about the size of a little finger, extending through the central core of the brainstem, from the upper spinal cord, through the medulla oblongata and pons Varolii, into the midbrain. For the most part, the RAS is not distinctly identifiable as a discrete system of CNS nuclei. Rather, it communicates, via networks of *interneurons*, with (1) afferent sensory pathways that course through this anatomical region, (2) sensory nuclei and motoneuronal cell groups located in the brainstem, and (3) neural pathways that operate through the autonomic nervous system – all of these forming, collectively, what is known as the *metameric nervous system*. In addition, the RAS has elaborate connections with the thalamus and hypothalamus. In other words, it is its own "web."

The interneurons of the RAS are very short, so that messages can be relayed quickly from one nerve cell to the next. This allows it to function as a sieve, continuously sifting through the wealth of incoming data. Only those sensory inputs that the RAS deems to be essential, unusual, perceived-to-be-dangerous, and/or in some sense "action-provoking" are selected as appropriate for further processing and forwarding to the higher levels of the brain. Thus, filtered by the RAS, only a few hundred stimuli, at most, actually make it through to cerebral regions above the brainstem.

Furthermore, information does not actually enter the CNS as a result of the individual firing rates of single nerve fibers. Nerves form *neural networks* (trillions of them), wherein there may be as many as ten thousand synapses (nerve junctions) associated with each and every neuron in the "net." One therefore speaks more relevantly of a *processing capacity* of a neural network, rather than a maximum transmission capacity for individual nerves. This, also called the *coding capacity* of the net, defines the rate at which it can transmit information after integrating the collective inputs from all of its contributing-member synaptic junctions and collecting sites (i.e., hubs), each of which can receive inputs from many neurons. The limiting factor affecting the coding capacity of the CNS is the input rate of post-synaptic, compound action potentials derived from neural networks, so that far less net information than the potential 100 million bits per second actually gets processed to elicit a response – more like 5–40 bits per second (called the information-processing resolution rate) (Schneck and Schneck 1996).

In fact, studies (e.g., Woody 1982) suggest that for most types of sensorimotor tasks of daily living, processing rates of around 20–25 bits per second (50–40 milliseconds per bit) will usually suffice to produce accept-able results. Thus, most of the time, the sensory cortex of the brain, in an awake state, is probably not receiving *processed* (as opposed to raw) informa-tion any faster than that. Slower processing speeds, up to several hundred milliseconds per impulse, are associated with more complex tasks, like rec-ognizing printed words; and one moves up the scale to faster processing speeds (i.e., a smaller number of milliseconds per bit) as the sensory inputs and/or motor tasks become more simple. One also moves back to slower processing speeds, perhaps 300 milliseconds or more per impulse, where there are physiological problems with sensory integration pathways, such as may be the case with "slow learners," or autistic children. If the information comes in faster than they can process it, some of it gets lost and a state of confusion may result. In engineering signal theory, these are called *dropouts* or *aliasing errors*, the problem resulting from an inadequate sampling rate of the incident adequate stimulus.

Dropouts gravely affect the significance of the information contained in the transduced signal. For example, they are the reason why one sees a wagon wheel "rotating backwards" when viewing it on a movie film, even though the wagon in real life is moving forward. Clinicians must be espe-cially cognizant of these phenomena, to the extent that they influence the dose–response effectiveness of therapy interventions in general, and those employing music in particular.

Finally, mean processed, integrated impulses, time-averaged over a "typical" day, for a "typical" individual, often cluster around 10 bits per second (100 ms/bit, rather than 40–50), and they generally are the result of information gleaned from synaptic networks containing between 10,000 and one 100,000 synapses. That is, every 10,000 to 100,000 to synapses in a neural network yield, on average, only 10 integrated, processed pieces of information per second. In fact, some of this information might not even make it to the reticular formation. That is to say, there are many so-called *spinal reflex pathways*. These are round-trips – from sensory inputs, to the spinal cord, to motor outputs from the spinal cord – which take place entirely along a path that is completely self-contained *within* the spinal cord, never reaching the RAS or higher regions within the brain. Responses derived from spinal reflex pathways are thus totally independent of "higher processing" (Schneck 1992), and help to minimize the total flow of unnecessary information to the brain.

Thus, all sensory perception is constrained by all of the factors that ultimately determine (1) the adequate-stimulus sampling rate, (2) whether or not neural network outputs reaching the CNS are intercepted entirely within the spine, never making it to the reticular formation, and (3) the CNS information-filtration and information-processing resolution rates.

### The fourth set of constraints

The fourth set of constraints that affect the processing of sensory information involves the hierarchy of three pathways, in series, through which the information passes on its afferent journey through the CNS. That is to say, complementing the five *Gestalt* laws governing the perceptual organization of sensory information is the prioritization of this information as it tracks through three processing levels above the spinal entry points.

## Hierarchy of information-processing channels in the CNS

The first level of information-processing, the reticular formation, was addressed above. Recall that, en route to the central nervous system, afferent sensory action potentials travel through a web of neural networks, where they are progressively assembled into integrated, compound action potentials that deliver to the CNS a "state-of-the-controlled-system" message. Those messages destined for further processing arrive first at the reticular activating system, the "port-of-entry" into the brain. Recall further that the primary function of the RAS is to prevent information overload by acting as a preliminary, coarse sieve, a *filter* that serves to avoid overburdening the brain with "garbage."

Next, information that makes it through the reticular formation travels up the *spinothalamic tract*, to be "greeted" at its arrival in the brain by the thalamus – a large, oblong mass of gray matter located towards the back of the forebrain. The thalamus is the chief sensory reception center of the encephalon, welcoming (like customs agents at geographic ports-of-entry) all information coming in to the CNS, except that derived from smell. The latter goes directly to the rhinencephalon, or "smell brain." As part of its role as a welcoming committee, the thalamus evaluates incoming information in order to establish a preliminary *classification* for it. In fact, certain areas of the thalamus are specialized to receive particular kinds of digitized information (Ornstein and Thompson 1984). Once classified, this information is immediately dispatched to two generic places: (1) the sensory regions of the cerebral cortex, where it will be processed further, and, possibly, eventually stored elsewhere following *delayed, conscious perception* (Libet 2002, 2003; Shevrin, Ghannam, and Libet 2002); and (2) the limbic system ("emotional brain") of the paleoencephalon, where it undergoes *immediate, subconscious perception* to effect instantaneous responses to potential threats.

In the limbic system, the second level of information-processing, sensory inputs are fine-tuned through the process of *stimulus-coding* (Berger 2002; Berger and Schneck 2003; Schneck 1997; Schneck and Berger 1999). The coding "tags" the information to give it temporal/sequential significance for subsequent filing away in memory, and for recall (the *somesthetic cortex* will use this information later). More importantly, however, the limbic system *evaluates* the data that the thalamus has classified, to determine its potential threat to the safety of the organism. For the latter purpose, the data travels in series pathways, first through the amygdala, and second through the hippocampus. If the amygdala senses "threat," real or imagined, it issues forth a distress message, an "SOS" error signal, that mobilizes corresponding controlling systems into action; it also truncates any further processing by the hippocampus. These distress signals are in the form of outgoing *motor* (as opposed to incoming *sensory*) compound action potentials. Motor signals travel via hypothalamo-hypophysial and hypothalamo-autonomic pathways to trigger the release from target organs and tissues of corresponding neurotransmitters and hormones that elicit a "fight-or-flight" response (Chapter 5).

Only when the amygdala sounds an "all clear" does information track next through the hippocampus of the limbic system, for additional stimulus-coding and processing en route to the "higher" centers in the cerebral cortex (Berger 2002; Schneck 1997).

There are three important things to remember, especially when evaluating the role of music in the human experience.

1.    The road to higher cerebral centers travels *first* through the older paleoencephalon and, within the latter, *first* through the amygdala of the limbic system. In the words of Ornstein and Thompson (1984, p.24), "Emotions were here before we were."

2.    As long as the amygdala is in "alert" perceived-threat mode, all roads lead to "fire stations, rescue squads, emergency services, and hospitals." Indeed, when active, the amygdala actually *inhibits* the activity of the hippocampus (but not the other way around), causing it to start to self-destruct (degenerate) if the amygdala-driven alert mode of information-processing persists for extended periods of time (Damasio and Moss 2001).

3.    As long as the amygdala is in alert mode, all roads through the hippocampus to "universities, libraries, Institutions of Higher Learning," and cognitive cerebral centers are completely blocked. It is an exercise in futility to try to reason with anybody in a perpetual alert state. Instead, one must emote with a person in this state, which is why music is so effective as a driving function that "kicks" the system out of its perpetual fight-or-flight mode.

If the amygdala signifies that all is well, information filtered by the RAS, classified by the thalamus, and evaluated and prioritized by the limbic system passes on through the hippocampus to the cognitive regions of the cerebral cortex. Here, the final stop in the hierarchy of information-processing channels *may* be storage in tertiary memory, because the body always reserves the option to discard unwanted information at any step along the processing pathways. Once the information is in final memory, however, it is there *forever*, barring physical damage to the brain in the region where that data is stored.

To further the effectiveness of all physiological function, the body also operates according to two guiding principles (Schneck 1990, 2003a). First, it attempts to economize on energy expenditure. The more scientists learn about the physiology of the human body, the clearer it becomes that this organism operates according to a minimum-energy principle, an optimization scheme. All metabolic processes, mechanical outputs, feedback/feedforward control mechanisms, and so on, take the path of least resistance in an attempt to optimize performance and at least minimize the *rate* of loss of usable energy.

Second, the body attempts to economize on the utilization of *space* for the storage and handling of raw materials and/or information. This it does in basically three ways:

1.    It stores *ingredients,* not *products.*

2.    It draws upon *fractal principles* to create complicated geometric shapes and configurations that fit neatly into tight quarters, yet maximize their functional capacity.

3.    It *discards* any and all information for which it has no perceived need. Unlike many, the human body is *not* a pack rat.

All of what has been discussed in this chapter, the body does for one ultimate purpose: survival – of both itself and its species.

"All well and good," you might say. "That's great: 7-6-5-4-3-2-1, all in a neat package. But what happens if the organism's operating set-points somehow go awry? What if a person's perception of reality causes his or her body to be in a perpetual, amygdala-driven, fight-or-flight mode of operation? How does a clinician 'get through' to such an individual? How can he or she apply effective means of intervention to break that destructive behavioral mode? And, how can *music* help?" Read on!

Chapter 5

# Fear and the Instinct for Survival: What Happens When the Set-points Go Awry?

The only thing we have to fear is fear itself.

F. D. Roosevelt, in his Presidential Inaugural Address (1933)

## Introduction

Borrowing the rhetoric from Shakespeare's *Hamlet* (Act III, Scene I), but attributing it to the amygdala rather than to the Prince of Denmark, the inquiry addressed in this chapter is, "To flee, or not to flee? That is the question." Before attempting to answer that question, however, some words of caution are in order.

Always keep in mind, as you read through the material in this book, and as you evaluate the scientific literature related to this subject, that the state of the art, at its current level of development, professes to describe what the "typical" human organism *should* (anatomists think) look like; how it *should* (physiologists think) work; and how the two, anatomy and physiology, are related (morphologists think) to one another; which is to say, how anatomical structure is *typically* configured, *most of the time*, on the basis of its *intended* physiological function. Even though the medical establishment would often have you believe otherwise, scientists are a long way from completely understanding the structure and function of the human body, most especially in those situations where it has apparently ceased to perform in accordance with expectations – such as when it is encumbered by diagnosed conditions like autism, Cornelia de Lang syndrome, Alzheimer's disease, osteoarthritis, muscular dystrophy, multiple sklerosis, cancer, stroke, and so on.

Given this level of ignorance, one should hesitate to use, especially in the clinical environment, the word "normal" to describe the anatomy, physiology, and morphology of the human body. "Normal" has yet to be defined in a rigorous, quantifiable, operational sense; and "normal," by extrapolation, implies (or at least infers) "*ab*-normal." But if "normal" cannot be defined, then one certainly cannot define what "abnormal" means, much less the word "appropriate." The best that can be done is to identify certain *diseases*, being anatomical/physiological/morphological conditions that can be diagnosed as being a threat to health; and/or certain *behavior* or conduct that suggests the organism is not performing according to expectations. But *whose* expectations: society's, the medical community's, or the individual's?

Indeed, to be entirely accurate, "abnormal" as diagnosed by an outside observer is normal to the person actually living inside the body that is experiencing one of the various states cited above. Furthermore, given the plethora of still other "conditions" (diagnosed or otherwise), diseases, pathologies, genotypes, phenotypes, archetypes, etc., that have been identified in *Homo sapiens*, one could develop a strong argument to support the idea that, when it comes to physiological function, the exception is more common than the rule (Schneck 2001a). In fact, there really are no rules per se; which is why, when asking a question about "normal" versus "abnormal" physiological function or human behavior, the answer one is most likely to receive, most of the time, is "It depends!" Each of us is a minority of one! (Schneck 2001a).

That being the case, perhaps it would be better to avoid using words like "normal" and "abnormal," in favor of more quantifiable, statistical terminology – such as "statistically, *most common*," or "apparently, *quite typical*" – to describe more precisely the states of affair that one is likely to encounter (within limits) most often when studying the human body. In statistical terms, one can quantify anatomical, physiological, and morphological *norms*. These are average quantities that allow generalizations to be made about what one can expect to encounter *most of the time* when examining the structure and function of the human organism. Keep in mind that, in this text, norms (which quantify what one is *likely* to find, on average) and normal (which connotes what is considered to be the *standard*, in terms of appropriate and acceptable) are not used synonymously.

Carrying this reasoning to its logical conclusion, then, there is also no such thing as "abnormal." Here, too, statistical language might be more appropriate, such as "statistically, less commonly encountered; rare; not come upon as often; mathematically unlikely; alternative response; on the basis of probability, less likely to be experienced regularly," etc.

The key is not to fall into the all-too-common tendency to equate the word "often" with "normal," because it is a gross injustice to the multidimensional, unique nature and diversity of the human experience. "Different" does not necessarily equate with "pathological"; these two words – like normal and norms, or therapy and therapeutic – are also not used synonymously in this book.

Having said that, keep in mind the further thought that music impacts the entire human organism, from the individual atoms, molecules, and cells to the most complex tissues, organs, and systems. Music transmits its vibrational acoustic information to all levels of structure and function, penetrating the body throughout, and eliciting holistic, integrated responses. The conscious mind is often not even aware until much later that such responses have taken place (e.g., changes in biochemical reactions, blood flow, breathing rate, hormonal expression, body temperature). That is to say, preceding cognition, in the sense of conscious awareness (i.e., the psycho-emotional "me"), there is reaction, in the sense of subcortical responsiveness (the inherently reflexive "me"); see, for example, Libet (2002, 2003) and Shevrin *et al.* (2002).

In order to discuss and appreciate these subliminal interactions between music and basic physiological function, especially if they are to be used as a clinical intervention, one needs to extend the material presented in Chapters 1–4. In particular, one must understand the various levels of organization of the human body in terms of how it receives, processes, and responds to sensory stimulation *when that stimulation is perceived (real or imagined) to be threatening to the survival of the organism.* This chapter addresses that perception.

Furthermore, it is important, if one is to intervene effectively, to appreciate the hierarchy of pathways through which the body goes about satisfying its fundamental need for survival, including the hard-wired "fight-or-flight" response to perceived threats. Perhaps the best way to pursue such understanding is first to examine several case histories, and to attempt to answer questions such as: "What's going on here? What is different among these various cases? What is the same? What is the body trying to do?" and "How can music help?"

## What is different and what is the same?

*Case studies*

ROBERT

Robert, age 14, enters the music therapy room with rigidity. His fearful eyes dart about as if looking for someplace to hide. He never stops circulating about the room, now here, now there, grunting and speaking non-stop; now gibberish, now incoherent, non-sequential questions and statements, touching everything in the room. The young boy references the therapist constantly as he agitates about the room, as if searching for a specific item, comment, location, or permission to undertake something or other.

Robert's demeanor is distrusting, agitated, nervous, as if anticipating that the worst is about to take place. His body moves with rigidity as if ready to flee the room; arms stiff and held down in a self-conscious manner. His head moves from side to side, his arms swinging, reaching out, never still. "I wanna play drums ...no, cn ah'sk y'a quesun? Kn I play these [indicating the chiquita maracas]?" he asks, as he somewhat frantically reaches for and already holds them in his hands before completing the request. Then, pointing to the xylophones, "Kn I play these?" "How 'bout the small drum ...what's ih called?" he queries, referring to the bongo drum, as if he's never seen it before. He repeats words in almost a stutter-like manner, although his medical report does not indicate a language stutter.

To describe Robert is to describe a frenetic, panic-stricken person unable to pace or control his reactivity to an environment. Rather, he appears always to be expecting a catastrophe, or punishment at any given moment, and afraid to stop talking in case something dreadful were to fill that empty, quiet space. He defies or rejects any and every request from others, whether or not a suggestion might actually be something in which he would like to engage. His inability to accept a suggestion, command, or directive is supported by his inability to modulate away from disappointment or desire to do something "his" way, or that he would like to undertake. Robert is completely self-absorbed and defiant, a demeanor which has become a source of punitive measures taken by schools, caretakers, and others, serving only to reinforce all the more his distrusting demeanor.

LAURA

Laura, age 38, enters the music therapy room smiling, looking directly at the therapist, grunting (she is completely speechless), and nodding her head "yes" as if to induce the therapist into agreement, approval, or acceptance of her behavior and being. Laura, too, darts about the room, although in a less frenetic manner than does Robert. With each curious investigation of items about the room, Laura refers back to the therapist for agreement and/or approval. In fact, Laura appears to be in constant need of positive stroking and reinforcement. Although she has absolutely no expressive language ability whatsoever, she remains visually connected and agreeable to being directed in and out of activities, but always with a somewhat fearful glance, as if at any moment she expects to be reprimanded for an action. Laura's body and rhythmic pacing appear to indicate that she is "on alert" for some threatening event.

BUCKY

Bucky is 8 years old. When he enters the music therapy room, it is with extreme caution and slowness, as if he is walking in his sleep or on a dangerous, partially frozen lake, or a very dark house. He stops at the entrance to the studio, looks slowly about, waiting, listening. Although verbal communication is not an issue for him, he speaks very little, and very briefly. "What are we doing today?" he queries, as if whatever occurs could be a heavy chore for him to undertake. When activity suggestions are offered, or he is asked for his choice and interest, he responds with inquiry, very slowly and deliberately, "why…do we have to…do…that?" or, "I… don't…know…you… tell…me." There is a long pause, then "you… decide."

Having been declared "legally" blind, Bucky's physical demeanor and environmental responses are akin to those of a visually impaired person. He moves extremely cautiously, touches everything, has keen hearing and listening skills, and is in a constant state of inquiry. "Why is the keyboard not working? … Why is the drum on this side of the room instead of the other? … Why do I have to do anything? … How does the speaker work? … Which button did you push on the keyboard? … Is it time to go yet?" And each response is greeted with another "why," "how," "when," and so on.

Bucky's self-motivation to undertake or design any activity of interest for himself in the environment is practically non-existent. In addition, he appears always to be "practicing" his cognitive information at the expense of trusting his instincts and "letting go" long enough just to have a good time in a permissive setting. Being constantly on alert, every undertaking has to have a reason, a complete explanation of why and wherefore, and in the end, Bucky usually prefers not to participate in any "creative" manner, but tends to evacuate from a situation by behaving in silly, infantile ways totally antitheti-cal to what had been suggested. In general, Bucky assumes a total avoidant behavior.

## RHEA

Rhea is 5 years old. She enters the music therapy room screaming, satelliting about, avoiding direct contact, crouching in corners, shutting her ears to sounds. Her eyes dart about and become tear-filled easily, lower lip quivering in preamble to crying spurts. Rhea prefers distance and total avoidance of any contact with another. During most sessions, Rhea touches this or that instrument, predominantly drums, and retracts herself from any further par-ticipation until some ten minutes prior to the conclusion of a 45-minute session, when she finally becomes calm enough to enjoy the environment and relax her stressed system.

## RACHEL

Rachel is a 31-year-old, attractive, well-dressed and quite verbally articulate woman, finding herself in a situation in which she feels she does not belong. She has been admitted to the Women's Intake Ward of the psychiatric hospital, and has been there for several weeks. As the days wear on and her distress escalates, Rachel decides to partake of music therapy sessions because she loves music. She enters the room with darting eyes, and an abundance of self-conscious mannerisms: self-embracing often, incessant hand-wringing and complaining of constantly cold hands and feet, unable to remain visually focused on the person with whom she is speaking. Rachel continually adjusts or flips her hair, and complains of having been errone-ously sent to "this place where I don't belong... I don't know what I'm doing here!"

To describe Rachel is to describe a person continuously enraged and "on edge." Partially due to the medication, but mostly as an ongoing state of anxiety, her clinical notes indicate she has "some nervousness about her movements, as if being chased by some evil person." Rachel constantly scans the room and comments on distant "noises" coming from the halls. Tears are never far from her disposition.

## Assessments

Consider this: What do these five people have in common? Why would they appear in the same chapter of this book? The answer is that even though each case represents a totally different diagnosis, each individual's inherent behavior mannerisms derive from the exact same emotion: *fear*. The symptoms of fear, as embedded in the "fight-or-flight" survival response discussed later in this chapter, manifest themselves in all five cases. In each case, the person's individual physiological response to the environment and circumstance is driven by the need to address a self-perceived threat, real or imagined, to the most fundamental of all human drives: *survival*.

## ROBERT

Robert is diagnosed with Asperger's syndrome. His fear responses emanate from faults in his sensory information-processing system, which, for whatever reason, does not provide him with an accurate assessment of the environment. Thus are generated misleading error signals that, among other things (such as taxing the intricate control loops that respond to these error signals), cause him to have a need to question constantly. As a result, his fear response is manifest in his literal need to "flee" the environment. Perhaps this is because his system finds it overwhelming; perhaps threatening; perhaps confusing (see discussion of the *Gestalt* laws in Chapter 4); perhaps subjecting him to sensory overload; perhaps all of the above; perhaps none of these. The fact is that not enough is really known about all of these possibilities, and the research to explain it is just in its infancy; much more needs to be done. The bottom line is, however, that Robert's perceived inability to be *in control* – the fourth most fundamental of all human drives, after survival of the self, survival of the species, and spiritual fulfillment – i.e., to "fight," causes him to "flee" rather than suffer the consequences of his perceived threat to survival.

## LAURA

For Laura, the fear of being punished or otherwise abused remains constant. Laura is an autistic adult, with no expressive language capability. Her physiologically perceived threat to her own survival, more than likely, derives both from: (1) her physiological inability to accurately "read" another person's body language in order to predict, with a reasonable (to *her*) degree of certainty, what might be on the mind of "the other" (this is a *transduction* misinterpretation); and (2) her inability to coordinate efficiently and effectively (within *her* system) the myriad sensory inputs with her cognitive executive brain and thought processes, in order to derive a feeling of comfort (survival) and reason inside her skin (this is an *integration* malfunction).

BUCKY

Bucky's inability to see well, coupled with his extremely low muscle tone and various other sensory coordination and information-processing deficits, cause him to be cautious, question everything, be on constant "alert," and approach every situation in a deliberate manner. Bucky's physiological deficits emanate from his having had strokes *in utero*, and it is still unclear to what extent these have had physiological implications to his functioning, in the sense of the feedback control paradigm developed in Chapter 4. Currently, his ambiensomatosensory limitations severely restrict his ability to obtain an accurate description of his own body, his body in space, the dimensions of the space, the sounds emanating from places he cannot see, and so on. Error signals are running rampant throughout his system and, together with many other physiological impediments, all of these restrictions result in his body assuming a perpetual fear of moving and responding quickly in a situation that could prove to be somehow threatening.

RHEA

Rhea's diagnosis, Down syndrome with autism characteristics, results physiologically in her inability to receive or properly decode and/or coordinate sensory information. This factor, coupled with the alien acoustic, multisensory environment into which she enters, presents a profound threat to her survival instinct, thus triggering a classic fear response. As a consequence, she is thrust into a continual fight-or-flight, avoidance behavior, which her system has not yet learned to modulate. Thus, she races from instrument to instrument, to corners and walls about the room, to cowering, until her system ultimately modulates to secure sensations and "comfort zones."

RACHEL

Rachel is diagnosed as schizophrenic. Physiologically, the state of schizophrenia includes excessive flow of epinephrine, norepinephrine, cortisol, and other potentially harmful chemicals, which is a classic symptom of a constant state of stress and anxiety. In addition to the physiological symptoms already in place, the flow of stress hormones is enhanced by inaccurate information-processing, both sub-cognitive (which results in emotional hormonal upheavals), and cognitive (through inappropriate assessment of reality, which further contributes to emotional upheaval) (Andreasen 1997; Cowley 2003; Dolan 2002; Goldman 1996; Holden

2003; Javitt and Coyle 2004; Rainnie *et al.* 2004). These misconceptions sustain her in a perpetual flight–fight mode. Her state of anxiety is exacerbated further by her perceived "incarceration," which, again (as in Robert's case), removes her free will to control her environment and her destiny. Rachel's continuous fear is that she will not survive in "this place," and that the deprivation of her right to self-determination will result in her extinction.

Although in each of the above five cases the clinical diagnoses are quite different, as are the anatomical/physiological conditions for which each of these individuals is being treated, the underlying symptomatic cause of the diagnosed behaviors is the same: all five have the exact same element acting to elicit their respective behavior. In all five cases, as is true for all animals and humans, the major emotion driving behavioral symptoms and responses is *fear*.

## Fundamental human drives and the physiology of fear

The point cannot be stressed enough:

> *The key to understanding what this thing called "me" is – and, therefore, how music affects physiological function, and how its role in the human experience can be exploited for clinical purposes – is to accept the fact that "me" is, above all else, an emotional creature! Not cognitive. Not intellectual. Not reasonable or rational. Emotional, first and foremost!*

All animal behavior is driven by emotion (Berger 2002; Berger and Schneck 2003; Damasio 1999, 2001, 2003; Damasio and Moss 2001; LeDoux 1998, 2002). Humans instinctively react first, and think later (an "afterthought" in the truest sense). To prove this to yourself, just imagine what would happen if you yelled "Fire!" in a crowded room. It would quickly become apparent that in one's emotional, amygdala-driven, instinctive states, behavioral reactions result from the most primary of human needs, survival of the self.

The survival instinct is pervasive in all living creatures, and is the most fundamental of all human drives. Survival of the self and survival of the species comprise the two most critical responsibilities of physiological function, both brain and body collectively. The entire feedback control paradigm developed earlier has these two considerations as its primary objective, because survival depends on the maintenance, within narrow limits, of physiological variables fundamental to the sustenance of life. This results in the need to sustain continuously the previously defined condition known as *homeostasis* (Berger and Schneck 2003; Schneck 1990).

Fear, and the accompanying "fight-or-flight" responses to fear, are the physiological reactions to an event (transduced by the body's information-processing systems into an error signal) perceived by the central nervous system (the command center) to be threatening to survival. Fear emerges as the single, strongest behavior-driving human emotion (Berger and Schneck 2003; LeDoux 1998, 2002). The fear response causes extreme physiological conditions to occur in the organism, which ultimately prepare it for the fight-or-flight response, which is examined further below.

## The physiological response to stress

Usually, homeostatic control mechanisms can routinely handle the pressures (in the form of disturbances to quasi-equilibrated states) derived from the activities of daily living. However, these mechanisms are constrained by upper limits, beyond which the "usual" becomes the "extraordinary," and those homeostatic mechanisms no longer suffice to maintain control of body chemistry, temperature, blood pressure, and so on. That being the case, when the central nervous system receives sensory-transduced alarm signals (error signals called *stressors*) that are perceived, rightly or wrongly, to be a threat to its survival, the organism shifts into an amygdala-driven mode of emergency operation. In the vernacular, this shift is commonly called a "fight-or-flight" response, often referred to also as a *stress response*. Still more accurately, in physiological jargon it is identified as the *general adaptation syndrome* or GAS (Tortora and Grabowski 1993). The GAS *temporarily* resets the body's operating reference parameters to values that are more suited for handling the perceived emergency, and more easily controlled by feedback/feedforward anatomical mechanisms. Administered by the hypothalamus of the limbic system, the GAS first produces an immediate, acute response (the instantaneous *alarm reaction*), which is followed by a longer-lasting, delayed *resistance reaction*.

The alarm reaction works through both the sympathetic branch of the autonomic nervous system and the adrenal medulla of the endocrine system, to excite visceral *effector organs*, such as the liver, the lungs, and the spleen. Responses to autonomic stimulation result mainly from the release, by the sympathetic nervous system, of the adrenergic neurotransmitter called *norepinephrine*; while responses to endocrine stimulation derive primarily from the release, by the adrenal glands, of the adrenergic hormone called *epinephrine* (adrenaline). In the alarm reaction, the liver pours huge amounts of glucose (fuel) into the blood, the lungs add a great deal more oxygen, and the spleen supplies additional stored blood to help carry that air/fuel mixture. The goal of these responses is to supply huge amounts of fuel to the organs that are most active in warding off danger, that is, the brain (which handles alertness and control), skeletal muscles (which allow one to fight or flee), and the heart (the fuel pump). Under a *temporary* state of alarm, then:

- one's heart rate can potentially quadruple, and the force of cardiac contraction, as well as blood pressure, can increase by orders of magnitude

- blood flow can be re-routed away from the skin and non-essential viscera to organs and tissues that are vital to the emergency response

- respiration rate can go way up, almost to panting levels, and breathing is much deeper

- the pupils of the eyes dilate (part of the increased alertness)

- blood sugar levels skyrocket

- one's mouth goes dry as saliva production virtually ceases

- gastrointestinal symptoms (such as a "queasy stomach", appear as digestive activity slows

- urinary and reproductive activities are inhibited.

This is all for the sake of survival of the self!

As opposed to being activated primarily by neurotransmitters that produce immediate, localized, short-term responses, the delayed *resistance reaction* is activated by the hypothalamic hormones growth-hormone-releasing hormone (GHRH), corticotrophin-releasing hormone (CRH), and thyrotropin-releasing hormone (TRH). These act on the anterior (front part of the) pituitary gland. In turn, the latter releases the hormones adrenocorticotropic hormone (ACTH, in response to CRH), thyroid-stimulating hormone (TSH, in response to TRH), and human growth hormone (hGH, in response to GHRH). ACTH causes the adrenal cortex to release cortisol and a variety of glucocorticoids and mineralocorticoids, some of which act on the kidney; TSH causes the thyroid gland to release thyroxine and triiodothyronine; and hGH acts directly on the liver. The resistance reaction basically takes over where the alarm reaction leaves off.

Thus, responding to these so-called stress hormones, disruptive inflammatory responses are mitigated; *cellular* biochemical reactions promoting additional fuel supplies are enhanced (although blood chemistry, especially sugar levels returns to essentially pre-stress values); acid–base balance is stabilized; one experiences increased sweating (to get rid of the additional heat generated by increased metabolism); emotional crises are addressed through cognitive pathways (after the fact!); and the body basically continues to respond to the stressor, in anticipation of its being shortly resolved and things soon returning to their pre-stressed condition.

But, what if they don't? What if the stress persists continuously? Recall that the operative word in describing GAS was "temporary." The heart was no more designed to beat continuously at 240 cycles per minute than was the musculoskeletal system to sprint at high speed through a 26.2-mile marathon race! Neither was the pancreas designed to handle sustained periods of elevated blood sugar levels without succumbing to a sequence of disturbances that could potentially thrust the body into a diabetic state. One cannot continue to breathe at panting rates for sustained periods of time. Indeed, those very hormones and neurotransmitters that were so helpful when they were needed to handle an emergency situation now become potentially toxic if they are permitted to hang around for extended periods. They were manufactured only to act for brief periods of time, to address a momentary perceived threat to survival, an emergency.

Thus, the flooding of the entire organism with excessive hormones can eventually become pathological if allowed to prevail. If, for the sake of survival, body rhythms are escalated in order to produce:

- either over-focused or extreme peripheral vision
- ambient hearing
- redirected blood flow from the extremities to the brain and certain skeletal muscles required to "fight or flee" (hence the corresponding feeling of cold hands and feet)
- evacuation of waste
- temporary abatement of digestion

and additional physiological responses that are "crisis-oriented" (increased heart rate, and so on), and if such escalated body rhythms are endured for more than brief, intermittent periods of time, then the body is in trouble! Indeed, among the plethora of consequences that may derive from prolonged stress responses are gastritis, ulcerative colitis, irritable bowel syndrome, peptic ulcers, hypertension, asthma, diabetes, anxiety, rheumatoid arthritis, migraine headaches, fibromyalgia, depression, chronic disease/infection, tension myositis, slow wound healing, total exhaustion. The list is virtually endless, and at the extremes there can result heart attack, cancer, stroke, and other seriously debilitating, often fatal, afflictions. In fact, one can say with a great deal of certainty that it's not really the heart attack, or cancer, or stroke that causes death – it's the stress, manifesting itself in all of these consequences, that kills (Schneck 2002).

Most important from the point of view of clinical intervention is that stressors soon cause the shutdown of cognitive function. The physiological reaction to fear preempts thought and dispenses with the need to analyze, discuss, scheme, calculate, etc., in favor of going directly to the business of preserving the system from possible destruction. When fear derives from uncoordinated, inaccurate, or systemically miscoded sensory information, as the five case examples introduced earlier suggest, the amygdala, thalamus, and hypothalamus of the old brain (paleoencephalon) immediately thrust the organism into a fight-or-flight emergency survival behavior. Worst of all, the temporarily re-set reference values, if allowed to persist, can become permanent, as we shall see in the next section. If the perceived threat is continuous, such altered behavior becomes the "norm" for that system. In other words, the operating set-points will have been *conditioned* to be the expected homeostatic response markers for that system (Berger 2002; Berger and Schneck 2003; Schneck 1990; Schneck and Berger 1999).

In a feedback control sense, homeostatic operating set-points for those individuals suffering from perpetual fear have been put in place to evoke continuous fight-or-flight reaction cycles for those systems. These are responses in which behavior and actions become governed by surges of endocrine hormones and sympathetic nervous system discharges (Berger and Schneck 2003; LeDoux 2002; Schneck 1997; Schneck and Berger 1999; Tortora and Grabowski 1993). Consistent repetition of stress-hormone-driven modes of physiological operation becomes a self-sustaining, conditioned response ultimately resulting in systemic toxicity and dysfunctional adaptations, as described below.

In all of the cases described above, the observed behaviors typify *dysfunctional adaptations* resulting from perpetual fear stressors. Whether those stressors emanate from ineffectual sensory processing, imagined situations and events, inability to process cognitive information, language and learning delays, incapacity to understand, anticipate, or decode the body language of others, or drug-related signal distortions, the ultimate response is the same: *fear*. How do persistent fear disturbances to the controlled system that is the human body permanently change its operating set-points? The answer is that it happens through the physiological process called *functional adaptation* (physiological Attributes 4, 5, and 6 introduced in Chapter 4).

## Physiological accommodation

Driving the body with a continuous disturbance (forcing function) activates the organism's ability to *accommodate* – which is to say, to alter either its operating set-points, or the transfer functions of its various sub-systems, or both, in response to a persistent stimulus (disturbance to a quasi-equilibrated state). Recall that operating set-points define the homeostatic reference quantities toward which the body tends to quasi-equilibrate, driven there by its numerous feedback/feedforward control systems. Recall further that transfer functions are the input/output properties of the respective sub-systems with which the body is anatomically endowed. "Driving the body" (i.e., practicing, as is common knowledge among musicians and athletes) propels the body to new levels of performance, which levels become the physiological norm, if the stimulus that triggered the accommodation process is persistent enough to be dealt with in a long-term sense.

As an example of how accommodation works, try this experiment. For one entire day, force yourself (i.e., disturb your quasi-equilibrated state) to neither say, nor do anything negative, no matter what. Make no derogatory comments about anyone; let unfavorable remarks made to or about you go by passively, without reacting; avoid confrontations; do not engage in arguments. Make a deliberate effort to find an admirable attribute of any situation in which you might find yourself, and magnify, out of proportion, the positive aspects of that situation; ignore the down-side of anything and everything and concentrate only on the up-beat side. Fail to notice if things are not going exactly according to plan. Launch no offensives; be harmless; find no fault; "turn the other cheek;" look for a reason to compliment – make one up if you have to.

We can already hear you saying "That's both ridiculous and impossible! Not practical; not realistic; naive; purely hypothetical; not 'normal'; contrary to 'instinctive' tendencies – no way!" And we totally agree. Such behavior is *not* "typical," because on a day-to-day basis one is bathed in negatives, such that the systemic operating set-points and corresponding transfer functions are specifically coded to "protect and defend" against anticipated attack. This is a classic example of a *perceived* reality, a "gloom-and-doom" forecast that *expects* threats to survival. Indeed, one is programmed, both genetically (nature) and experientially (nurture), to always be "on guard," and to be prepared to go on the offensive (or flee) as necessary. The 'average' person is taught to treat everyone, and every situation, as a potential threat to his or her safety; one must be suspicious, dubious, cautious.

One of the first words everybody learns is "No!" Every day, newscasters open their broadcasts with the words "Good morning" – and then proceed to tell their audience why it isn't! In fact, one prominent American television news network journalist has been quoted as saying, "Hear no evil, speak no evil, see no evil, and you'll never be a television anchorman." Society seems to function according to the Law of Murphy: "If anything can go wrong, it will." And, according to the Principle of Peter, "Mediocrity is encouraged by our consistently promoting people to their level of incompetence." Many religions preach that everybody is, by nature, a sinner and thus in need of divine salvation.

So, are humans *conditioned* to think in negatives? Apparently that is exactly the case; and, for the same reason, we are also conditioned to try to survive and to fear perceived threats to survival. The wiring, the hardware, the anatomical neural networks to perceive otherwise are basically not there, or are suppressed. Certainly, if not encouraged, such suppression is a classic illustration of the generally accepted "use it or lose it" principle in physiol-ogy, which is the very basis for the process of accommodation. That's why we (the authors) agree that it is hard, *at first*, to go through a 24-hour period without succumbing to the tendency to accentuate the negative and eliminate the positive. Of course it is! That's exactly why, in your first attempt, you have to force yourself not to succumb to that tendency.

However, although we might agree that your apprehension is perfectly justified, we do so only to a certain degree, because we also know that the "use it or lose it" principle works in reverse as well. Thus, while the sustained *absence* of a continuous disturbance can cause the body to lose its responsive-ness to that form of stimulation, continuous driving functions – such as those embedded in the elements of music – can exploit the body's ability to accommodate in order to do just the opposite, which is to say, "use" the stimulus as a way of re-coding the system's homeostatic operating set-points.

Each time a particular sensory or motor signal to which the body is responsive passes through a sequence of neural pathways, these pathways become more capable of transmitting the same signal the next time it comes through. This is a physiological process called *facilitation*, or "memory of sensation."

At first, the disturbing signal might need to be "forced" through an anatomical region having the ability to generate new neural pathways that are possible, but not yet existing. In that sense, forcing functions can "blaze" new information-processing channels. Alternatively, the stimulus might have access to already-existing but dormant tracks, "overgrown with weeds," so to speak, from lack of use. The latter will frequently exist as one or more *collateral* branches of a nerve axon, in which case one might think of facilitation as a "clearing of the tracks," opening them up for subsequent use.

In the first case (i.e., forging new information-processing channels), one could think of facilitation as a type of *programmed learning*, akin to writing the software that commands a computer to do a specific task it has not done before. But, unlike a computer, the human body has the ability to convert software into hardware. It can build new "tracks" (neural networks) through an anatomical remodeling capability known as *plasticity*. But it does so only if the disturbing signal is persistent enough to be reckoned with. That is to say, the nervous system *remembers* both how, and how often, it responded in a certain way to a certain stimulus. Thus, subsequent responses to that same stimulus, if it is repeated enough times (practice!), become routine and "second nature."

Through the physiological property of plasticity/anatomical remodeling, then, the processing of information through facilitated pathways eventually evolves into a *conditioned reflex network* (as opposed to an inherited *instinctive* one). The result of this conditioning is that the systemic response to a persistent disturbance (originally in the form of a software program, or some other type of forcing function) now takes the form of a newly generated anatomical neural network (hardware) that defines a new systemic operating set-point toward which the body is driven through its various control mechanisms. If the new reference set-point defines some behavioral pattern (like not finding fault, in the simple experiment suggested earlier), the individual involved finds that he or she can manifest that behavior more easily, and it eventually becomes a *habit*.

Once that has happened – once the new (or rejuvenated) neural networks are in place and the new homeostatic reference quantities are established – the system is said to have *adapted* to the persistent stimulus. In most cases, this physiological process reaches the point where the original stimulus that started the adaptive process is no longer necessary to elicit the response, for reasons discussed later in this chapter and in Chapter 6. This is because such stimulation has been replaced by a new operating set-point that serves the same purpose. That is to say, the body's desire to function at that new reference level results in its being forced to do so by its own inherent control systems; it no longer needs anything else (a separate forcing function) to remind it of what to do.

As the adaptive process relates to the little experiment we are proposing you try, no doubt at first you will have to work at overriding existing temptations (reference set-points already in place) to be negative. But remember that you also probably fell off your bicycle the first time that you tried to ride it; and great performers did not succeed the first time they picked up an instrument; and superior athletes did not materialize overnight. Keep that in mind as you realize also that the music therapist, in the five examples cited earlier in this chapter, is faced with five individuals presenting with operating set-points that have gone awry. He or she, then, must approach the clinical intervention with the confidence that, to the degree that the "new way" is practiced, over and over again, and to the extent that the therapist persists and doesn't give up, he or she will prevail. In those five cases – and in the case of your original apprehensions regarding the little experiment – the physiological process of functional adaptation will eventually prove that it *can be done*: your original doubts were wrong!

As time goes on, if you persist in overriding your body's "errant" set-points, you will find that you no longer have to work at seeing the best in situations and/or people. It will become natural for you to be that way; you will have evolved into a new person, and you will have done it by exploiting your body's inherent ability to adapt to a persistent stimulus. You will have "practiced to make perfect." That is precisely the technique that the music therapist must employ to effect change in his or her clients, as will become more apparent as you read the material in Chapters 7–12.

Going one step further, if children are taught to develop these same habits, and they teach their children, then generations later, what started out to be just an "experiment" in your particular lifetime could possibly wind up being inscribed into your family's genome. In other words, what began as a disturbance-driven, forced response that became *entrained* (Chapter 6), triggering the physiological process of functional adaptation, could very well evolve into a set of instructions permanently etched into the genetic code of your progeny, several generations down the line.

To be strictly accurate, it should be noted that the foregoing is currently an unresolved issue in the field of genetics, so that it remains somewhat speculative, although feasible. As of this writing, a specific mechanism to explain how the somatic line of DNA can permeate the genetic line of nucleic acids has not been discovered, nor has enough experimental evidence accumulated to support the idea that such a mechanism even exists. Thus, the prevailing conventional wisdom dictates that *acquired* traits, such as through functional adaptation, cannot be inherited, except as the result of mutations that derive from the effect on DNA of external forms of radiation, ultrasound, X-rays, etc. In other words, current thinking is that the *genetic* line of *inherited* attributes, and the *somatic* line of *acquired* attributes, derive from separate processes. However, not all such processes have yet been investigated sufficiently to make this a definitive conclusion.

The above caveat notwithstanding, should further research show that at least some acquired traits *do* turn out to be inheritable, then, with respect to *those* traits, and their associated homeostatic operating reference quantities, not only will the latter be completely re-set in your great-great-great offspring, but also, the very organic transfer functions (input/output characteristics) of the physiological systems that are responsible for the behavioral patterns instigated in your generation will have been totally overhauled. As an inscribed code, then, less *control* will be needed to achieve those patterns, so the feedback/feedforward control mechanisms will not have to work as hard in order to elicit the desired responses, which are now genetically guaranteed. Keep in mind that subjecting the body to inident sound energy through the elements of music, as discussed in Chapter 6, *is* a form of external "radiation" that affects *both* somatic and germ cells, so what is proposed here is not as speculative as it might appear. Moreover, should it turn out that there *is* a mechanism for somatic adaptation to be inscribed into the genetic code, then this might be a better way to look at Charles Darwin's theory of natural selection. In other words, those species who "survived" were those best able to adapt to their changing environment (continuous disturbances), and were thus the "fittest" in that sense (i.e., effectively responsive and able to inscribe that response).

Be that as it may, at least in your generation, the important thing is not to get discouraged with early failures at attempts to learn something new, like riding a bicycle, or change particular behavioral patterns through professional therapy, or whatever. One needs to get out of the programmed "I tried

– it didn't work – I give up" mindset, replacing it with trust and faith in the physiology of functional adaptation. The process must be given time to "do its thing," and not truncated after a mere token attempt, only to be abandoned. Indeed, physiological accommodation is fundamental to the process of learning *anything*, in that learning is most effectively accomplished only by persistent repetition, by practice. Precedents clearly prove that it works in a given individual, regardless of whether or not behavioral changes can be inherited.

Furthermore, functional adaptation is not exclusively confined to the domain of consciously instigated driving functions. For simplicity we chose, as an example, alterations in operating set-points that were motivated by a conscious desire to change. However, from the point of view of the process of accommodation, it does not matter whether the continuous disturbance is deliberate (cognitive, verbal, etc.) or subliminal (subconscious, emotional, musical, etc.). The *process* by which change is effected, through physiological entrainment, facilitation, conditioning, adaptation, possible inscription, and so on, is the same, whether it be the result of a conscious effort or one that is subconscious. And the *effect* is the same. The human body can be "driven" just as easily by subliminal stimulation, such as through music, as it can by mindful stimulation, such as through cognizant efforts. In fact, in many ways, subliminal stimulation is even *more* effective in driving the system, because it does so through subconscious pathways that are less likely to encounter conscious resistance. That is why, for example, the fear response can be so devastating if one gets caught up in it. On the other hand, that is also why music can be so effective in reversing the fear spiral, compared with other methods of clinical intervention.

In a way, we feel almost silly making a point of this. Anyone who has ever studied an instrument, or participated in a sport, or learned to ride a bicycle, or swim, or whatever, knows and appreciates the value and importance of practice as a means to an end. It seems almost too inherently obvious to be writing about, especially considering that the physiological examples of functional adaptation are many. We can mention the remodeling of bone tissue under sustained stress (this is Wolff's law: a piezoelectric phenomenon that actually reverses in a sub-gravity environment), and the ability of the cardiovascular system to (reversibly) acclimate itself to high or low altitudes, involving the kidney's control of the production of red blood cells and the evolution of gravity-driven balance and equilibrium reflexes (Schneck 1990).

That being the case, it should be equally obvious that music therapy takes *time* to produce results, in a not-yet-quantified, dose–response sense. The process of functional adaptation does not manifest itself overnight. The forcing function that is music must be continuous and maintained at threshold levels for extended periods in order to effect significant, measurable, and permanent changes, most especially when those changes require first truncating the *fear spiral*.

## Caught in the fear spiral

As discussed earlier, humans have always initially responded sub-cognitively, intuitively, and spontaneously to sensory stimulation, by means of genetically inscribed, emotionally driven instincts. Indeed, emotions were with us before self-awareness. The instinct to survive in the face of *perceived* threats is the engine that propels physiological function. *Thought* (based on the cognitive awareness of internal and external events) is a luxury afforded as an "after"-thought, whereby the event(s) enter consciousness long after (as much as 500 milliseconds) a response to the event has already taken place instinctively (Berger and Schneck 2003; Damasio 1999; LeDoux 2002; Libet 2002, 2003; Shevrin *et al.* 1992). In other words, in a moment of perceived danger, first the heart races, hands sweat, stomach cramps, breathing hyperventilates, etc., before one knows the reason why. It can also be that any given event might never even enter (via the hippocampus) the conscious arena, but rather remain in the subconscious memory of the amygdala permanently, so that the slightest subliminal reminder – a scent, vision, *déjà vu* circumstance, etc. – will trigger palpitations and sweat without the person ever understanding why this is occurring.

Since fear derived from a perceived threat to survival is the underlying emotion driving human behavior, it follows that in problematic sensory systems, where stimulus encoding of sensory information is distorted or otherwise inaccurately processed, the human system will be thrust into a perpetual state of fear, and survival behaviors will be manifest as norms for that system. Such systems will routinely operate in fight-or-flight mode, characterized by internal hyperactivity, ambient or over-focused vision, and the rest of the fear aspects described in the above five clinical cases. As already explained, when the body is thus conditioned, fear responses will always predominate, eventually becoming self-sustaining habits (pathological set-points) even when one might never be fully aware of the fact that this behavior is continually being perpetuated by recurring (subconscious) fear. Thus, the sequence flows as follows:

*fear* ⟶ *stress* ⟶ *response* (sub-cognitive) ⟶ *desired result* (safety, survival, comfort, etc.)

Stress could subsequently become consciously attenuated, through the cognitive pathways of the neocortex, by adaptive mechanisms which, over time, could serve to modulate fear responses to certain stimuli. Of course it is hoped that this modulation would take the form of minimizing, redirecting, or totally eliminating former fear responses. In fact, functional adaptation through cognitive attenuation of fear responses is probably one of the ways by which the human organism has managed to survive to its current stage of evolution. But in order to comprehend this process, one must understand the organization of the human system as *nature* engineered it, while attempting to fit that understanding into those paradigms that human engineers have conceptualized in order to envision, develop, and build human-made designs and control systems that are formulated from nature's role models.

Should the fear factor survive mitigation by the amygdala, and somehow manage to reach higher levels of cognitive processing and conscious interpretation, then what one might refer to as "psychologically induced" stress manifests itself as a conditioned *attitude* of fear. For example, as illustrated in Figure 5.1, the roar of a jet engine, or merely seeing the picture of a jet aircraft on a billboard, can trigger the response of fear of flying in a person who has a distinct attitude toward the idea of flying. In other words, this person's operating set-point has become a persistent attitude of fear. Through the *instinctive* fear-response mechanisms, a cognitively derived attitude of fear now reinforces and amplifies the *conscious* stress-related fear response. Cognition has stepped in after the initial occurrence that triggered the original response, and has taken over in an attempt to explain previous, spontaneous responses that were originally the result of feedback to subcortical instincts.

At this juncture, the fear responses become further fortified (learned) and are now fed forward to create states of fight-or-flight even when the original stimulus is no longer present, as in Figure 5.1. Just the thought of the event triggers increased pulse, stomach cramps, and so on. Consequently, instinctive reactions become even more conditioned by a feedback/feedforward, give-and-take exchange (a sort of "dance") choreographed by the cognitive brain's awareness of fear (Berger and Schneck 2003; Damasio 1999, 2003).

*Figure 5.1 The birth of pathological fear. When sensory input (in this case, the sound of a jet airplane) is interpreted as threatening to survival through neural pathways that course through the amygdala and other subcortical brain structures, the body is instinctively diverted into a fight-or-flight response mode (sweating, quickened heart beat, shortness of breath, etc.). This state of high alert is exacerbated when related inputs are further interpreted, both sub-cognitively and cognitively, as threatening. Once fear takes hold, it can escalate, become automatic, and even spiral out of control in response to similar or related situations, whether actual or suggested, as in this case, when the individual happens to pass a suggestive travel billboard.*

Interestingly, as Joseph LeDoux (1998, 2002) and others point out, a fear event that has once occurred – even if there was no conscious realization of it at the time because the event bypassed cognitive channels in favor of being tracked and processed by instinctive ones – can still become permanently recorded into the memory of the amygdala. The event need not ever have reached the hippocampus for further coding and cognitive processing. Instead, it remains inscribed into the archives of the subconscious (the amygdala). Once there, even the slightest reference to the original event will be immediately perceived as a threat, and thus elicit the fear response sub-consciously. This could then trigger panic attacks, hyperventilation, and a state of agitation common to the fight-or-flight response. Meanwhile, the person to whom this is happening wonders what is going on, and why, not being particularly conscious of the fact that something is wrong. Caught up in the fear spiral, the person's state of defensiveness escalates out of control. No sense of reason prevails. Emotions dictate all behavioral responses, which are entirely instinctive reactions to *perceived* threats to survival. This, more often than not, is what the therapist must "work through" in developing sys-tematic protocols for clinical intervention.

What's more, if the fear event *has* reached the conscious mind, then the clinician must also deal with the added *attitude* factor, which will alter the previous instinct-derived paradigm of fear response. What results, then, is an infinite cyclic *do-loop*, to use a computer-language phrase, which escalates further, beginning with the initial cycle:

*fear* ⟶ *induces* **perceived threat stress** *(mediated by the amygdala, thalamus, hypothalamus etc.)* ⟶ *which triggers* **instinctive responses** *(flight-or-fight symptons)* ⟶ *which create* **desired results** *(safety and survival)* ⟶ *followed by* **cognitive recognition/attitude** *(changes in memory, thought and condi-tioned/learned responses, mediated by the hippocampus etc.)*

This is reinforced over and over again as the cycle repeats, as shown in Figure 5.2. So, when cognition enters the scene, the fear cycle becomes an escalat-ing spiral that is extremely difficult to redirect once cognitive recall and "thought" have imposed themselves as integral parts of the system.

Any form of *sensory misrepresentation*, whether in diagnosed populations or typically functioning individuals, can operate within such a spiral. The process begins with uncoordinated sensory information tracking, process-ing, and encoding, which leads to inaccurate assessments of survival condi-tions, which leads to a constant physiological state of fear, which leads to a

*Figure 5.2 Schematic representaion of the fear spiral*

continual survival behavior mode derived from operating set-points gone awry, which keeps academic learning, memory, and social accommodation limited, which precipitates social "disapproval" and negativity, which is perceived by the victim of the fear response as a further threat to survival, which further exacerbates those fear responses. As you can see, the fear spiral is as exasperating as reading through the above paragraph.

Eventually, neither meaningful academic learning, nor effective clinical intervention, can take place while the organism is in this perpetual fear–response spiral. One cannot deal effectively with an individual whose conditioned responses have set the system's feedback/control reference signals to a continual emergency alarm configuration. The brain is simply too busy protecting the body from what it has erroneously concluded to be an environmental situation in which existing elemental conditions are threatening to its survival (Schneck and Berger 1999).

## To change, or not to change?

The person caught in a fear spiral may not be aware of the state of physiological stress and anxiety that his or her system is enduring. In fact, fight-or-flight behavior might be so deeply instilled that it feels like a familiar and perhaps even "comfortable" way for that "me" to be. After all, how would the brain know that the information it is processing, or cannot process, is not the norm? How could the brain know that it does not know something, or that it is not processing information accurately? Indeed, how does a brain know what it does not know? Inputs received from the sensory systems is the only information that the brain perceives and can act upon. And if that information is processed as being unsafe, action will be called for accordingly: sound the alarms!

Before contemplating interventions designed to alter responses in an individual, one must carefully consider his or her reason(s) for wanting to do so, not the least of which involves answering the question "For whose benefit are adaptive changes being sought?" Disregarding societal, educational, psychological, or intellectual reasons for seeking to alter perpetual fear responses (all of which are often of more interest to the clinician than to the recipient of the treatment), one of the main reasons for the need to truncate the fear spiral is its constant assault on the system by surges of hormones elicited by anxiety and stress. As discussed earlier in this chapter, these hormones, if allowed to "hang around," can damage organs, tissues, and brain areas, so it is important to control or reduce such continuous chemical surges. The fight-or-flight stress response is intended to be triggered only occasionally, and to last for just short periods of time; if it persists, the hormones elicited can, and do, become toxic to the organism. Thus, for physiological reasons alone, it is critical to modify homeostatic set-points that have gone wild.

In order to break the infinite "do-loop," or reconfigure the escalating fear spiral, the system's inscribed emotional/instinctive responses to perceived fear threats must be systemically reprogrammed. Such reprogramming will allow comfortable, functionally adaptive processing and evaluation of sensory information to proceed relative to calmer homeostatic reference points that replace those derived from criteria of fear. This means that the sensory system must be targeted for more effective integration and functional coding of information. As sensory integration and response reprogramming begin to take hold (adaptation), feedback/feedforward control responses will change and be better able to be redirected to the higher level cognitive processes that might also have been contributing to the chaos. Only after the system has been relieved of the emergency alarm responses will the gates to thinking and learning fully re-open. Enter the role of music as a clinical intervention.

## The role of music therapy

As a physiological tool (forcing function) for triggering functional adaptation, music helps drive the sophisticated feedback control system that is the human body, to adjust its operating set-points (reference signals). This the body does through mechanisms of *entrainment* (discussed in Chapter 6) that, in turn, set into motion functionally adaptive processes. These processes can result in redirected physiological patterns, as well as psychological attitudes. In short, music can truncate the fear spiral!

Why? Because, as has already been suggested, music does not depend on semantic interpretation to be understood. Therefore, music does not need the "thinking brain" in order to reach and influence activity within the inner realms of the human physiological apparatus. Because music resonates symbiotically with instinctive physiological attributes, it has the ability to bypass the cognitive feedforward *attitude toward fear* aspect of the response spiral illustrated in Figure 5.2. Furthermore, precisely *because* music has no particular need for cognitive assistance in order to be efficacious, music therapy is one of the most efficient, effective, non-invasive, non-chemical, non-pharmaceutical applications for addressing and altering sensory perception difficulties at the subcortical, instinctive level of accommodation.

To summarize, the common factor in each of the five personalities described earlier in this chapter is that they are all victims of the fear spiral, with flight-or-fight responses permeating their reactions and behaviors. Each individual's homeostatic set-points have been set as that system's "response norm" to presenting circumstances, *as their brains perceive them to be.* These circumstances may be externally and/or internally derived. Therefore, each behavior becomes "normal" and perfectly comfortable for each individual system, which is precisely why music intervention works so well. Music is neither normal nor abnormal; neither right nor wrong; neither correct nor incorrect as it penetrates the system. Rather, it is a subtle, subliminal source for inducing physiological changes in the moment. The goal, of course, is the continued application (forcing function) of music elements, singularly or in complex combinations, in systematic and repetitive applications targeted to revise fear-inducing sensory information-processing by providing new response options to the brain. Given enough repetition (continuous disturbance, *practice*), it is possible to eventually alter homeostatic set-points, thus modulating anxiety and fear-induced behaviors. The mechanism by which this is accomplished goes by the technical term introduced earlier, and discussed in more detail in the next chapter – *entrainment.*

Chapter 6

# Physiological Entrainment

Musical training is a more potent instrument than any other, because
rhythm and harmony find their way into the inward places of the
soul, on which they mightily fasten, imparting grace, and making
the soul of him who is rightly educated graceful.

Plato, *The Republic*

## Introduction

In Chapter 5, the concept of physiological accommodation/adaptation was
introduced as the means by which the body can develop a tolerance to any
type of disturbance that it has to deal with on a regular basis. It does so by
fine-tuning its operating set-points and organic transfer functions, so that its
various control mechanisms concerned with homeostasis can be optimized
for better, or in the case of the fear spiral, for worse, in the presence of persistent forcing functions. The essence of accommodation is that human body
responses are information-based, and the body is always ready and receptive
to taking in and adapting to new information – "willing to listen," so to
speak. This aspect of physiological function provides the scientific underpinnings for the development of effective protocols to intervene clinically,
especially with music, in diagnosed populations. Physiological adaptation,
as a means for optimization of homeostatic control, is generally initiated by
the process of *physiological entrainment*.

The definition of entrainment reduces to a description of this phenomenon, rather than a formal meaning of the word. This description, in turn,
derives from an observation that has been emphasized throughout the earlier
chapers of this book, namely, that the human body has a natural predisposition
to connect with and respond to – via feedback/feedforward control loops –
both its internal and external environments. This is ambiensomatic percep-

tion. Such coupling and reacting are critical aspects of the organism's instinct to satisfy its fundamental need to survive.

Entrainment, then, is the word used to describe what is occurring when the human organism succumbs to a forcing function. "Succumb" connotes the body's becoming *synchronized* with the forcing function (literally, "boarding the train"), to the ultimate extent of allowing itself to be *driven* by it (letting the train take it to a specific destination), consciously or subconsciously. The driving to the point of actual entrainment is among the variables that ultimately "convince" the body to adapt (in a sense, "live" at the destination to which the train has taken it). Any form of clinical intervention, including music therapy, is ultimately trying to accomplish just such an adaptation, as a means for alleviating specific diagnosed afflictions.

Invariably, external forcing functions (*continuous disturbances*, in control-theory language), manifest themselves in the types of adequate stimuli to which the organism attends. Recall that these are just various forms of energy (heat, light, sound, etc.), several of which are embedded in the elements of music. In fact, the phenomenon of resonance (described in Chapter 3), wherein a system is driven at its natural frequency, is one specific example of entrainment. Another is what often happens at a pop concert. The on-stage performer (driving function) begins to clap his or her hands in a rhythmic pattern, encouraging the audience to follow suit. At first, there is a random response, and one hears irregular clapping with no discernible pulse. But as time goes on, order derives from chaos, and soon the entire audience is clapping in total synchrony, at a very distinct, steady, almost mesmerizing pulse, in perfect time with the rhythm of the music. *That's entrainment!*

There are several different types and mechanisms of physiological entrainment. As the process relates specifically to musical inputs, however, only five of these will be discussed. They are entrainment as it is accomplished through:

- neural excitation/inhibition/neogenesis (i.e., entrainment through the *nervous system*)

- gene expression/suppression/recruitment (i.e., entrainment through *genes*)

- enzyme kinetics/mobilization/deactivation (i.e., entrainment through *biochemical catalysts*)

- biasing of CNS information-processing networks (i.e., entrainment through *sensitization* of such networks to specific stimuli)

- the transport and utilization of energy (i.e., entrainment through *metabolic* pathways and energy centers).

## Entrainment through the nervous system

Neurotransmitters, synapses, excitatory versus inhibitory action potentials, and compound signals that derive from neural networks were discussed in some detail in Chapters 3 and 4. In the discussion of functional adaptation in Chapter 5, these principles were extended to introduce the concepts of:

- memory of sensation (*facilitation*, under the influence of repeated stimulation)

- anatomical remodeling (*neogenesis*, affected by the attribute of neural plasticity, acting through potential tissue spaces)

- collateral networking (*re-routing* signals through alternative branch points along neural pathways)

- conditioned reflexes (*habits* that result from persistent forcing functions).

Entrainment, through its action on the nervous system, exploits all of these mechanisms, gaining access to the body through central, peripheral, and autonomic nerve pathways. This it does in basically two ways.

The first method is by selectively inhibiting or exciting *existing* neural pathways. That is to say, a sensory input can be entrained by the body when it activates physiological mechanisms that determine *which* nerve is firing, at what firing *frequency*, and with what barcode-like *firing pattern*. These are all functions of the specific adequate stimulus involved (i.e., type of energy to which the nerve responds), its intensity (related to the *threshold* firing frequency of specialized nerves, discussed further below), history (as it relates to *accommodation*), and rate of change (as it relates to the *speed of recovery* of the responding nerve). The sensory input determines also the corresponding *amount* of inhibitory/excitatory neurotransmitter released at synaptic terminals, as well as the *number* of synapses in the particular nerve network.

The second method of entrainment can operate through processes that can be described as *discriminatory innervation*. By this is meant those techniques whereby the body entrains sensory inputs by activating mechanisms that affect:

- the specific anatomical/morphological shaping and/or branching configuration of neurons

- the building of new nerves (commonly known as *plasticity*)

- the elimination of neurons that are either not used routinely (which follows directly from the "use it or lose it" principle), or are otherwise obsolete.

A perfect example of discriminatory innervation is what happens if, during infancy, one eye of an animal is kept deliberately shielded from the outside world. If the cover is subsequently removed from the shielded eye, that animal will be completely and permanently blind in that eye, even though the eye itself may be functioning just fine! The problem is that the normal eye has entrained all visual inputs, to the point of developing enough neural fibers to completely occupy all of layer IV, the input layer of the visual cortex of the brain. Thus, in a competition for space, the normal eye will have "won" over the closed eye. The former will have evolved exclusive access to, and activating "privileges" for, nearly all of the cells in layer IV of the visual cortex; while the latter has "lost out," not being "allowed in" to the visual cortex (see a complete description of this process in Ornstein and Thompson 1984). The reason why the lost vision is permanent is that adaptation in the central nervous system is very slow, most especially when it is constrained by space limitations. Thus, in this case, it either does not occur at all, or, if it does, it is not fast enough to take effect within the lifespan of the animal, so it remains blind for all of its life.

There is much that remains unknown about the details of entrainment – the hows, and whys, and operational definitions of selective neural inhibition/excitation. Nor do scientists have all the information they need to understand discriminatory neogenesis (de-novo growth of new tissue) and/or necrobiosis (degenerative death of tissue) under the influence of persistent forcing functions. Indeed, these are but some of the many areas of systemic information entrainment, transport, and processing that are so badly in need of further research, especially as they relate to the processing of musical inputs. But here are some of the things that *are* known.

A most natural response of the human body to music is a synchronization of anatomical movements and other physiological/psychological functions with musical rhythms. That is to say, the first and perhaps most important (from a physiological point of view) element of music that the organism instinctively detects, attends to, and entrains through neural mechanisms is rhythm. In fact, perhaps the very nature of the pulse and rhythm of music was originally derived from, and is an external expression of, physiological periodicity. If that is truly the case, then the close relationship between the rhythms of the human body (biorhythms) and the rhythms in music render the latter most effective in capturing the brain's attention through neural entrainment. The system is definitely "interested" and responsive to the syntax of rhythm.

For example, a growing number of studies (e.g., Thaut *et al.* 1999) confirm that, when people listen to music, various aspects of their body rhythms display a dynamic embodiment of the temporal structure inherent in the musical rhythms they are encountering. Furthermore, electromyographic (EMG) studies of the electrical activity of muscle function show that auditory cues (driving functions) can arouse and raise the excitability of spinal motor neurons. This excitability is mediated by auditory-motor neural circuitry at the reticulospinal level. In particular, these findings have implications in clinical situations where motor planning is a problem (Berger 2002).

Also, in those instances where "mood adjustment" is an appropriate clinical intervention, electroencephalographic (EEG) studies of the electrical activity of the cerebral cortex of the brain show that auditory cues can capture one's attention. Such attentiveness results in brain waves becoming synchronized with the *binaural* beat frequency (repeating pulse; Chapter 7) – not to be confused with *dissonant* beat frequencies (Chapter 9). This synchronized brain activity seems to establish a "pleasing resonance" that captures the entire range of human emotions. The mechanism of action of this cerebral resonance was investigated in a National Institute of Mental Health (NIMH) study (Fries *et al.* 2001).

NIMH researchers discovered that synchronous firing of neurons in the brain (likely resulting from sensory entrainment) followed a subject's making a deliberate effort to *pay attention* to a particular sensory stimulus, while ignoring all other distractions. The investigators suggested that the resonance phenomenon following entrainment could be the brain's way of amplifying the volume of brain signals representing behaviorally relevant stimuli. Such amplification would boost the intensity of these particular stimuli above the level of the surrounding "noise." That is to say, entrainment, leading to brain-wave synchronization, leading to resonance, leading to amplification, might be the brain's way of paying attention to a particular stimulus, over and above surrounding distractions. This would allow it to concentrate on that sensory input, perhaps because it is perceived to be a threat to survival.

The results of these NIMH studies could also explain why, in a crowded room of people, talking in disparate voices, a very few of them singing in unison can quickly drown out the surrounding noise. In quantifying their findings, the investigators found that cerebral neurons excited by specific attributes of the attended stimulus conspicuously synchronized their activity in the gamma (40–90 Hz) range of the EEG, indicating extremely strong brain activity.

Other studies (e.g., Iwanaga 1995a, 1995b) reveal that subjects listening to music express a desire to hear it at "preferred tempi" (musical pace). Moreover, if the music is "familiar," these preferred tempi seem to have a simple harmonic relationship to (i.e., are directly proportional to) the individual's normal heart rate (70–100 cycles per minute). On the other hand, when exposed to simple, "unfamiliar" repeating patterns of "pure" tones, delivered machine-gun-style (like a 440-Hz, 60-decibel "concert A"), the subjects were found to prefer tempi in the somewhat higher range of 105–200 cycles per minute. What all of this means awaits further investigation.

## Entrainment through stimulation or inhibition of genetic material

In Chapter 4, under Attribute 7 of the "musical countdown paradigm," the functional unit of the human genome was identified to be the gene. It is that part of a chromosome that has the ability to elicit a specific anatomical trait, morphological characteristic, or behavioral pattern. Genes may be thought of as recipes for *proteins*. Proteins, in turn, are complex organic (carbon-containing) compounds constructed from 20 "standard" *amino acids*, which one may think of as the individual ingredients contained in the genetic recipes. These amino acids are linked together (mixed, according to the instructions in the recipe) in a *specific sequence* determined by the corresponding sequence of base-pairs (the recipe) in the DNA chain. Thus, different sequences code for different proteins; and different proteins serve different functions. Here are some examples:

- Proteins coded to serve as biochemical *enzymes* promote and speed up specific metabolic reactions.

- Proteins intended to serve as *neurotransmitters* relay the messages encoded in action potentials.

- *Contractile proteins* form the excitable elements of muscles.

- Proteins serving as *hormones* control the activity of "target" organs and tissues.

- *Structural proteins* act as scaffolding to establish the anatomical framework of the body. One such protein, the most abundant in the human body, is collagen.

- *Antibodies* are proteins specifically designed to ward off disease.

- *Hemoglobin* is a protein that helps to transport oxygen, as do other *protein carrier molecules,* which transport substances like glucose (carried by *insulin*) and various fats (carried by *lipoproteins*).

- *Receptor proteins* located along the surface of cell membranes provide sites to which substances having a geometry congruent to the receptor protein can "dock." Some of these substances, like hormones, activate a response from the particular cell to which they bind, while still other receptor proteins (such as *human leukocyte antigens*) serve as cell membrane "markers" to uniquely identify you as being *you.*

- *Sensory proteins* are responsive to adequate stimuli (various forms of energy).

- *Histones* are *nucleoproteins* that surround genes to protect them from mechanical harm and to ward off toxins and radiation.

Proteins are the inherited code over which one has little or no control, the set of building blocks that endows you with what is *possible* – your *nature.*

But in order for proteins to be manufactured and elicited, the portion of the DNA molecule that codes for them must be activated in a process called *gene expression.* That's the *nurture,* the actual, what becomes real, from what started out to be possible; and this process is one over which one does have quite a bit of control. Again, enter music!

Gene expression is mediated right on the DNA chain itself by specific command centers called *control genes.* These, too, can be excited or inhibited – for example, by corresponding neural stimulation, such as through the elements of music, as described below. Thus, some control genes *activate* gene

expression; others do exactly the opposite, they *suppress* protein production. In fact, most of the body's operating set-points are both established
and adhered to by the level of activity of *suppressor* control genes. These
regulate the activity of expression control genes that are responsible for the
manufacture of specific proteins, such that, when the suppressor gene is "on,"
gene expression is dormant. When the suppressor gene is "off", gene expression is activated, thus eliciting the type of "desired" physiological response
that is called for. In other words, only when the suppressor control gene is
deactivated does the desired response called for by the corresponding
operating set-point manifest itself, and vice versa. Entrainment exploits this
type of control, gaining access to the body through its effect in activating or
deactivating suppressor genes. This it does in ways that are described below.

But first, it is important to emphasize that the level of activity of suppressor control genes is especially significant when it involves the production of
stress hormones – which, as was mentioned in Chapter 5, could be harmful if
their presence is allowed to persist. Fear *inhibits* stress-hormone suppression,
which leads to stress-hormone *expression*, which leads to corresponding
fight-or-flight responses, which keep the body in a constantly mobilized
state in an attempt to protect it against perceived threats to survival. Fear
accomplishes this by acting through the amygdala to cause the release of
fear-induced neurotransmitters. These attach to and geometrically reconfigure (distort) the suppression control gene, thereby deactivating it. The
expression control gene for the manufacture of stress hormones can thus
function unabated and unregulated.

When such responses are legitimate – which is to say, when they derive
from a *real* threat to survival – the activity of the controlling elements/
signals, acting via the autonomic nervous and endocrine systems to trigger
emergency behavior, is totally justified; indeed, necessary! That's why such
responses evolved in the first place. But when the situation is otherwise, or
when the fear persists for periods of time that are much more than
"temporary," such responses, as discussed earlier, are entirely unjustified, and
potentially quite damaging. That's why, as a matter of routine, there are
active sensory signal-processing neural networks that actively suppress the
expression of stress hormones. A state of fear inhibits these; while music,
there is ample evidence for us to believe, has the ability to excite them.

That is to say, it is entirely feasible to propose that the elements of music
are a source of information that communicates directly with the body's
genetic material. Just as food communicates with the body through *biochemi-*

*cal* pathways, music communicates with it through *energy* pathways. Research is now under way (see below) which points clearly to the fact that the physiology of the human body is *harmonically ordered*, through the response characteristics of the human genome. That being the case, it follows that the elements of music may very well have the ability to excite stress-hormone-suppression genes (and perhaps even others) on the DNA molecule. Moreover, to a reasonable degree of scientific certainty, it is entirely possible that music can thus help to re-set malfunctioning system reference parameters that act to maintain the body in a perpetual fear state. The mechanism of action could be through entrainment of musical elements that resonate with these control-gene suppressors.

Lending credence to this theory are at least two recent, very interesting, studies, one reported by Alexjander and Deamer (1999), and the other published by Bittman *et al.* (2005). The former examined the vibrational frequencies at which the four DNA bases (adenine, cytosine, guanine, and thymine) resonate, when exposed to infrared radiation. They then transcribed these characteristic resonant frequencies into the audible spectrum and discovered a readily identifiable acoustic pattern! In fact, using microtonal scales derived from this pattern, one of the authors of the study (Susan Alexjander) was actually able to compose a piece of music which she called, appropriately enough, *Sequencia*. The other author (David Deamer) composed *Molecular Meditation*, based on a synthesizer translation of the nucleotide sequence of an antibody gene.

In the Bittman *et al.* (2005) investigation, a rather novel technological approach to analyzing gene expression was used in a study of the effect of a music-based clinical intervention in mitigating stress responses. The results obtained provided clear evidence that there may be a "highly-individual response to stress, in terms of gene expression changes, and a common pattern of reversing those gene expression changes in responding to a stress-reducing intervention." The authors emphasized the *individual-specific* nature of the responses, which, again, points to the need for dose–response criteria that can be tailored to a specific patient or client. To date, no such criteria exist.

Be that as it may, by extrapolation, these two very sophisticated studies strongly suggest that the body of any given individual may have a way of "recognizing" in music his or her unique electromagnetic pattern, a *musical DNA-print*, if you will. Perhaps through mechanisms of *melodic entrainment* (paralleling the previously discussed rhythm entrainment), or *harmonic entrainment* (see Chapter 9), or whatever, music can synergize with a specific and unique DNA-base-pair sequence that is encoded into that individual's nucleic acid chain. If the musical code (perhaps a unique melodic line) corresponds to the genetic code (a unique base-pair sequence), one has a "match," and entrainment follows, generating the appropriate resonant response – which, incidentally, could affect germ cells, as well as somatic cells, apropos to the discussion of physiological accommodation in Chapter 5.

Generalizing this reasoning still further, various anecdotal inferences suggest that, similar to the concept of "enneagrams," which define *personality* types on the basis of instinctual drives, certain *behavioral* types can be defined in terms of their physiologically derived musical preferences and their responses to different key signatures. Thus, for example, it is quite possible for someone to have a "C-major personality," or an "A-minor personality," and so on, paralleling the well-established psychological norms that define such things as "type A behavioral patterns" (Friedman and Rosenman 1974). Indeed, there is even evidence (based on a British study reported in the 9 March 2001 edition of the *Roanoke Times*, and published in a subsequent issue of *Science*) that "tin ears," too, may have a genetic origin. That is to say, these investigators found that about 80 percent of one's inability to recognize "fractured melodies" is an inherited characteristic.

We can mention two other mechanisms by which genetic entrainment could affect physiological function:

1.  Since only about 10 percent of the DNA chain is genetically "active", there could be activation (known as *recruitment*) of parts or all of the remaining 90 percent of that chain, which contains recipes that rarely, if ever, get used and which, too, can play a major role in the process of accommodation. These parts of the genome are there in reserve, as potential resources that can be enlisted as needed, not only for such purposes as accommodation/adaptation, but perhaps as well for evolution.

2.  The creation of genetic *mutations* can, perhaps through natural selection, deactivate growth suppressor genes, while activating others. The former is one viable mechanism that might help to explain the proliferation of cancer cells. The latter, depending on the type of mutation and the portion of the DNA chain affected, can have both positive and negative consequences. But the bottom line is, as was the case for entrainment through neural excitation/inhibition/neogenesis, that much still remains unknown, and there is ample scope for much more research,

most especially as it relates to music therapy. The same is true for entrainment through biochemical kinetics, discussed below.

## Entrainment through biochemical catalysis

The previous section addressed how musical stimulation of nucleic acids that function as control genes in the central nervous system can activate (or inhibit) the synthesis of specific proteins such as neurotransmitters, hormones, and enzymes. In the language of biochemistry, these proteins are called *first messengers* because they are the prime movers that act directly on target organs and tissues to affect specific physiological responses. The responses, in turn, derive from the first messengers' ability to activate *second-messenger* systems located within the cells of the target organs and tissues themselves. Such activation either: (1) mobilizes these systems to manufacture, via appropriate *enzyme kinetics* processes, more chemicals, more hormones, or more receptor molecules (affecting the *response thresholds* of the cells); or (2) does just the opposite, that is *deactivates* specific cellular processes. Second-messenger systems can act also on the genetic material (the DNA) located within specific cells (like neurons), to cause long-lasting, even permanent changes (Ornstein and Thompson 1984).

For example, first-messenger stimulation of the pituitary gland results in its secretion of opioids (*endorphins*, from *endo*genous mo*rphin*es). These cause about half of typical adults, listening to their favorite (that's the operative word here) music, to report experiencing a feeling of "chills running up and down their spine" – the so-called excitatory thrill effect (Goldstein 1980; Panksepp 1995). Opioids are protein stimulants manufactured in response to musically induced control-gene expression and have been shown to relieve pain and the suffering that accompanies stress, and to induce euphoric feelings of pleasure – presumably to counteract those anxiety sensations that result from stress (Gerber 1996; Jourdain 1997; Patrick 1999). Indeed, pain and pleasure are among the most compelling forces that drive human behavior. Thus, an ability to control these clinically through, for example, music therapy presents a significant means for medical intervention.

Also affected by the activity of second messengers is the body's immune system. In an interesting study conducted by Drs. Robert Beck and Thomas Cesario at the University of California/Irvine (2001, as reported on the UC Irvine website), it was found that professional choral singers experienced raised levels of immune system proteins important for fighting off

disease-causing agents after performing Beethoven's complex choral mas-
terwork *Missa Solemnis*. Researchers looked at singers' levels of immune
system proteins, including immunoglobulin A (IgA) and the stress hormone
cortisol, in saliva before and after two rehearsals and the performance. The
researchers concluded that "choral singing, particularly in performance,
appears to stimulate the immune system to fight disease." Admittedly, this
was not a double-blind, randomized, carefully controlled investigation, but
it is anecdotal evidence that suggests the need for further scientific study.

And the list goes on, with rather comprehensive reviews of the relevant
literature appearing in Hodges (1996b) and elsewhere (e.g., Bartlett 1996).
Suffice it to say here that second-messenger protein stimulants, manufactured and released in response to musically induced control-gene expression,
and acting primarily through the hypothalamic–pituitary–adrenal (HPA)
axis, the autonomic nervous and endocrine systemsm, have been shown to
have significant effects on:

- the cardiovascular system (heart, blood, blood vessels)
- the neuro-musculoskeletal system
- the respiratory system
- the renal system (kidneys)
- metabolism/bioenergetics and biochemical processes
- the integumentary system (skin)
- body temperature (both core and peripheral)
- the hepatic system (liver)
- the immune system (immunoglobulins, leukocytes)
- the central nervous system (brain and spinal cord)
- balance and equilibrium (vestibular responses)
- proprioception
- sexual activity.

These effects can be classified, generically, as being:

- excitatory (i.e., enhancing function)
- inhibitory (suppressing function)
- sedative (quieting)

- stimulative (arousing)

- aesthetic (providing an entertaining diversion)

- therapeutic (remedial – which, as shall be made clearer in the last section of this chapter, we distinguish from *therapy*, the latter connoting the actual re-setting of the body's operating set-points and transfer functions)

- ameliorating (making "better," or at least tolerable)

- abrasive (i.e., actually *producing* stress)

- biasing (affecting response sensitivity, which is discussed in somewhat more detail below).

## Entrainment through biasing of information-processing networks

In order to understand how entrainment works through the mechanism of biasing, consider the following physiological constraints, and refer back to Figure 4.1 in Chapter 4.

### *The depolarization potential and biasing*

Before a nerve will fire (generate an *action potential*), its electrochemical activity must be brought from a resting state (called the *resting potential* of the nerve, illustrated in Figure 4.1a) to a threshold level (called the *threshold potential* of the nerve, illustrated in Figure 4.1c). This process is called *depolarization*. It ensures that only adequate stimuli of sufficient strength will trigger a nerve response, so that the nerve will not be bothered by inconsequential "background noise" (Figure 4.1b). The difference between the threshold potential and the resting potential of a nerve is called its *depolarization potential*.

In order to get a nerve to fire, it must be depolarized from its resting level to its threshold level. It follows that the closer the resting potential is to the threshold potential (i.e., the smaller the depolarization potential), the more sensitive the nerve will be to the strength of the adequate stimulus. If the two are very close – a physiological state that can be achieved either by raising the resting potential or by lowering the threshold potential, or both – the nerve will be quite sensitive and fire very easily under the slightest provocation (Figure 4.1d). In other words, a small depolarization potential results in a nerve that is on the verge of firing.

Conversely, the more apart the two potentials are, the more resistant will be the nerve to any form of excitation (Figure 4.1b) because the large depolarization potential required to trigger a response will protect the nerve from firing too easily. Fine-tuning the depolarization potential of a nerve is one example of a process called *biasing*. In an everyday sense, biasing is understood to mean a predisposition to responding in a particular way, to a particular set of circumstances, oftentimes irrespective of the reasoning involved.

## Catalysis and enzyme activation

In order for biochemical reactions to take place at speeds consistent with the maintenance of life, nothing can be left to chance; the reactions must be carefully choreographed and enhanced. Such enhancement is called *catalysis*, which is accomplished by biochemical matchmakers called *enzymes*. While remaining themselves unchanged, enzymes ignite the participants (substrates) upon which they act to unite, at rates billions of times faster than they would otherwise. It follows that having the right enzyme, in sufficient quantities, in the right place, at the right time, in the right *state of activation*, are all crucial to ensuring the success of the biochemical reaction that the particular enzyme involved catalyzes.

Having the proper amount of the right enzyme, in the right place, at the right time, are mainly functions of genetic considerations previously discussed. But the state of activation of such enzymes is quite controllable. "Right state of activation" means that the enzyme is geometrically configured to be identically congruent (in a jigsaw puzzle sense) with the shape and size of the substrate molecules upon which it operates. That congruency (or lack thereof) is critical to proper enzyme function, and it depends on many factors independent of genes.

For example, because of the effect of heat on the geometry of molecules, extremes of body core temperature (hyperthermia or hypothermia) can seriously render enzymes incapable of performing their catalytic duty. The latter is referred to as *denaturing* the enzyme. The activity of these catalysts can also be seriously impaired by: (1) physiological states of excessive alkalinity or acidity; (2) the absence of certain important vitamins (*coenzymes*, like the B-complex vitamins thiamine and riboflavin) and minerals (*cofactors*, such as the inorganic ions magnesium and iron); and (3) malnutrition. There is a long list of other variables.

The bottom line is that activation of an enzyme is, to biochemical reactions, what depolarization threshold is to the generation of action potentials. Thus, fine-tuning the state of activation of enzymes is another example of biasing. But this time, biasing can cause biochemical reactions to "lean toward" completion, which is analogous to nerves "leaning toward" firing. Or biasing can do just the opposite: inhibit biochemical reactions to the point of not taking place at all, and thereby disrupting metabolic processes.

## Receptor sites

Before a target organ can respond to a neurotransmitter or hormone, it must have "docking sites" for that chemical substance. Like the activity of enzymes, this docking process involves geometric considerations. In a lock-and-key sense, the neurotransmitter or hormone gains access to a target cell by docking to it in a manner not unlike that of a space ship docking to a space station, or a jigsaw puzzle piece fitting exactly into its proper location. Docks, in physiological terms, are called *receptor sites*, "ports of entry," so to speak. It follows that both the presence on a cell membrane of receptor sites for a particular biochemical species, and the number of such sites, determine the *responsiveness* of that target to that species, be it a neurotransmitter, a hormone, or whatever. Thus, fine-tuning the presence and number of receptor sites on a cell membrane is a third biasing mechanism by which entrainment acts to affect physiological function.

## Other biasing mechanisms

The list goes on:

- The responsiveness of muscles is regulated by gamma-innervated neural biasing of striated skeletal muscle spindles (Schneck 1992); a fact of particular importance to individuals suffering from performance anxiety or "stage fright" (Berger 1999).

- The reticular activating system (RAS) can be biased, like controlling the mesh size of a sieve, to selectively determine *what* information gets passed on to the brain for further processing. This biasing mechanism merits our further consideration.

Many of the effects of the RAS noted earlier can be attributed to music's effect on how sensory inputs are handled by the reticular activating system and the brain. In acting like a sieve, the RAS is biased to allow to pass through it information that is perceived to be threatening and/or which it perceives to be otherwise of some interest to the central nervous system, which it activates. Thus, by regulating the "sieve size," one can effectively bias the RAS in order to further control its sensitivity to various threshold stimuli, along a continuous spectrum that ranges from coarse to fine. Exercises such as meditation, praying, chanting, guided imagery, and music therapy, acting through mechanisms of entrainment, can bias the RAS, shifting its threshold sensitivities one way or the other, to let more or less information pass through to higher centers.

In physiological terms, regulating the sieve size means controlling *which* neural networks the RAS will respond to and at what threshold frequencies, and so on. The entrainment and response mechanisms involved are sometimes considered under the topic of "transducer-filtration theory." In the limit, such regulation and the theory on which it is based could help to partially explain the existence of different levels of consciousness, and perhaps things like "enhanced" or (preferably) "extra-sensory" perception. That is to say, different states of one's awareness about the world could result from a hierarchy of levels at which sensory information is filtered out (i.e., biased), allowing some individuals to be more perceptive than others. Thus, individuals endowed with a heightened awareness can "sense" things that others cannot. Again, more research is needed to confirm or refute this theory.

At higher levels, a person's ability to originate or react to a particular *rhythm* depends, as discussed in Chapter 4, on his or her innate cerebral infor-mation processing rate. This one's inner psychobiological clock. How that clock is affected by environmental factors greatly affects how one responds to rhythm. Environmental biasing of this clock through entrainment is discussed at some length in Schneck (2003a) and Schneck and Schneck (1996). Related to this biasing are studies like those of Ikeda, (1992), which show that music that elicits *pleasant* emotions causes the listener to (1) under-estimate the passage of time, (2) lose track of time, and (3) exhibit the ability to concentrate and stay focused, while displaying increased cerebral alpha-rhythm (8–12 Hz at about 50 microvolts on the EEG) that is associ-ated with a relaxed state of physiological tranquility.

Moreover, Cossu, Faienza, and Capone (1994) and others (e.g., Faienza 1994) have shown, through power spectral analysis, an increased activity in the delta-wave (1–5 Hz at 20–200 microvolts) and theta-wave (4–7 Hz) regions of the EEG of infants when they are processing musical as opposed to verbal inputs. Delta-wave activity is associated with deep sleep, theta-waves with various states of drowsiness. These authors go on to note that specific differences in EEG responses confirm that different computational processes (information-processing modes) are associated with the brain's handling of musical inputs versus verbal inputs such as speech and language. It is important to note, however, that the processes involved are not *necessarily* consistent with a left-brain/right-brain lateralization paradigm (see also Ornstein and Thompson 1984).

Music does, indeed, have a profound influence on how information tracks through the brain. It is able to alter the *route*, from amygdala-centered neural networks associated with emotional fear responses, to hippocampus-centered networks associated with more rational, cognitive responses (Berger and Schneck 2003; Schneck 1997; Schneck and Berger 1999). Finally, through mechanisms of entrainment that involve biasing of neural networks, music can also affect processes of *sensory integration*. The latter refers to how the brain organizes and interprets (in accordance with the *Gestalt* laws) inputs arriving simultaneously from multiple sensory modalities, such as sight, sound, smell, taste, touch, heat, pain (nociceptive), etc. Once such changes are effected, former ways of responding to a condition give way to new response options, including changes in metabolism, inflammatory responses, reactions to fear and stress, the flow of hormones, neurotransmitters, toxins, anti-toxins, and other life-supporting biological events.

## Entrainment through the transport and utilization of energy

There is a type of physiological entrainment that manifests itself in the way the body handles the transport and utilization of the "energy of life," most especially as it relates to anatomical pathways that affect the physical and emotional vitality of the entire organism. An ancient Oriental system of therapy tracks the flow of this energy (*chi*) through the body along pathways called meridians. There are twelve major meridians, two complementary ones that encircle the midline of the body in front and back, and many collateral minor ones. Conceptually, meridians are to the flow of energy through the body, what the vascular system is to the flow of blood, or what neural networks are to the flow of action potentials. Moreover, in a manner not unlike the way lymphatic channels encounter small, oval bodies called *lymph nodes* as these vessels course through the organism, meridians, too, congregate at various pressure or tonification points at regular intervals along their path. These tonification points form the basis for the medical practice of acupuncture.

Oriental meridians and tonification points work in concert with Hindu energy centers called *chakras*, derived from an ancient Sanskrit word for a disk, representing the sun and the cycle of years. Chakras may be thought of conceptually as receiving and sending stations (hubs) for the energy that flows to and through the body, and out from it, moment by moment (Prophet and Spadaro 2000, p.3). There are seven primary chakras and 144 secondary ones. All are associated with pathways (meridians) that course through specific organs and tissues of the body, essentially as follows:

- Ten of the twelve major merdians pass, respectively, through the spleen, stomach, lungs, large intestine, kidneys, bladder, liver, gallbladder, heart, and small intestines.

- The remaining two meridians relate more to function than to structure.

The seven major chakras are located as follows:

1. the base of the spine, affecting the adrenal glands

2. midway between the navel and base of the spine, affecting the organs and systems of elimination and reproduction

3. the solar plexus ("abdominal brain"), a nerve network located behind the stomach, affecting the liver, pancreas, and digestive system

4. the heart, also affecting the circulatory system and thymus gland

5. the throat, affecting the thyroid gland, lungs, and respiratory system

6. between the eyebrows, affecting the pituitary gland, pineal gland, and portions of the brain

7. the top of the head, affecting the entire central nervous system.

Of particular interest, in terms of the subject matter of this book, is the fact that each of the chakras is also identified with a particular musical instrument:

1. base of the spine, "root" chakra: drum or tabla

2. "seat of the soul": woodwind instruments

3. solar plexus, "abdominal brain": organ

4.  heart, "unbroken": harp

5.  throat, "pure": brass instruments

6.  "third eye": piano

7.  "crown": stringed instruments.

Could these ancient Hindu, Chinese, Buddhist, Islam, Jewish, and early Christian clinicians have instinctively known what modern medicine is just now finding out about the role of music in the healing process? These early investigators believed that the power to heal ultimately comes from within the body itself; and that when the free flow of energy is interrupted, or when one part of the body becomes over- or underactive, health-related problems result. These may be caused by an improper diet, lack of proper exercise (coupled with periods of rest and relaxation), disease and other inflammatory conditions, poor body metabolism, too much stress with the consequent accumulation of stress hormones and other mental and emotional toxins, and so on.

Given this state of physiological malfunction, manipulation of various tonification points and chakra sites could help the body restore balance and proper energy flow. Such restoration, it was (and still is) believed, derives from quieting or stimulating portions of (or entire) meridians, and/or, by "unblocking" clogged energy pathways. "When an energy center is blocked," say Prophet and Spadaro (2000, p.7), "we can experience fatigue or health problems, emotional imbalances and lethargy. When energy is flowing freely through an energy center, we feel energetic, creative and at peace." Modern Western medicine is gradually adopting this point of view because it is difficult to ignore the ever-increasing clinical evidence that verifies the effectiveness of acupuncture, transcendental meditation, guided imagery, music therapy, homeopathic medicine, and other forms of holistic clinical interventions, in helping the body to heal itself. The point is that all of these interventions are highly effective because they work *with* the body's innate physiological processes, rather than against them (as is the case with most forms of pharmaceutical remediation).

Helping to lend credence to the above is the theory that these chakras, being associated with energy, have (as explained in Chapter 3) certain vibrational attributes. By exploiting these attributes, one can *drive* the chakras and tonification points, using resonant frequencies to unblock the clogged pathways and restore normal biological rhythms. In this respect, music can help by "tuning" the body through various synergistic mechanisms of entrainment. The theory is quite plausible; the clinical evidence is certainly highly suggestive; the need for further investigation is definitely warranted; and the mandate is clear. What also needs to be made clear is the distinction we are making in this book between music as therapy and music as therapeutic.

## Music as therapeutic, or music as therapy?

That music is therapeutic is a given. Without exception, every culture on this planet has music. It is a phenomenon of rituals, spirituality, social unification, holistic healing, entertainment, and recreation. Its services are called upon to animate, or to quiet the human being; to excite or to calm; to bring joy or support sadness; to announce a happening or simply to become *the* happening. For therapeutic purposes, music is employed for the temporary relief of stress and anxiety, to enhance memory recall, animate under-active systems, help one to overcome insomnia, uplift the spirit, provide a diversion from mental concerns, and create a comfortable acoustic environment in which to work, play, study, shop, and perform activities of daily living.

There is, however, a difference between music as a diversionary thera-peutic succour, for temporary physical and psychological reasons, and music as a focused medical intervention – a *therapy*. As a therapy, the use of music is aimed at accomplishing longer-lasting, specific anatomical and physiologi-cal changes, and reparation of particular human conditions. Music therapy has as its goal the permanent re-setting of systemic operating parameters (set-points) and input/output transfer functions, in order to derive function-ally adaptive responses that result from mechanisms of entrainment. Music used for clinical therapy involves not only an immediate, in-the-moment relief of a circumstance, but also the setting of long-term goals for inducing permanent changes in physiological and psychological functions that are being addressed by the intervention. In this respect, music used as therapy assumes a role not unlike other forms of clinical intervention for diagnosed populations.

Stated another way, while *therapeutic* music temporarily alters a state of being or level of consciousness, in the here-and-now, music *therapy* seeks to alter states of function permanently, both in the here-and-now and in the hereafter, by instigating actual changes in conditioned responses that had been maintained through previously established, errant homeostatic set-points. The consistent application of music as therapy can potentially force alterations to these homeostatic set-points.

The consistent (continuous forcing function) application of music as therapy has the ability, by driving physiological systems to the point of forcing them to comply through various mechanisms of entrainment, to force the systems to re-set their operating parameters and transfer functions. They are made to *adapt*. This implies that once such changes are achieved, former ways of responding to "adequate stimuli" give way to new response thresholds and options, including, but not limited to, changes in:

- hormone flow
- the activity of neurotransmitters
- the elimination of toxins
- the expression of anti-toxins
- the flow of cytokines (chemical messengers that are to the body's immune system what hormones are to its endocrine system, or neurotransmitters are to its nervous system)
- mechanisms associated with gene expression
- other life-supporting biological events.

Keeping in mind all of the material covered thus far in this book, it is now time to take a closer look at how these principles can be applied clinically, by examining separately each of the elements of music, beginning with the most fundamental one – *rhythm*.

Chapter 7

# Rhythm in Music and Physiology

When the music changes, the dance step must change also.

Minianka proverb

## Introduction

Having explored various aspects of physiological function, general music characteristics, functional adaptation, sensory information-processing, and the very important process of physiological entrainment, we now are in a position to take a closer look at the individual elements of music, and how each of these, in its own way, drives anatomical systems, causing them to resonate with properties of music, entrain them, and thereby derive changes in homeostasis that result in functional adaptation.

Rhythm, as already emphasized, is found in every aspect of cosmic and physiological function. Therefore, it is not surprising that music embodies and is driven by rhythm, which is the first attribute instinctively detected by the brain and body. In fact, it is likely that the very nature of music's pulses and rhythms evolved as external expressions of those very pulsating properties of physics and physiology, and continue to do so even today. The close relationship and interactions among the rhythms of nature and those of the human body are analogous to the rhythms of music, and thus render the presence of music's rhythmic element as one of the most effective methods for capturing the brain and body's attention.

## What is this thing called "rhythm"?

*Periodicity*, the tendency of an event to recur in cyclic intervals, is one of the basic foundations upon which physiological function is sustained, and is an inherent characteristic in music. It is within the timed relationship between sound events, often driven by a consistent pulsation of energy, that an overall musical form takes shape. Rhythmic pulsation embodies a consistent symmetrical balance of energy output, of fall and rebound (the bouncing ball of Chapter 3), of tension and relaxation. Rhythmic vibration in music involves the same steady stream of force–rest–force–rest, of systematic strong and weak impulses, of alternating *flexion* (contraction), *release* (relaxation), and *extension* as is the case for paired and coupled muscular behavior, including that of the heart. Rhythm drives a physiological process that is ultimately capable of accomplishing purposeful activity.

As stated in Chapter 3, energy must vibrate. Cyclical events, both large and small scale, are the manifest characteristics of energy, the vibrations of which correspond to alternating periods of energy conversion: balance (potential) and imbalance (kinetic). The fall and rebound activity of the dropped ball in Figure 3.1 is not unlike the fall and rebound rhythm that characterizes the act of human walking, which is an equilibrated, balanced state momentarily disturbed by a shift in center of gravity as body weight is transferred from one foot to the other. That shift results in an act of propulsion. The body is actually in a falling position as gravity (the "adequate stimulus" in this case) attempts to pull it down. Kinetic energy and momentum take over. But located in each mammalian ear is a specialized set of sense organs that are responsive to linear motion of the organism, to angular motion, and to vibration. Known collectively as the *labyrinth* or *vestibular organ*, these special transducers are responsible for the *kinesthetic senses* that are intimately connected to postural reflexes that orient the body in space (Schneck 1992).

The labyrinth provides feedback information to the brain via the vestibular branch of the eighth cranial nerve, concerning the kinematic relationship of the organism to its environment. It consists of two major parts:

- the *semicircular canals*, of which there are two sets of three – one set on each side of the head, oriented at right-angles to one another to sense rotation of the head around an orthogonal coordinate system

- two *otolith organs*, the saccule and the utricle, which sense translation movements along each axis.

The sensory information fed back to the brain forces it to establish a motor plan in the form of control signals fed forward *from* the brain. The result is that a leg is thrust forward to catch the body before it actually succumbs to gravity and falls. Thus, in reality, walking is the process of *almost* falling,

some 80 times per minute (Schneck 1992). In diagnosed populations exhibiting faulty feedback–feedforward motor planning, or in situations involving
accidents in which an unexpected interfering element, such as a stone in the
path, suddenly and unexpectedly interrupts balance, the body will tend to
become unsteady or to trip and fall. In effect, the unprepared "motor plan" is
taken by surprise and insufficient corrective motor responses yield to the pull
of gravity – gravity wins. It is to our advantage that our living, responsive
bodies do not bounce on impact, as does the inanimate ball discussed in
Chapter 3.

Concurrent with the rhythms of human propulsion and motor activities
are a complex array of compound rhythms simultaneously taking place
within our physiological systems. For example, there are the pulsations of
heartbeat; there are the myriad rhythmicities of neurons firing in the brain
which, according to neuroscientist Rodolfo Llinas (2002), produce an actual
humming (background signal) of constant electrical impulses which fire
rhythmically across synapses in the brain, mostly at about 40 Hz, in the
gamma range of the electroencephalogram. It is observed that neurons
entrain to each other's rhythms via synchronized action potentials as they
communicate with one another. Neuronal activities appear to be contingent
upon coherent rhythmicity and resonance (Llinas 2002, p.10). In a private
interview, Dr. Llinas ascertained that the oscillation in the gamma range of
40 Hz of neuronal rhythms in the brain, when amplified in his laboratory,
actually emitted hum-drone audible sounds. This finding calls to mind the
DNA studies of Alexjander and Deamer (1999) referred to in Chapter 6.
Recall that when the resonant frequencies of the four DNA bases were transcribed into the audible spectrum they produced readily identifiable acoustic
patterns. Now one wonders: do we resonate with certain music, and/or *create*
certain elements in music as a result of our instinctive entrainment with, and
need to reflect back to ourselves, our own body's rhythmic sounds?
Although we do not hear these biorhythms, do we somehow sense them
within our innermost sensory matrices? Could it be that some diagnosed populations with highly sensitive auditory issues actually do hear internal
sounds? Future research related to these questions may yield some answers.

In heart muscle, the kind of rhythmic pa-thump, pa-thump ("lub-dup,
lub-dup" in the physiology realm) pulsation of heart muscle cells, which are
all rhythmically entrained to pulsate in unison, is an indicator of wellness or
vulnerability. In fact, the heartbeat consists of a complex set of *polyrhythms*, a
multiplicity of concurrent rhythms in non-static, constant states of fluctuation,

depending on other physiological variables (not the least of which is the firing rate of the autonomic nervous system) and body activities (such as gastrointestinal rhythms, motor activities, states of body function, stress factors, etc). Contrary to what one might think, a heartbeat is actually a continuous metric adaptation to the functional requirements (metabolic needs) of the organism, called for as a result of messages received by the brain through internal and external monitoring by the sensory systems (Schneck 1990, 2003b, 2003c).

A team of research scientists at the Rey Laboratory of the Harvard Medical School in Boston, Massachusetts, directed by Dr. Ary Goldberger, Associate Professor of Medicine, developed an interesting project called Heartsongs. These scientists probed what they refer to as "fractal" features common to both music and the compounded (and complex) rhythms of the healthy heart (Gardner 1992; Goldberger 1996a, 1996b; Hsu and Hsu 1990; Peng et al. 1993, 1995). Fractals is a term applied to geometric objects or processes that have structure on multiple scales of space or time, and which are self-similar, meaning that larger scale structures are directly proportional to corresponding smaller scale structures, differing only by a common scale factor. The geometric shape of a snowflake is an example of a fractal.

According to the findings of several researchers (Goldberger 1996a, 1996b; Hsu and Hsu 1990; Taylor, Micolich, and Jonas 1999), many biological structures and physiological fluctuations operate in rather complex fractal patterns. These fractal patterns of physiological function were found also to appear in a wide range of human creative works of art, particularly architecture and music. Goldberger (2000, 2002a, 2002b) further asserts that disease and aging are associated with degradation of fractal structures and processes of the body.

Of particular interest to us is the aspect of the Heartsong project which is analogous to the work of Susan Alexjander and her colleagues (1999). This time, however, the investigators undertook to actually create musical compositions, the melodies of which were derived from electrocardiogram (ECG) rather than DNA information. ECG electric signal frequencies were translated into pitches and digitally recorded. Heartsongs contain the musical notes (melodic contour) which are mapped from the heartbeat data, including the rhythmic intervals of beats which, when digitally recorded and translated into pitches, actually form a melodic contour. A composer combined these melodic contours of the heartbeats with harmonies and rhythm patterns to make musical compositions. Information and samples of the actual music can be obtained at http://reylab.bidmc.harvard.edu/heartsongs. Goldberger notes that heart rhythm anomalies and potential heart diseases can be determined, perhaps even forestalled, through this clinical analytic procedure that translates heartbeat patterns into audible melodic contours. Imagine adding one's very own baseline heart tune to the previously suggested musical DNA-print, and using these as a reference to which future body tunes can be compared for clinical purposes!

In Germany, Dr. Gunther Hildebrandt has devoted most of his research and medical life to investigating what he terms "chronobiological aspects" of music physiology. His writings discuss biological rhythms in humans and their counterparts in music (1976, 1986, 1987). His work tracks rhythmic structures within human disease physiology, including such elements as rhythms of pain sensitivity (nociception), activity rhythms, cosmic rhythms, endogenous rhythms, muscular rhythms, pain-wave rhythms, rhythms of blood circulation and respiration, rhythms in sleep, breath, heart, and others. In combination with the musical skills and talents of his colleague, composer Peter Huebner, the two have set out to develop musical scores specifically designed as clinical treatment modalities applied to resonate with malfunctioning physiological rhythms in efforts to alter diseases through alteration of rhythmicity. Dr. Hildebrandt calls the therapeutic process "chronomedicine," and maintains "digital pharmaceutics," with specific music interventions developed through digital recordings of biological rhythms which are then orchestrated into larger music compositions (see www.digipharm.com).

One can add to all of the above the fact that auditory stimulation (adequate stimulus), applied in a persistent manner (continuous disturbance) induces *neuronal activation* (entrainment, followed by functional adaptation), as measured by neural tissue oxygen consumption in the frontal lobes of the brain. This is similar to what occurs in the visual cortex of the occipital lobes under the influence of photic stimulation (Ornstein and Thompson 1984). Then, too, there are the *cognitive* elements of rhythmicity, such as the rate of cognitive cerebral information-processing, the rhythmicities of speech articulation, language (syntax) perception, and semantic interpretation of verbal syntax. So, what, more precisely, *is* rhythm?

## The three "P"s of rhythm

We have established, conceptually, that rhythm is in some sense associated with vibrating energy, periodicity being everywhere; and that human physiology includes a complexity of compound polyrhythms. As a key element of the physical universe, the physiological system, and this thing we call "music," rhythm is not one single item but, rather, a complex combination of three distinct and interdependent properties working simultaneously. In order for something to be identified as having rhythm, it must display at least two of the three attributes "pulse," "pace," and "pattern."

## Pulse: the music clock

For the most part, when one refers to rhythm in music, one is actually referring to the ongoing, steady, underlying *pulse* (like that of a beating heart) that organizes musical events and provides order to acoustic information. Pulse is the first attribute of this complex musical component that captures one's attention; it is immediately noticed and perceived by the ear and *entire body* alike. Music's pulse is a driving repetition of strong and weak "beats," the primary component of rhythm that the body entrains, and to which we tap the foot or clap the hands. Pulsating sound vibrations are immediately detected not only by the auditory system, but also by the *tactile* (exteroceptive) and *proprioceptive* (interoceptive) systems. Our bodies "feel" pulsations, both externally through our skin receptors (Meissner's corpuscles, Merkel's disks, pacinian corpuscles, hair follicle receptors, tactile disks, and Ruffini endings), and internally through receptors in muscles (muscle spindles and Golgi tendon organs) and joints (pacinian corpuscles, Ruffini endings, Golgi endings, and free nerve endings). All of these buzz with the vibrations and pounding beats of the drum, while the ears identify the sound through its frequency, amplitude, and timbre, and locate its source. Persons with various levels of impaired hearing, even total deafness, still have the ability to sense rhythmic vibrations, since sound vibrations disturb the air pressure, which is sensed by the tactile system. They can clap hands in synchrony with a pulse. In her "Hearing Essay" (available at www.evelyn.co.uk_hearingessay.com) world-renowned percussionist Evelyn Glennie, who happens to be totally auditorily incapacitated since age 8, explains her ability to hear music with her body. The National Theater of the Deaf, in Connecticut, makes use of unique sound/vibration-producing sculptures for cueing deaf actors. The Helen Keller School and Center in Long Island, New York, uses a vibrating floor, beneath which are speakers providing music vibrations for sensing through the feet and body. More on Ms. Glennie in the next chapter.

Pulse is the ongoing, relentless, steady, *evenly spaced*, ticking-clock element of rhythm, referred to in music as "the beat." It is the attribute of music that gives it the dimension of time; which is to say, it is the time-keeper that controls most of what transpires within the music. It is the unifying factor, the pace-maker that propels forward the component parts of a musical composition (Berger 2002; Berger and Schneck 2003). The pulse of a piece of music directly impacts the rhythmic entrainment potential of the human body. It can mobilize neurotransmitters, hormones, enzymes, opioids, and a myriad of biochemical messengers to bias responses of the motor planning systems, organizing muscular contraction and relaxation in time with the music. Most readers are probably aware, and may even have experienced the fact, that aerobic exercises are most effective when undertaken in synchrony with the strong beat of loud and repetitive rock music, which tends to support high-energy exertion, driving the rate of exercise (we entrain to the beat and, too, to the speed of a tune). The music of John Philip Sousa compels audiences to "march" or clap rhythmically to a 4/4 beat. The name Johann Strauss conjures up music with the 3/4 waltz beat. Who can resist rocking back and forth to the pulsation of the Beatles (in duple-meter 2/4, 4/4). Songs of the Gypsy Kings cause hips to wiggle in Latin pulsations. Entire groups of people can become organized and unified, entrained to each other and to the beat, conforming to shouts of pulsating political rhetoric and slogans.

The ability of music pulse to provide musculotropic stimulation may be due in part to the very close, influential proximity of the brain's auditory cortex to the motor cortex. For the purpose of survival, this is quite an expedient evolution, since the acoustic information of a lion's roar, or the fast-pulsed sounds of a galloping onslaught of elephants, would require immediate transduction into a flight response. Pulse factor in music also appears to cause entrainment to the beat of other bodily muscles, including conforming changes in heartbeat (Standley 2000).

## Pace: the speed of the clock

If pulse is the systematic spacing between one "tick" and the next "tock," followed by the next "tick" and the next "tock," and so on, then an additional rhythmic element emerges: the *duration* of that time space between ticking events. That is, the *pace* determines the amount of space between one tick and the next, which in turn establishes how many tick-tocks will take place in a given period of time. Music pace denotes the *tempo* of the pulse; how fast, how slow the next beat comes. For instance, it is standard practice to pace a march tempo to a speed of 120 "ticks" per minute. That is, the metronome is set at 120, the number of times per minute (frequency) at which each "tick" clicks off one beat, and hence how fast the beats are moving along in time. If a clock beats at 60 ticks per minute, for example, then a march tempo beats twice as fast as a clock.

For the music therapist's physiologically targeted clinical intervention, these two major rhythm characteristics – pulse and pace – are critical to the effectiveness of the music dosage being applied as treatment for the results being sought. Referring back to our discussion of the fear cycle in Chapter 5, we ascertain that, in the majority of diagnosed populations, regardless of age or disturbance, the pulse and pace of those systems generally function from the perspective of a fright-fight-flight demeanor, which is *frantic-furious-fast*. That is to say, the "fear spiral" chemistry (adrenalin, norepinephrin, cortisol, *et al.*) resulting from faulty sensory information-processing is producing an atypical response to the perceived circumstances. These fear behaviors can take the rhythmic form of either faster-paced (flight), or slower-paced (cautious and deliberate) adaptations *different* from those considered to be typical for the given conditions. As long as the amygdala and the emotional system, which is fixated on survival, perceives danger – even if that perception stems from faulty information derived from a diseased state, developmental delays, erroneous information-processing, pain, or anxiety – the fear-cycle physiological behavior will be the "norm." Therefore, it is obligatory for the music therapy clinician to be skilled in identifying behavioral symptoms on the basis of possible physiological causes in order to determine how best to employ rhythmic pulse and pace (among other elements) for the purpose of achieving a desired outcome.

### Pulse and pace elements in music therapy

When we suggest that the element of rhythm in music has the power to elicit systemic entrainment, whether it be to subdue or to animate the system, or to trigger adaptive responses, we allude to its intrinsic attributes of slow or fast beats and tempos. It is (at least in part) to the pace and pulse of music that the body's elaborate entrainment mechanisms respond and, if persistent enough, eventually adapt. Therefore, these two characteristics of rhythm stand out as the major physiological influences of music in clinical interventions.

The pulse is metrically indicated in music as being in counts of twos (2/4, two beats per measure, with the quarter note getting the beat), threes (3/4), fours (4/4), sixes (6/8, six beats per measure, with the eighth note getting the beat), or more. The pace is often indicated quantitatively by metronomic suggestions (quarter note = 80 per minute, eighth note = 120 per minute, etc.); and qualitatively by Italian words (*allegro* = happy and fast, *presto* = very fast, *lento/adagio* = slow, and others).

The music therapy profession is familiar with the effects of pulse and pace on motoric entrainment in the bodies of physically rehabilitating populations. In addition to the field of vibrational medicine mentioned earlier, and to the studies and situations discussed above, the emerging field of neurological music therapy, spearheaded by Professor Michael Thaut and colleagues at the Center for Auditory Research at Colorado State University, focuses exclusively on the use of pulse and pace for gait training in victims of brain traumas, Parkinson's disease, cerebral palsy, and other diseases affecting movement (Thaut 1997a, 1997b; Thaut *et al.* 1999). Through this work, and that of others specializing in movement rehabilitation, it has been shown that music's pulse and pace are invaluable clinical applications for retraining gross motor movements in paralyzed victims (Miller *et al.* 1996; Pachetti *et al.* 1998; Thaut *et al.* 1996, 1997). In some rehabilitation centers, physical therapists have been using metronomes (in the absence of a music therapist) to encourage paralyzed victims to sustain a walking pace (entrainment) to the continuous ticking of the beat at a predetermined speed.

Music therapist Myra Staum (2000) of the State University of New York, New Paltz, has put together an impressive compendium of nearly 50 years of literature and research on the impact of music therapy – particularly the elements of rhythm – for physical rehabilitation, as applied to the development of efficient neuromotor patterns, respiration, fine and gross motor skills, muscular relaxation, locomotion, balance and posture, endurance, muscle tone, digestion, and more. The cited research indicates that the beat and tempo of music have been observed to redirect or diminish physical impairments such as hand tremors and involuntary movements of the limbs in victims of Parkinson's disease, cerebral palsy, and various types of brain damage from strokes, Alzheimer's, and other afflictions. Staum's survey provides an extensive bibliography of research on the applications of music rhythms in various diagnostic and rehabilitation settings.

Pulse and pace are of service to conditions well beyond those of brain trauma and motor diseases. They are also major contributors to emotional rehabilitation, serving to redirect the amygdala away from the fear mode in both diagnosed and undiagnosed populations. Because the meter (time signature) and tempo of a piece of music can alter the level of stressors within the body, it is necessary to consider how these rhythm characteristics can be employed as part of the music therapy treatment.

Recall that all the individuals introduced in Chapter 5 displayed the same physiological behavior, characterized by the textbook elements of the "fear cycle," although each person bore a different diagnosis. In the case of Robert, age 14 years, diagnosed with Asperger's syndrome, his defiance, his frenetic, panic-stricken inability to either pace or control his reactivity to the environment, and his erratic behavior suggest excessive autonomic and endocrine function, leading to intense, fast-paced motor impulses that had become, by now, standard to his systemic function. In other words, his chaotic responses had become *his* "normal" mode of operation. His body had adapted to these reference set-points. He was stuck in fear's flight-or-fight cycle. His behaviors represented his body's accommodation to his system's idiosyncratic sensory information-processing. His parents reported that Robert even agitated when asleep, reinforcing the idea that his body was functioning "on automatic," driven by the stress-response set-points. Was he sentenced to spend the rest of his life in this state?

If Robert's behaviors are to be taken as indicators of constant fear or stress, then the fear emergency signals must be quelled before any of his other problems can effectively be addressed. In fact, perhaps with the quelling of the fear symptoms, other sensory processing issues might simultaneously be remedied in the process. Therefore, the first clinical music therapy intervention applicable to Robert's situation would be an endeavor to revise the system's modus operandi by *slowing it down* through focused rhythm interventions. These would employ strong, steady pulses and slow-paced tempos that could provide new response options to the amygdala and supporting brain regions. Here, the clinician confronts questions of *protocol* and *dose–response*. How slow? How much? How often? Which meter (duple 2/4, 4/4, or triple 3/4, 6/8, etc.)? What activities can drive entrainment/functional-adaptation mechanisms in order to re-set this system's aberrant homeostatic set-points? Which musical instruments would serve this purpose best? What type of music could permanently kick this system out of the "fear cycle?" And finally, how often and how long before results are observed and maximum medical improvement of the patient is declared? We will return to these questions; but first let us sample part of Robert's music therapy prescription:

GOAL: Alteration of body rhythm for re-pacing and slowing body tempos, including speech, movement, breathing, listening and hearing,

TREATMENT PROTOCOL (PARTIAL)

- One hour per week (minimum) of one-to-one contact, two half-hour sessions preferable.

- Begin session with activity to control and slow breathing: long blows on recorder, slow humming into a kazoo, etc. Supporting music: native American flute and other non-rhythmic, unilinear music. If necessary, decrease visual stimulation by dimmer lights, concealing instruments, and limiting number of choice possibilities, depending on assessment of fight-or-flight response level.

- Slow-paced rhythmic gross motor movement activities to sustained tempos with a metronome setting below 100. Marching, galloping, rise and fall, for developing rhythmic-based motor-planning skill. Preferable meters: slow 3/4 alternating with 4/4 to alter fall/rebound movement and quell body's impulse toward speed.

- Drumming activities to strong, slow-paced, repetitive beat and consistent pace over varying rhythmic patterns (played by therapist, and participant when possible), to maintain interest and concentration.

- Singing by participant: of simple, familiar, age-appropriate songs of participant's choice, while simultaneously beating percussion, or other instrument(s) of choice.

- Conclude session with relaxation activity undertaken to slow, quiet sounds. Include deep breathing, imaging, toning, and similar activities.

Although the addressing of ancillary sensory integration and emotional issues are also part of Robert's prescription (omitted above), the dominant focus of therapy is the enabling, through rhythmic entrainment, of his system to experience and learn new ways of responding: to substitute "fear" stress with calm pacing. The rippling effect of this approach tends to reorganize and revise basic sensory issues as well, including those of the vestibular, visual, proprioceptive, and tactile parameters.

His reaction? At first, Robert's system continuously repelled and rejected these new behavior modalities, although he would reluctantly defer to the therapist's choices when turn-taking for preferred activities. Because his system's operating set-points had been firmly established, his stubborn physiological resistance to systemic rhythmic changes remained active for many months. In this regard, it is important to realize that adaptive reprogramming to establish new reference parameters takes time, in a dose–response sense that has yet to be quantified.

Robert's least favorite activities were the blowing of slow and sustained breaths into a recorder and/or kazoo, decelerated and prolonged slower-paced drumming, and the concluding relaxation segment that involved imaging, further deep breathing, and the maintenance of a quiet, non--movement state of being. Now, three years into music therapy as this book is being written (three years of driving his system with entraining stimuli) Robert's body rhythms and his ability to be aware of, and to control, his movements have clearly progressed for the better; so much so, that clinicians in related therapy modalities have consulted with the music therapist on how to apply the above processes in their specialties, as well. Robert's erratic, combative fight-or-flight behavior is basically extinguished in most of his daily settings (not just music therapy), and his academic cognitive skills and his sleep and other erratic habits have improved (according to school records). His eye-tracking has slowed, enabling improved reading and math skills, and he is much more aware of the tempos of his music of choice. Indeed, Robert's body has adapted to new operating parameters, driven there by sensory entrainment, operating through *feedback/feedforward* information-processing pathways nested within one another.

Robert's receding fight-or-flight mode resulted in his having more patience to reason and better negotiate with peers, elders, and persons in authority. His musical taste has progressed from the very fast, very loud, rock-and-roll groups he originally fancied, to more controlled, rhythmically slower but more actively varied groups in which lyrics and orchestrations are much more stabilizing and understandable. (Listening to, and playing along with, a tune from one of his favorite CDs concludes each session.) Considering what we have learned about body speeds and entrainment, Robert's change in musical preferences reflects corresponding changes that have occurred within his internal biorhythms. As with gait training and other rhythmic objectives, changes in musculotropic behaviors can become permanently homeostatically re-set, and can also impact on a variety of other sensory issues.

Getting back to the questions of protocol and dose–response, there is here an urgent need for much more rigorous music therapy research. In Robert's case, on the basis of 40 weeks, one hour per week for a three-year period, a quick calculation reveals that he has been exposed to approximately 120 hours of music therapy, with progress becoming noticeable at nearly the completion of the second year (some 80 hours later). Is his case just an anecdotal peculiarity, an exception to the rule, or *the* rule? Is 120 hours of music therapy, spread out uniformly over a three-year period, enough to produce permanent functional adaptation in a more generic sense? Would that same 120 hours, compressed into one year, have been more effective in eliciting adaptive responses? Would 80 hours have been enough if administered in an even shorter period of time, but with complementary dietary restrictions? How can all of these variables (and other related ones, some not even defined yet) be measured objectively, assessed realistically, and *directly attributed to the specific effects of his music therapy* (which raises the issue of controlled, double-blind, randomized investigations)? Will termination of his treatments at this point cause regression? Will continuation reach a plateau beyond which no further progress will be observed? That is to say, is there a point of diminishing returns, which suggests that his treatment protocol can, in some sense, be optimized? Will increase of service create more or faster positive adaptations?

There is one answer to all of these and many more questions, and that is: it depends, and investigators really don't know yet on what, or how (dose–response). Moreover, the answers may very well be individual-specific, depending on such things as the individual systems being treated, their learning styles, speed of information-processing, body mechanics, and other variables. Much more research on the subject of dosage is required.

Be that as it may, the rhythmic elements of pace and pulse as applied to Robert over the 120 hours did seem to yield changes and positive results. Similar prescriptions for the use of pace and pulse can be applied to other cases in which evidence of the "fear" fight-or-flight response is noted, whether or not the behaviors involve quick movements or recessive demeanor, and regardless of whether the diagnosis is one of depression and schizophrenia, autism, language and learning delays, attention deficits, psychological distress, and/or many other problems. Music's pulse and pace designed to slow down and retard a system such as Robert's can also be pre-scribed to produce exactly the opposite effect: to quicken breath control, animate the system with fast music, and so forth. These were applied in several of the other cases described in Chapter 5.

For Laura, our adult autistic participant, the act of pounding several drums and cymbals to the steady beat of the music not only organized and animated her connectivity with the musical activity, it also resulted in redi-recting her fearful suspicions, and kept her mentally and emotionally alert – focused away from fear and insecurity for extended periods. This type of activity also served to limit many of her perseverative, stereotypical autistic behaviors (spinning, self-stimulation, impulsive actions such as twirling a stool or drum, etc.). Aides verify that for several hours following her basic rhythmic music therapy interactions, Laura remains focused, comfortable, trusting, and calm. Her therapy has only recently begun: to the date of this writing, she has had thirty-six 45-minute sessions, one per week, totaling some 27 hours.

In the case of 5-year-old Rhea, who would enter the room screaming and crouching in corners, a modified prescription of the above elements served to immediately organize her system, calming it down, and enabling her to participate productively in specific activities designed to redirect fear, and reorganize sensory information-processing.

For our 31-year-old schizophrenic woman, Rachel, the prescription of slow recorder blowing, calm pulse and paced xylophone playing (having a mesmerizing impact), slower songs, and many other interventions were applied over a period of six months of daily 45-minute sessions, five days per week. This appeared to quickly redirect not only her fight-or-flight responses, but also her erratic and illusionary thought processes. Psychotropic medication was also part of Rachel's treatment, which meant that the music therapy interventions would need to be carefully balanced between slow pacing and animation, in order not to contribute to possible labile mood shifts. Here, again, the concept of drug/therapy interactions is one deserving further research. The paced drumming activity of music therapy helped to redirect both Rachel's erratic mood shifts and the dyskinesia effects (tremors and tics) that she experienced as a result of the psychotropic drug she was ingesting.

In Bucky's case – the extremely slow-paced, unmotivated youngster – the goal was to entice his system to speed up, just the opposite intervention to that applied to Robert. Fast drumming, fast running, constant changes in speed and beat, contributed to his ability to entrain to fast responses. In fact, the objective here was actually to stimulate the flow of epinephrine (adrenaline) and call upon fast fight-or-flight responses as a way of suggesting to his brain that between his lethargy at one extreme, and this adrenaline-induced excitable behavior at the other, there could be a happy medium of controlled animation devoid of fear. It would be okay and safe to be excited. In Bucky's case, a fluctuation between high and low moods would be a welcome change to the consistently slow, frightened demeanor. And indeed, as Bucky's therapy continues at one 45-minute one-to-one session per week, more enthusiasm and less fear is starting to emerge. He is into his fourth year of music therapy, and only recently has begun to show improvement in his demeanor. His system is finally learning how to organize information more quickly, while his amygdala is learning to trust the environment as being safe and inviting. He smiles more, questions less, displays more initiative in task organization, and trusts his remaining senses to guide him where his vision is impaired.

The pulse and pace factors of rhythm remain two of the key ingredients in treating fear behavior. Once these are understood physiologically, and implemented musically, mechanisms of entrainment can be activated through targeted music therapy interventions. It is also important to determine when and how to implement some of the standard music therapy processes, such as that of musically mirroring someone's behavior by playing music that is reflective of that behavior (e.g., running music to reflect the running action of the person being treated). If the behavior connotes a fight-or-flight response (symptom), and the music therapist is not sensitive to the physiology involved, then music "mirroring" of the behavior could actually be counter-productive, increasing the stress and advancing the fear response rather than redirecting or subduing it. In effect, the intervention is addressing, and perhaps even reinforcing, the behavioral symptom. Meanwhile, the actual *cause* of the fear response might not be addressed. Does an already animated, fearful (fight-or-flight) system require animated, fast-paced, imitative rhythm? For what purpose? What is it expected to accomplish? Similarly, does a morose, depressed system need quiet, slow rhythm? When is it applicable, when not, and for what expected result? These and many other questions relative to treatment encompassing rhythm's pulse and pace beg rigorous research. But that's not all. There's one more essential aspect of rhythm that needs to be addressed: *pattern.*

## Pattern: the "language" of the clock

We now arrive at our third "P", and the most complex characteristic of rhythm: pattern. A pulse by itself, at any speed, expresses a very limited amount of musical information. Indeed, the ticking of a metronome is nothing more than an ongoing, monotonous, light-sounding, beating clock announcing nothing more than the passage of time. The brain has a tendency to "tune out" such repetitive information once it has determined that it is non-threatening, just as it tunes out the ticking of a clock and many other repetitive background noises. Recall, also, that *sensory adaptation*, in the form of alterations in resting, threshold, receptor, and depolarization potentials, accomplishes the same thing even at levels below the brain, so that non-threatening, persistent stimulation gets tuned out right at its source, before it ever reaches the central nervous system (Coren and Ward 1989; Schneck 1990; Tortora and Grabowski 1993). A pulse, in and of itself, is not a pattern, in the sense of conveying information. Thus, compound action potentials that are the *net* output of sequences of nerve networks are in the form of *pulse trains*, within which are contained pulse patterns that do encode specific pieces of information. The stop/start, long/short, Morse-code-like (as in communication systems) or barcode-like (as in product identification systems) messages carry with them cues that call for (excitatory) or suppress (inhibitory) physiological responses. Indeed, alpha-motor-neuron excitation of striated skeletal muscles utilizes just these types of pulse-train patterns to command certain responses from the tissue (Schneck 1992), and sensory feedback systems, too, relay information in patterned pulse trains (Schneck 1990).

The rhythmic pulse can be *made* to convey information by endowing it with a variety of rhythmic interjections, variations of fast/slow–stop– start rhythmic events, and other patterns that create a form of "dialogue," in order to communicate information to the central nervous system. This dialogue is often organized in ways that bring about attention, anticipation, and the brain's interest in upcoming music events that may occur over a steady pulse and speed (Berger 2002, p.116). Syncopations (beats and off-beats, as opposed to synchronization) in jazz are examples of patterns "teasing" the strictness of a pulse. Patterns can be repetitive, so small pattern sets can be repeated over and over within an overall pulse and tempo, as in for example: "I beat my drum...I beat my drum..." (short–long...long–short... short–long...long–short...). They can also be self-similar, in the "fractal" sense discussed earlier.

Patterns can take an expanded route over, between, against, or parallel to a tempo and pulse, as in for example: "I like to beat my drum…when I march around…because it makes me feel so good…it makes me smile and sing…." Or, they can also be compounded when, for instance, the above two sentences are spoken or sung simultaneously by two different persons, over the same underlying pulse and tempo. In other words, whereas beats must remain steady, patterns can be freer, alternating fast and slow material, providing illusions of fast and slow speed changes, in spite of an ongoing slow-paced pulse. For example, say this pattern of words: "Mississippi… Mississippi…Mississippi…River-boat," while clapping your hands once with each word. You will notice that the beat (your hand-clapping) is not fast, but the words are spoken quickly, causing an auditory illusion of speed.

Although the exact mechanisms by which the body entrains various rhythms are still not clearly understood, rhythmic patterns do play an important role in maintaining the brain's attention to acoustic information, because, getting back to the *Gestalt* laws of perception discussed in Chapter 4, the brain does look for, and enjoys the stimulation of, ever-changing information. It is always in a state of attention, waiting in anticipation for the next event to occur, expecting to make sense out of what it is perceiving. No doubt, the steady ticking of the metronome is useful in treating gait problems, attention deficit hyperactive disorders (e.g., listening to, and learning to respond in time to the metronomic pulse), and as rhythm training for music students. However, for the most part, the brain will attempt to "tune out" this kind of repeated, droning information devoid of changing patterns. In a sense it knows intuitively that, in the words of Heraclitus (c.540–475 BCE), "there is nothing permanent except change," and so it looks for it. In fact, it actually takes much effort and concentration for the brain to stay attuned to the boring beat of a metronome. But when pattern interacts with the beat and speed of rhythm, interest and attention remain high. Combined with the pulse and pace, the element of pattern completes the musical rhythm-scape.

Rhythmic pattern alone has become an invaluable aid in speech pathology. The breaking down of words into their rhythmic syllable patterns continues to be employed by music therapists as an ideal intervention for aiding the development and rehabilitation of receptive and expressive language. The brain (which we now know loves patterns) will tune in and instinctively call for the verbal imitation of well-articulated, slow-paced, patterned words. In fact, syllables may have *originated* from the brain's love of rhythmic patterns as a form of communication. Since the patterned syllables of words tends to slow down verbal communication, while involving various related brain regions in the process, music therapy's rhythmic interventions serve well to support language/speech development.

During treatment, Robert was often asked to clearly enunciate each spoken word within the rhythmic beat, usually while clapping a tambourine or taking breaths in between. He was also asked to break down the words into their rhythmic syllable patterns. This eventually slowed his speaking tempo to a great extent (something he resisted vehemently), and eventually he could make himself clearly understood, with good pronunciation and oral motor articulation, rather than his usual rambling drone of unclear speech. It has taken the better part of two years to achieve these results.

This activity is not unlike learning to speak and understand a foreign language. In that process, speech is slowed and words reduced into rhythmic utterances in order to identify the beginnings and endings of words. When a foreign language is spoken by a native of that country it tends to be quite fast, and this is the reason it is difficult to catch the words and derive meaning. When we speak to a foreigner, we tend to slow our speaking pace considerably in order to be understood. For many impaired populations it is important to adopt slower speaking methods because, not only might the language sound like a foreign tongue to them, but they could also very well be having problems with the information-processing rate, causing drop-outs, aliasing errors etc., that could be quite confusing. The slowing down of speech patterns through rhythmic enunciation of words is an effective music therapy practice for enhancing spoken language development. The rhythmic patterning of words into rhymes and limericks, as in the songs "This old man" or "One, two, buckle my shoe," will often be more readily repeated and recalled than if the same words were to be spoken without rhythmic context. This, perhaps, is because the slow tempo and pace of the sentences leave ample space between words, so the brain can absorb and retain the information more easily.

Studies and clinical music therapy work drawing upon rhythmic patterning for the purpose of speech rehabilitation confirm the efficiency and effectiveness of rhythmic pattern, combined with pace and pulse, for either slowing down or animating speech production, and improving oral motor planning, articulation, vocal intonation, breath control, and other issues related to aphasia, dysarthria, language comprehension, and related problems (Adamek, Gervin, and Shiraishi 2002; Berger 2002). The use of pattern along with pace and pulse to achieve positive language results is employed in all of the cases introduced in Chapter 5.

Both Rhea and Laura are severely aphasic, having very little, if any, language ability. Literally, the word "aphasia" (sometimes referred to as "dysphasia") means "without speech and language abilities" (or, in the case of dysphasia, replace "without" by "impaired"). It is a communication disorder that affects one's ability to engage in symbolic processing, including the representation of thoughts in symbols. Thus, aphasic (dysphasic) patients have trouble reading, writing, dealing with arithmetic symbols, speaking, articulating thoughts, listening, understanding what other people are trying to communicate to them, and even interpreting various bodily gestures.

Laura, an adult, can do nothing more than grunt and occasionally vocalize short, non-consonant utterances. Rhea, age 5, has the ability to imitate enunciations when motivated to do so, but otherwise will not use language. In both cases, the task of slow-patterning the word syllables uttered while simultaneously beating the same word pattern on a bongo drum together with the therapist – a technique referred to as "drum-speak" by Berger (2002) – has enabled better word recognition and imitation. In addition, in Rhea's case, oral motor articulation has been improving through this rhythmic drum-speak, wherein she imitates the words spoken/beaten by the therapist. Because playing on the bongo drum (which sits in between therapist and participant) is a motivator causing the brain to attend, drum-speak word rhythm has altered the language skills of a great many non-verbal, fast-speaking (e.g., Robert), or slow-speaking persons (e.g., Bucky) receiving speech and language therapy.

In the case of Rachel (schizophrenia), drum-speak served as a form of spontaneous communication, speaking/drumming the first things that came to mind. This became available as indicators of her inner impulses and compulsions. Drum-speak for Rachel served as an analytic component through which her spoken sentences, drummed out simultaneously with the utterances, immediately reflected back to her those thoughts and emotions behind her words, opening the path to self-reflection. Because Rachel enjoyed drumming, she relinquished her fear response and could freely flow with her thoughts verbally, almost without censoring them, but rather hearing them rhythmically. She was then able to "hear" her rhythm, review her words/thoughts, and analyze her state of being. This is akin to writing song lyrics, except more immediate and spontaneous. Meanwhile, her fight-or-flight responses abated, and she took delight in her ability to drum her thought patterns.

The power of rhythm pattern as therapy cannot be overestimated. Not only does it provide interest to keep the brain at attention, it also adds an important dimension to the element of rhythm: the depth of multiple rhythmic events taking place within, over, under, and/or in synchrony with a highly controlled system of beat and tempo. And these three – pulse, pace, and pattern – are most effective because of an aspect of rhythm that we have alluded to throughout this chapter, and that is *repetition*. As a concept, repetition connotes a *continuous disturbance*, a non-stop, relentless, *repetitive forcing function* which drives and compels the listener to notice the beat. It is not so much an attribute, per se, of rhythm, but of the way that rhythm is applied persistently (a fourth "P", if you will) in order to achieve a desired result. Of all the music elements we are covering in this book, the main feature that is consistent, stable, non-changing, and reliable – the stimulation that keeps the brain and body connected, and drives a piece of music to its conclusion – is the non-stop repetitive pulsing of the meter. The patterned excitement of the piccolo tune in John Philip Sousa's "Stars and Stripes Forever," blown at a pace of 120 beats per minute, would make no sense were it not for the repetitive nature of the 4/4 march meter that remains constant throughout. While the pace can have its variable fast and slow moments, "The Beat Goes On" sang Sonny and Cher in the 1970s, and rhythmic music therapy interventions that consist of drumming groups of geriatric populations, or general drumming circles consisting of various African and Eastern populations (such as those described and conducted by Yaya Diallo and Mitchell Hall in *The Healing Drum* in 1989), depend on the persistent repetitive nature of the pulse for sustaining group participation. Moreover, *despite* the non-repetitive nature of ever-changing polyrhythms that evolve in a group drumming circle, the fact that such random rhythms are superimposed over the steady, repetitive pulse of the "mother drums" to which all adhere sustains the brain's attention and brings about entrainment to the point of euphoria. This universal group entrainment with the repetitive rhythmic pulse is one of the key reasons that drumming causes the release of physical and psychological tensions. Participants are "lost in the repetitive pulse," mesmerized by the complexities of the compound patterns, and driven by the momentum of the pace. Such is the effect of music's element of rhythm.

## Summary

We note that indeed, "when the music changes, the dance step must change also," as our chapter's opening quote suggests. The "dance steps," in our case, is a metaphor for impaired sensory information-processing, the "fear" spiral, language and cognitive deficits, and physical limitations that are observed to be changing. The "changing" results from music therapy treatments that employ the attributes of rhythm to achieve specific goals. In this chapter, we have investigated several ways in which the "dance step" can and has changed in our five sample case histories. The power of rhythm as a clinical intervention is that, in order for it to be administered and effective, it does not require any special training on the part of the participant. We noted that two of the three basic characteristics of rhythm, pulse and pace, immediately vibrate within the physiological system, causing entrainment that contributes to systemic organization, consistency, rhythmic pacing and internalization, and various types of rehabilitation that result in adaptive responses. When methodically applied as music therapy interventions, the pulse and pace of drumming, song, or instrumental music assists physical coordination because of rhythm's unrelenting, driving momentum. Polyrhythms and compounded rhythmic events – patterns – add information, dimension, and interest to the basic beat. Pace, the speed in which the beats and patterns operate, is a factor in animating or subduing a behavior symptomatic of the fear response, and it sustains one's connection to the necessary physical rehabilitation task. The need to "keep pace" with the music is activated by the persistence of the driving beat. The understanding of physiological function, and how rhythm's three main characteristics both *reflect* physiology and contribute to *altering* it, yields effective music therapy treatment modalities.

If rhythm were the *only* effective element of music that contributed to efficient and effective clinical treatment interventions, it alone would suffice to bring about physiological and emotional rehabilitation, driving the body to functionally adapt. But, to our benefit, there is more to the music landscape than just rhythm, just as there is more to the emotional animal than the thinking brain. As complete and self-contained as the element of rhythm appears to be, it is but one of six interactive music components that exist in a hierarchy which uniquely distinguishes this art form – not only as an aesthetic vehicle for communicating emotion but also as a powerful medical treatment modality for stimulating functional adaptation. Thus, in addition to rhythm, five other vital elements (and variations thereof) synergize with, and depend on, rhythm, and on one another, to evoke the passionate forces of human physiology. One of these, and the next one to be considered, is the element that intones the drama of human emotion within its domain – *melody*.

Chapter 8

# Melody: The Pitch
# of Human Emotion

Music has a poetry of its own, and that poetry is called Melody.

Joshua Logan, Broadway writer and director

## Introduction

"Whenever I feel afraid, I hold my head erect, and whistle a happy tune so no one will suspect I'm afraid," sings Anna in Rogers and Hammerstein's musical *The King And I*. She continues with the conclusion that "The results of this deception are very strange to tell. For when I fool the people I fear, I fool myself as well." Enter the effect of music on the fear spiral!

We have all used a tune to quell our fears, those inner physiological fight-or-flight responses that define humans as emotional beings. Antonio Damasio (2003) explains that the thinking brain recognizes and translates as "feelings" (cognitively) those emotional, physiological responses that have already transpired at the instinctive, sub-cognitive level (Libet 2002, 2003). The labeling of "feelings" occurs at a later stage in the hierarchy of information-processing. As explained in the fear spiral discussion of Chapter 5, the recognition of "feelings" can trigger instinctive fear responses, which are again identified as "that feeling," which again causes stress, and so on up the spiraling anxiety scenario. Placating those feelings with words takes time and semantic clarification. Diverting and even extinguishing those feelings with melody is immediate.

Rogers and Hammerstein knew whereof they spoke. The master element of music's emotional content lies within the nature of its tune, the melody. Implicating rhythm, timbre, harmony, dynamics, and form, the tune can depict, divert, and *convert* emotions and feelings, because it immediately and directly resonates with inner physiological operations that do not rely on semantic interpretation of cognitive logic and language in order to function. In short, melody gets right to the point; it immediately engages one's basic emotional instincts. Donna Williams (1998) claims that the autistic system that can sense things without dismissing anything is actually more able to make sense of the planet because instinct and intuition have not yet been lost, and perhaps, also, that integrated sensing through cognitive channels has actually limited human intuition and instinctive responses. For many diagnosed populations, the tune speaks louder than words in tapping into inner physiological functions.

In *The Symbolic Species: Co-evolution of Language and the Brain*, Terrence Deacon (1997) conjectures that language development may have diminished the instinct for using human calls to convey emotional states and needs, since humans could now articulate verbally (though less accurately) what a call, or calls, would have symbolized. The more the neocortex expanded for cognition, the less became the need for instinctive (and non-verbal) communication. How unfortunate – for while language absolutely *requires* cognitive processing (see Chapter 2 in this book), melody does not; and while cognitive processing is comparatively slow and prone to misinterpretation, melody makes immediate sense to human instinct and intuition. Deacon notes that human calls continue to remain limited to only six basic forms, and variations thereof, while speech employs many vocalizations to elucidate emotional "pitches" of word meanings.

Speech inflection is a form of emotional vocal communication providing parallel channels to verbalization. One understands, but often can misinterpret, the meanings of foreign language words largely because of the emotional content derived from their inflected pitches, which can as often be *mis*understood as understood. In spoken language, vocal intensities change, attitudes permeate within inflection, pitches rise and fall, and one intuitively seems to comprehend meanings, regardless of whether or not words are recognized ("reading between the lines," so to speak). An infant will surely recognize the intent behind an adult's loud shriek long before he or she learns the meaning of "No!" Deacon (1997, p.418) suggests that "Though tonal shifts [in prosodic emissions] can be used as phonemes, the changes in tonality, volume, and phrasing that constitute prosodic features are most often produced without conscious intention." Prosody and inflection might also be instinctive and culturally dependent. So, too, with melody.

Thus, given that human calls developed as symbolic communicators of emotion and feelings, it is more than likely that melody – particularly

instinctive vocal discharges of notes linked in relation to one another –
preceded language (as Charles Darwin speculated) in symbolically conveying
states of mind and emotions. Coupled with human rhythmic drives, the phenomenon of extended vocal incantations as pre-language – in essence, the
human being's *first* language – could be why it is often thought that humans
are genetically pre-programmed to process music as symbolic communication of human emotional experiences. As evolution progressed, vocalizations became extended and amplified through various instruments, such
as bone or hollow reed flutes, animal horns, and other vibration-
producing wind and percussion instruments, precisely imitating and
expanding on human calls.

## What is this thing called "melody"?

Just as some of the most fundamental principles of physics derive from
concepts of *periodicity* (recurring cycles, as described in Chapter 3), so do
some of the most fundamental principles of cerebral information-processing, including the *Gestalt* laws discussed in Chapter 4 and the fear spiral
described in Chapter 5, derive from the human brain's affinity for *tracking*
and *linking* pitches in search of meanings that could make the difference
between safety and danger. Deacon (1997) argues that, millennia before
speech evolved to its present state, and before the neocortex evolved to its
current size, the uniquely human form of social communication, and the
symbolic expression of feelings and needs, took the form of extended vocalizations (see Berger 2002, p.119). Yet, however strange this may seem, of all
animals, humans are the most limited in their repertoire of vocal "calls."
(Could music have evolved to expand upon an otherwise paltry set of calls?)
As Deacon points out, two of the basic human calls are *laughter*, which
involves a rhythmic exhalation of breath and vocal sound, and *sobbing*, a
rhythmic inhalation of breath and sound. He conjectures that perhaps these
two calls are two sides of one coin.

In support of the paradigm presented in Chapter 1, we theorize here that
melody, as an element of music, undoubtedly *is* the symbolic extension of
these calls – laughter being encoded in music as an expression of joy, and
sobbing being reflected in music as an analogue for sorrow. For example, the
musicologists among our readers will note that analyses of the liturgical
works of J. S. Bach are found to contain melodic and rhythmic patterns that
are deliberately repetitive, composed precisely to simulate the rhythmic
breathing and intoning of sobs and moans that lament the sorrow of the

crucifixion. Or, as in some of Bach's other works, similar patterns represent the despair of sinners, human misery, or contemplation of death, depending on the text or nature of the work (Marshall 1989).

Along with laughter and sobbing, the limited repertoire of human calls include: screaming with fright; groaning in disapproval; sighing as an expression of sadness and weariness, fatigue, or relief; and crying with pain, fear, and/or remorse. These six human calls and their variants are exclusively available to all human animals. Given the extensive enlargement of the human neocortex, it is strange that the human species is still limited to only these six calls. Diagnoses and dysfunctions of any kind seem not to impede employment of these basic symbolic calls, except in cases of severe damage to the amygdala (Chapter 4), one of the brain's emotional regions, which can impair a victim's ability to react emotionally (Damasio 2003).

The element of melody, as with rhythm (Chapter 7), also embodies at least four interrelated characteristics (four more "P" words), and their influence on the function of the human auditory system. Melody's inherent characteristics include:

- pitch

- prosody (literally, "speech song," conveying rhythmic patterns, pace, and other features that characterize the emotion inherent within a series of linked pitches)

- phrase (a musical sentence)

- profile (the shape of a melodic flow, referred to as *melodic contour*).

These four characteristics interplay with the element of rhythm by superimposing onto rhythm's overall panorama those additional patterns which are inherent in a melodic stream. The processing of melody by the brain depends directly on the manner in which the human auditory system (described below) functions and transmits auditory information, which introduces a fifth and most important "P" – *perception*. How the brain and body receive and perceive tonal information is directly related to the accuracy with which the attributes of melody are distinguished, organized, and coded by auditory mechanisms, by ancillary subordinate sensory processes, and by the brain. These are by no means simple, straightforward processes. Indeed, the subject could, in and of itself, fill several textbooks, assuming one even knows all there is to know about it (another area for further research). For the purposes of this book, however, suffice it to say that the first step towards understanding sounds as melody requires that one examine at least some fundamental aspects relevant to the *discrimination* of pitch, one of the most complex processes of audition.

## Pitch: the music ladder

The discussion in Chapter 3 about the principles of physics from which the elements of music are derived noted that all energy must vibrate in order to sustain itself. Furthermore, depending on the frequency of those vibrations, energy is perceived in various forms – light, heat, mechanical vibrations, and so on. In order for the human auditory system to detect energy as *sound*, that energy must vibrate within the 20–20,000 cycle-per-second range (20 Hz to 20 kHz). What the human auditory system perceives when exposed to energy vibrating within this range, the *auditory spectrum* of frequencies, is called the *pitch* of the sound. Vibrations at the slower end of this frequency spectrum are perceived as lower-pitched sounds, and those at the faster end of the spectrum are discerned as higher-pitched sounds.

In general, pitches that can be sung encompass the range of the human voice, which is roughly four octaves. An *octave* refers to the pitch perceived when a fundamental frequency is doubled (yielding "an octave *above* the fundamental frequency") or halved (yielding "an octave *below* the fundamental frequency"). Thus, four octaves for the range of the human voice starts at a fundamental frequency of approximately 65–80 Hz for a male basso profundo, and increases by a factor of sixteen, to 1040–1280 Hz, for a female coloratura voice. The normal range of speech sounds is usually from around 300 Hz (low-pitched whispers) to 3000 Hz (extremely high-pitched screams).

Auditory perception and pitch discrimination (hearing one pitch as being different from another) depend on the *resolution ability* of the auditory system, as discussed later. Questions immediately arise. Does everyone hear the same pitch frequency, that is to say the *same* sound, in the same way? And is it possible that, as with color perception, each person hears only approximately the same sounds? Actually, this is entirely likely. For example, a string player will keenly discriminate the difference between a concert A frequency of 440 Hz and one played at 438 Hz, while the lay listener will hear the pitch as just an A. A trained ear can resolve differences in pitch frequency down to 2–4 Hz. In addition, when an A pitch is played, one listener may perceive that A as being at 440 Hz (the exact "concert A"); another, an A that sounds "sharp" at 442 Hz; and still another, an A that sounds "flat" at 438 Hz; and so on. A French horn player might discriminate the exact same A pitch in a totally different manner, perhaps as being even lower. *Timbre* (Chapters 2 and 9) and *overtones* unique to a rendering instrument or voice will impact upon one's ability to discriminate pitch. Moreover, an A played on a piano may be perceived differently from the same A played on a xylophone or saxophone. The ears/brain can play many tricks on the listener, including enabling one to hear pitches that have not even been presented. Therefore, one cannot, and should not, take for granted that everyone hears a concert A, or anything else for that matter, in the same way – or even at all.

## Pitch and the act of hearing

The physiological act of hearing, known as the sense of "audition," comprises a very delicate, highly complex series of processes, which begin with the three distinct parts of the ear (see Figure 8.1):

- The outer ear is the receiver, including the pinna and auditory canal.

- The middle ear is a relay station that transmits sound waves from the primarily air-filled auditory canal into the fluid-filled inner ear.

- The inner ear is where receptor cells receive fluid oscillations (transduced sound energy) and, in turn, convert (transduce) these into electrochemical signals called *action potentials.* These are dispatched through the afferent nervous system to the brain (Berger 2002; Brown and Wallace 1980; Dallos 1986; Hudspeth 1997; Schneck 1990).

The tympanic membrane – the ear's outer drum, similar to a loudspeaker diaphragm – forms the boundary that separates the air-filled outer ear from the liquid-filled middle ear. Sound traveling along the auditory canal eventually bumps up against the tympanic membrane, setting both it and a very tiny bone (the malleus, or "hammer") attached to the middle-ear side of it into vibratory motion. This activates a vibrational chain reaction as the malleus drives two other tiny bones, the incus ("anvil") and the stapes ("stirrup"). The three bones of the middle ear are referred to collectively as the *ossicular chain.*

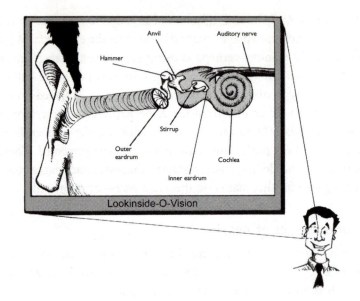

*Figure 8.1 The human hearing apparatus: from the receiving outer ear drum, through the impedance-matching bone architecture (hammer, anvil, and stirrup) of the middle ear, to the transmitting inner ear drum and cochlea (inner ear), from which the auditory nerve (shown only schematically) emanates.*

The ossicular chain mechanically amplifies the tiny vibrations of the *outer eardrum*, while at the same time ensuring that the sound energy inherent in the vibrating air molecules will transfer smoothly into liquid molecule vibrations (a process called *impedance matching*), rather than being reflected right back out of the ear. At the end of the chain, the stapes bone is attached to, and therefore sets into corresponding vibratory motion, a second much smaller *inner eardrum* that guards the entrance to the inner ear at the "oval window." Once this inner eardrum begins to vibrate, it sends transduced sound waves flowing through the fluid of the cochlea in the inner ear.

The cochlea is a tubular structure coiled two-and-one-half times into the shape of a snail (hence its name). This tube, into which sound vibrations gain access at the oval window, is divided in cross-section (by two membranes that extend through its entire length). This forms three separate channels: (1) a lower, half-moon-shaped scala tympani; (2) a middle, pie-shaped scala media (or "cochlear duct"); and (3) an upper scala vestibuli that occupies the remainder of the cross-section.

The middle scala media chamber and lower scala tympani chamber are separated by the basilar membrane, a trampoline-like structure that spans across a diameter of the cochlea. It is this membrane that is set into motion by the waves generated in the fluid of the cochlea as it responds to sound waves. In turn, the scala media is separated from the upper scala vestibuli chamber by the vestibular (Reissner's) membrane, which also spans the diameter of the cochlea in its cross-sectional plane. However, Reissner's membrane lies at an angle of 45–60 degrees relative to the basilar membrane. The scala vestibuli, guarded by the oval window, is the first region to receive the vibrations transmitted to the inner ear by the stapes footplate bone.

The entrance to the scala tympani, the lowest of the three channels of the cochlea, is guarded by a "round window" which lies below the oval window. The scala tympani and scala vestibuli actually become continuous regions, since they meet at the apex of the cochlear spiral (i.e., the *helicotrema*), so both of them actually influence the basilar membrane. The pie-shaped (in cross-section) cochlear duct (scala media) is literally sandwiched in-between the upper and lower channels, bordered by them all the way around.

The basilar membrane is a gauzy strip of tissue, on the scala media side of which rests the Organ of Corti, often referred to as the "organ of hearing." Here reside *hearing receptor cells* – ciliated (hair) cell bundles arranged in several parallel rows running along the membrane. Like blades of grass swaying in a breeze, the hair-like extensions projecting out from the row of inner hearing receptor cells (thereby making contact with the basilar membrane) entrain sound wave vibrations generated by mechanical forces. The forces drive the basilar membrane; the membrane deflects the hair-cell receptors that are in contact with it; this deflection is transduced into corresponding *afferent sensory action potentials*; and the action potentials transmit the encoded information to the central nervous system via the cochlear branch of the auditory nerve (the VIIIth cranial, or *vestibulocochlear nerve*). The process of pitch discrimination relies on several properties of this anatomical configuration.

1. A pure high-frequency tone generates a wave that travels only a short distance along the basilar membrane before reaching its peak amplitude (maximum basilar membrane displacement from its neutral position). That is due to the fact that high-frequency signals dissipate ("burn up") much faster than do low-frequency signals. The reader may have experienced this fact in observing that the bass notes (lower-to-middle frequency) of a loud piece of music can travel through walls and be heard on the other side, but the treble (middle-to-upper frequency) notes disappear. Thus, the hair cells at the position of the peak amplitude "fire the

loudest," and the brain receives signals from the corresponding nerve fibers attached to those hair cells, which are coded to convey "high-frequency information."

A pure low-frequency tone generates a wave that travels much further along the basilar membrane before reaching its peak amplitude and deflecting the membrane a corresponding amount. Signals from nerve fibers connected to that region of the membrane evoke a "low-frequency" sensation in the brain. This has been called the "place theory of audition" (Békésy 1960; Békésy and Rosenblith 1951).

2.   Cilia bundles range in size from short to tall, thick to thin, and so are responsive to corresponding particular ranges of frequencies. Lower (slower) frequency vibration ranges are detectable by thicker, taller receptor cilia – to which are attached "low-frequency" nerve fibers – and so on up the scale of pitches as the cilia become progressively smaller and thinner. Simultaneous multiple-pitch vibrations (notes and chords) activate multiple cilia concurrently, providing the sensation of timbre (sound quality), consonance, and dissonance. (For a demonstration of various vibrational impacts on cilla in a webcast lecture on hearing, see Hudspeth (1997).

3.   A closer look at the basilar membrane reveals that it is actually made up of some 24,000 closely packed, tightly stretched transverse fibers ("strings," as it were) that are very short near the oval window at the entrance to the cochlea, and gradually increase in length (like the strings of a harp) as one progresses up the cochlea to its apex. Thus, the basilar membrane actually behaves like a miniature harp, with the shorter fibers being associated with high-pitched sounds, and the longer fibers corresponding to low-pitched sounds (Buser and Imbert 1992).

4.   Both the fiber density (number of fibers per unit length along the basilar membrane) and membrane stiffness decrease in the progression from base to apex in the cochlea, thus affecting its responsiveness to mechanical disturbance, and making it more "sluggish" as it progresses from base to apex (akin to loosening a violin string).

All of the above factors combine to make the base of the cochlea responsive to high-frequency sound vibrations, and the apex responsive to low-frequency sound vibrations. More specifically, traveling around the first full turn (about 25 mm) at the base of the cochlea, it is found that the basilar membrane responds to sound frequencies decreasing from about 20,000 Hz (door squeak, chirping of some insects) at the oval window, to some 1500 Hz (not yet down to the coloratura, high soprano range of the vocal register). In other words, the first full turn of the cochlea is not very responsive to musical inputs other than those emanating from the highest-pitch ranges of instruments like the piccolo, violin, flute, oboe, and clarinet. This is a fact that could be very useful to music therapy clinicians when treating auditory and behavioral issues related to sound.

Continuing around the second full turn of the cochlea (about 8mm further), the basilar membrane is responsive to sound frequencies progressively decreasing from 1500 Hz to 500 Hz, thus adding the higher-pitched ranges of the viola, trumpet, French horn, and cello to the arsenal of instruments, and the voice ranges of sopranos and altos. The human ear generally responds most acutely in the narrow range from 1000 to 4000 Hz; i.e., from just under two-thirds of the way into the first full turn of the basilar membrane, to just over one-third of the way into the second full turn of this membrane.

The final half-turn of the cochlea (the last 2 mm) is responsive to sound frequencies that decrease from 500 Hz to around 20 Hz. This portion of the basilar membrane is also *least* sensitive to relative frequency *changes*. Thus, it becomes progressively more difficult for a listener to discriminate changes in pitch as sounds move from high-pitched notes to lower ones, which emanate from bass instruments, tenor and baritone voices, and trombones, bassoons, tubas, kettle drums, and so on.

Once stimulated, the respective cilia send out rapid-fire, Morse-code-like electrochemical impulses (action potentials) through the 30,000 or so afferent fibers that innervate them. These action potentials identify the *frequency* (impulses per second), *intensity* (by the amplitude of basilar membrane displacement), *duration*, and *location* of a sound. Auditory action potentials commute along the auditory nerve, enter the brain, and track through the thalamus, pons Varolii (see Chapter 4), the hypothalamus, amygdala, and hippocampus, being eventually sent off to the auditory cortex situated close to the motor cortex. Along the way, the signals are encoded, compared, evaluated, referenced, etc., in accordance with information-processing considerations discussed in Chapters 4, 5, and 6. Ultimately, they might (or might *not*) be sent to the various "file cabinets" of the neocortical hemispheres for storage, and whatever else the cortex does with sensory information.

As noted earlier in considering one's hearing of a concert A pitch, given the complexities of auditory sensory processing (greatly simplified above), it should not be assumed that vibrations that are mechanically projected on to, and detected by, the ears will be *perceived* and *discriminated* in the same exact way by different persons receiving the same information. It is especially significant to keep this in mind when imparting acoustic information to any listener, but especially to diagnosed populations in whom auditory sensory function may be impaired.

Sound processing and pitch discrimination take place entirely within one's head and body. Neither the intake of pitches, nor their perception and discrimination, are observable to the eyes or ears of the onlooker. It is only through self-reporting and reiteration (accurate reproduction) of a pitch through one's voice or instrument that an approximation of accuracy in pitch processing can be ascertained; which is to say, whether the pitch that was *perceived* resembled the pitch that was *sent*. It is expedient to make no assumptions regarding anyone's pitch discrimination process.

There are some individuals who display "perfect pitch" memory, also known as "absolute pitch." These individuals have pitch memory and recall so astute as to enable them to exactly identify and reproduce a pitch simply upon verbal request to do so, without any further auditory cue; they just "remember" exactly what that particular pitch sounds like. For example, individuals with "perfect pitch" can immediately sing, play, or identify a note or scale as being a B-flat or F without further prompts or cues. The phenomenon is similar to perfect visual memory, known as a "photographic memory."

Although the skill of "perfect pitch" is nice to have, it can become an impediment in many ways, and a detrimental factor in the development of expressive language for many diagnosed children exhibiting absolute pitch memory. Since language includes *inflection* (varying intonations) and *rhythm* (prosody), a young child diagnosed with language disabilities could have difficulty identifying as being the same, those words intoned by two different persons with varying inflection and voice timbres. If the child's "perfect pitch" memory has already recorded (encoded) sounds/words according to the child's initial hearing of them, then those words may not be understood as being "the same" (i.e., generalized to other situations) even if those words are spoken in the exact same pitches and prosody, but by different persons and vocal timbres, or in circumstances different from those that prevailed the first time the child heard them.

"Absolute pitch" discrimination can become problematic in other ways. For instance, having first heard "Twinkle, twinkle little star" in the key of C major, and hearing it another time in the key of F major – or even in the same key but on a different instrument, as suggested earlier in describing the pitch sensitivity of different portions of the basilar membrane – the listener may experience great agitation and distress. Auditory defensiveness and anxiety often stem from the "perfect pitch" factor. Things appear to be out of tune, incorrect, in the wrong circumstance, and so on, especially in amplified and electronically reproduced versions such as on compact disc, television, and radio. Furthermore, as is often the case in autism, the need for sameness and repetition is violated when the person exhibits "perfect pitch" memory, and something is not rendered as it was initially recorded by that brain.

At the other extreme, there are persons considered to be "tone deaf," unable to "carry a tune." This is taken to mean not having the ability to discriminate and reproduce accurately the same pitches and sequences of tones transmitted to the ear. One may think of this as a kind of "tone blindness," akin to color blindness, which may be genetically inherited (*Roanoke Times* 2001). Reasons for pitch discrimination incapacity can vary from poor auditory receptor cell behavior, to distorted pitch perception, erroneous encoding, inaccurate pitch memory and recognition, inability of the larynx to reproduce the correct tone, and a myriad of other auditory processing problems. Here again, it is important for a clinician to consider the many variables and obstacles to pitch perception and discrimination, taking nothing for granted when implementing melodic interventions for particular anticipated results.

## Prosody, phrase, and profile

The second *Gestalt* law of the perception of sensory information (Chapter 4) suggests that, in order for musical notes to be sensed as melody, the stream of pitches must be sequenced such that they have a specific relationship to one another. They must flow linearly and horizontally across space and time, depicting, evoking, and referencing emotional contexts as the melody evolves. The *syntax* of melody is defined by those very relationships of pitches, one to the other, in what is ultimately perceived by the brain to be an orderly, coherent system of *tonal associations*. There are two basic types of pitch relationships. One takes the form of consecutive, step-wise movement of pitches flowing sequentially, from low frequencies to high (or vice versa), and back, in designated patterns having well-defined (close) step sizes (e.g., the tune "Frère Jacques"). This is referred to as a melody evolving in *scale-wise* (or "step") relationships (the word "scale" being derived from *scala*, the Latin [and Italian] word for ladder).

Indeed, the simplest type of scale-wise melody is the musical scale itself. Such melodic ladders can be built on tonal centers, referred to as *keys*, because of the key role that the tonal center plays in organizing the remaining pitches around itself. Among the many types of scales are: *pentatonic* (five-tone scales common in Oriental music); *modal* (as in Eastern and Middle Eastern music); *quarter-tone* (in Indian ragas); and the *major* and *minor* scales common in Western music. Major and minor scales are derived from Pythagorean overtone theory. Pythagoras, a Greek philosopher believed to have lived from 582 BCE until around 500 BCE, formulated some basic principles from which can be mathematically calculated the overtone series (harmonics) inherent in the sound generated by an "imperfect" source.

When a melody is not in a scale-wise mode and intermediate notes are omitted, the melodic line (contour) can evolve as a result of *intervals* rather than notes that follow a step-wise sequence. That is, the relationships among consecutive notes leap about rather than follow a close "scale-line" note-to-note motion, but they still remain centered within a scale (key) structure. For example, the tunes "Happy Birthday" or "Somewhere, over the rainbow" are more intervallic than is the scale-wise song "Frére Jacques." "Leaping" melodic lines offer a type of pitch relationship, mood, and emotional content different from that of the scale-wise melodic contour. Larger works comprise both scale-wise and intervallic melodic lines.

The syntactic pitch relationships of melody also include prosodic-like interactions, rhythmic associations of one pitch to another. That is to say, since every pitch has some inherent duration, and since duration is also associated with rhythm, it is almost impossible to completely separate melody from rhythm, or from the pace of the tonal stream. Thus, melody also includes *accenting* certain notes and beats (notorious in jazz), *repeating* them, and setting them to verse, in a manner resembling the rhymes, limericks, and poetic rhythms of language (such as poetry's iambic verses illustrated in the tune, "Itsy bitsy spider"). Prosody in melody, however, does not depend on lyrics and, in fact more often than not *suggests* lyrics by the very nature of the interactions taking place between melody's pitch and rhythm (e.g., the English lyrics that were added to the original melody in Brahms' *Lullaby*). Writing lyrics to existing musical compositions has been termed, by Jon

Hendricks as "vocalese" (-ese, not the -ize that defines a composition for voice *without* text).

Melodic flow generally complements and relies on rhythm's pulse, while often contributing its own diverse patterns. As demonstrated in Chapter 7, a melodic line that flows in quick-paced notes ("Mississippi, Mississippi, Mississippi") can give the illusion of speed while adhering to, and integrating with, rhythm's existing pulse and pace. In some cultures, as in Indian raga, certain music of the Orient, or of the Native American, melody may evolve more slowly than in Western cultures, containing brief phrases and prolonged spaces between phrase groupings, causing the music to appear to a listener (especially one more familiar with Western music) to be devoid of pulse and meter altogether.

Giving further meaning to the syntactic relationship of one pitch to another is the organization of melody into *phrases*, the beginnings, middles, and endings of melodic motifs. Similar to speech, melody states its musical "sentences," and it does so within an established rhythmic pulse and pace, which at times is implied rather than actual.

Melody is organized into phrases by the incorporation of such characteristics as breath stops (rests), long-and-short/loud-and-soft (barcode-like) pronouncements, accented pitches (prosody), dynamics (sound volume), question-and-answer-type inflection styles, repetition of statements, and more. These, coupled with high-and-low pitch patterns, and integrated with the element of rhythm, create a melodic contour or profile. The melodic contour is a soundscape, having peaks and valleys, high and low pitch streams, shapes and lengths of prosodic flow (including *where* and *when* accented notes materialize) – all features that can actually be seen on a written music score, or sketched on a piece of paper. It is within this melodic contour that meaning and coherence become part and parcel of melody's syntax.

## Perception of melody

The world would be a very simple place in which to live if all humans perceived things in exactly the same way. Such is not the case. And as with any sensory information-processing and perception, the processing and perception of melody, or any piece of music, is as diverse as the physiology of its listener. For instance, some listeners will perceive and entrain a melody's pitches, prosodies, phrases, and profiles (contours) so distinctly as to receive chills when listening to a particular or familiar melody. Another person, hearing the same melody, may shudder and perceive it to be abrasive or instrumentally unpleasant. Since melodies replicate human emotions and personalities, distinct "personality matches" between listener and melody take place routinely. But first the auditory system must perceive the acoustic information as being pleasant or unpleasant, friendly or hostile.

Psychology-of-music professionals continue to devote major research and study effort and time to the auditory processing of music information as it relates to auditory perception; that is to say, how and what one actually *hears* when in the presence of music (see, for example, Aiello and Sloboda 1994; Bregman 1999; Buser and Imbert 1992; Coren and Ward 1989; Deliege and Sloboda 1997; Hargreaves 1986; Hodges 1996b; McAdams and Bigand 1993; Seashore 1967; Slawson 1985; Sloboda 1985; Warren 1999). Before exploring the auditory processing of music, it is of interest to review some information discussed in Chapter 7 about rhythm. Recall that music in general, and the elements embodied in rhythm, pitch (melody), and dynamics (sound volume) in particular, are not only heard through the ears, but are also felt via the body's tactile sensors. For some individuals, such perception is actually *cross-processed* by other senses, predominantly visual, and occasionally gustatory (taste, another tactile-related sense).

The much lauded Scottish percussionist Evelyn Glennie referred to in the previous chapter (see page 140) does not hear music with her ears. Yet, she is an accomplished concert artist appearing as soloist with orchestras all over the world, performing concerti on xylophones and on an amazing assortment of other tonal and percussive instruments. A phenomenon? Not really. Recall that sound energy derives from vibrating sources, quivering at frequencies in the range 20–20,000 Hz. These sources cause surrounding air molecules to vibrate, which the ear picks up and converts (transduces) into neural action potentials (electrochemical signals). However, once set into motion, this vibrating air is not perceptible to ears alone. Other sensory systems that can respond to energy in the same frequency range, and that intercept the path of vibrations, can and *do* respond as well. Thus, in humans, vibrating air is also detected by the senses of touch and vision. For example, if you are at a pier when a huge ocean liner blows its horns for departure, it is very likely that you will not only hear the sound but also feel it. Indeed, the human being's sub-cognitive sensory systems really are holistic, in the sense of the fifth *Gestalt* law of perception (Chapter 4). In keeping with the concept of sensory integration, they are totally interdependent, working *collectively* to impart frequency details to the various areas of the brain. Unfortunately, more often than not, cognition fails (or forgets?) to process those feelings that are derived from acoustic vibrations.

As Glennie explains in her online discussion of hearing (available at www.evelyn.co.uk/hearingessay.htm), the human ear becomes rather inefficient when it comes to detecting very slow vibrations. Thus, in these low-frequency bass/baritone/ low-tenor ranges, other senses begin to compensate, especially the tactile (and sometimes the visual) sense. For some reason, typically functioning humans tend to distinguish, as being different, the hearing of a sound from the feeling of it within the body. Actually, it all happens simultaneously. But the "hearing population" typically desensitizes its tactile awareness of sound in favor of typically functioning ("normal") *audition*. This is not unlike the corresponding desensitization of human beings to *aural* consciousness of sensory inputs in the presence of typically functioning ("normal") *vision*. Indeed, various estimates suggest that as much as 90 percent or more of the environmental information that is received daily by the human organism enters the system through the 70 percent of the body's total sensory receptors that are clustered in the eyes (Schneck 1990). For most humans, seeing is indeed believing! Still, whether or not one can hear thunder, its sound vibrations will explicitly be felt by the bodies, windows, floors, etc., with which it comes in contact; and the brain may evolve fight-or-flight anxiety responses, whether the information has been heard or felt, or both.

Percussionist Evelyn Glennie, who became profoundly deaf at 8 years of age, had "perfect pitch" memory prior to that. She believes that deafness does not mean one cannot hear, but only that there is something wrong with the ears. Thus, from childhood, she devoted time to refining her ability to detect vibrations, and eventually managed to distinguish rough pitches of notes by associating where on her body she *felt* the sound (identified through her earlier sense of "perfect pitch"). Glennie hears low sounds by feeling them predominantly in her legs and feet. She distinguishes high pitches on areas of her face, neck, and/or chest, and so on.

In addition to feeling pitch vibrations and flow, a person can also employ his or her sense of *vision* to actually *see* certain items moving and vibrating – a drum head, for instance, or a cymbal, or leaves moving on a tree. It is thereby possible to sense accompanying sounds, some perhaps from one's virtual "imaginary reality" places of the mind.

These considerations could explain why people often prefer to attend live concerts, as opposed to hearing them on CDs, TV, or radio. Since music vibrations are perceived through the ears, the body, and multiple sensory processing modalities, it is reasonable to assume that a live concert exposure, as well as live music in therapy sessions, provides a more complete perception and enjoyment factor of this type of acoustic sensory stimulation (again, *Gestalt* law number 5).

Going one step further, "audition" perception is also an associative experience for listeners, regardless of auditory capacity. That is, just as Glennie perceives the crackling sound she hears in her ears, and the sensations she receives on her body, as being associated with the ringing of the telephone, some people who have no (obvious) auditory impairment associate auditory perceptions with corresponding experiences that have come to be identified with that particular type of acoustic information. One *associates* (links) pitch *a* with another pitch, *b*, and *c*, and *d*, etc., and recognizes it as a melody, *provided these pitches are received in time in a reasonable proximity to one another* (*Gestalt* laws 1, 2, 3) . But more than that, a melody (a string of pitches) is often *associated* with an event or memory, which may have been pleasant or hostile; and so on. What's more, such associative experiences are different for every listener. In this sense, when it comes to auditory perception, human beings may all be somewhat "impaired" – which is yet another reason to make no assumptions about what any given individual actually perceives when listening to a melody, and what "comes to mind" for that individual, in terms of the cognitive and/or sub-cognitive associations that he or she may make with that particular melody.

## Synesthesia: hearing, seeing, tasting, and feeling sound

An interesting aspect of sound perception, one that psychologists and neuroscientists have yet to research formally, is the most fascinating perception phenomenon called *synesthesia* (or synaesthesia). This is a phenomenon whereby sensory information is cross-processed by more than one sensory system. Thus, synesthesia provides a simultaneous perception derived from two or more separate senses: a musical note might be perceived to be a color, as well as a pitch. By and large, one takes for granted that sensory systems each process stimuli in separate ways, within discrete locations in the brain; and that, through a process of *sensory integration*, all of these simultaneous inputs ultimately allow the brain to derive a sensible, organized, seemingly accurate representation of events (again, *Gestalt* law number 5). There are, however, individuals who actually *see* what another is saying; individuals who literally "see what you mean"! This is a phenomenon whereby parallel sensory information-processing becomes cross-processed. Thus, for example, sensory processing of auditory vibrations might actually be translated into visual scenarios, or visual scenarios into taste or tactile sensations, and so on.

The word "synesthesia" derives from the Greek prefix *syn-*, meaning "together," and the word *aesthesis*, meaning "perception." In other words, a person with synesthesia senses information through unexpected and alternative systemic channels (Cytowic 2002). When dealing with perception of pitches, a person with synesthesia may literally be seeing the pitch or the melodic incantation, perceiving the sound vibrations visually as a particular color, or seeing them as a solid item such as brick, metal, or glass, or as some kind of picture. What is being discussed here is not merely an *association* of sound with color or taste (which many persons have) but the actual *transduction* of the auditory input, subcortically, as being color, taste, touch, and/or smell (Schneck 1990). In *The Man Who Tasted Shapes*, Dr. Richard Cytowic (1999) discusses several cases of crossed perceptions that involved visual stimuli perceived as sound, taste stimuli perceived as shapes, sound stimuli perceived visually, and more.

Dr. Cytowic relates that, in 1704, Sir Isaac Newton attempted to devise an actual mathematical formula equating vibrational frequencies of sound to corresponding wavelengths of light (1999, pp.52–53). Newton was unsuccessful, but later others did manage to invent musical instruments capable of converting acoustic vibrations into corresponding visual effects. Also according to Dr. Cytowic (1999, pp.54–55), the composer Alexander Scriabin (1872–1915) was a synesthetic who actually saw sounds, and incorporated his experiences into some of his compositions involving music and simultaneous light displays. The painter Vasily Kandinsky (1866–1944) was also apparently synesthetic, painting to music backgrounds, and exploring the "harmonious relationships between sound and color and [he] used musical terms to describe his paintings" (1999, p.55; see also Cytowic [2002] for further information on synesthesia). It is interesting to note that, although *any* of the senses can be "mixed," the auditory/visual crossover is the most common (Smith 1989, p.26). Moreover, synesthesia occurs to varying degrees in virtually everybody, but its manifestations in an everyday sense are suppressed for all of the reasons given earlier; i.e., vision at the expense of hearing, hearing at the expense of taction, and so on (Schneck 1990). In other words, synesthetic sensations become background noise.

To summarize, the peculiarities of pitch and melody *perception* can provide clues to determining behavioral causes possibly based upon how a diagnosed listener might be internalizing a music intervention. The clinician cannot assume that the *melody* he or she is playing is being *heard* as played, *perceived* as intended, or *associated* with some presumed experience. Precisely because this aspect of acoustic information-processing is so individual, it is advantageous to consider the problematic possibilities when presenting melody to diagnosed populations. For diagnosed, as well as undiagnosed, populations with apparently "normal" hearing, there are still further aspects of audition that need to be considered.

## Auditory scanning and tracking

### Auditory scanning

Auditory scanning refers to the brain and auditory system's ability to accurately scan the sequential flow of melodic syntax in order to receive, perceive, and discriminate the acoustic information in a one-to-one correspondence with the way it is being generated and transmitted. In vision processing, the eyes continuously scan a scene, determining those "resting zones" that attract attention, for whatever reason, be it their color, light intensity, shape, subject, etc. Essentially, the eyes are constantly surveying the landscape before them, usually with a rapid, almost imperceptible back and forth ocular movement. The auditory system undertakes similar scanning activities, despite the fleeting nature of acoustic information. The ears scan the acoustic landscape (observe those of a dog or horse, for example), so that the brain can determine its safety features, as embedded in the relationships among pitches. It, too, intermittently "rests" at certain points in sound, for whatever reasons those particular sounds are selected as focal points. Such scanning of constantly moving sounds relies heavily on short-term memory. Short-term memory enables the temporary holding of one sound long enough for the brain to reference it against another (scanning back and forth just as with visual information), in anticipation of the next associated sound event (Berger 2002; Schneck 1997; Schneck and Schneck 1996).

Auditory scanning, most especially when continuously linked sounds are presented (as is the case for melody), is a *cumulative* process. The more sound that is added to the auditory scene, the more the short-term memory compiles the information, and the wider the auditory scanning process becomes. Eventually, melodic sounds introduced at an earlier point in time will disappear, giving way to new incoming information, because the brain can hold on to only a limited amount of information at one hearing. This auditory scanning process is one reason why two people do not experience sound sequences in the same way, and why person A might dwell on a sound that escapes person B entirely. In fact, even when the same musical stimulus is presented to the same person on several different occasions, each hearing will produce different "scanning" resting points, and various other features will be noticed each time.

In addition to this, the more complicated and dense the music information is, containing complex harmonies, compounded rhythm structures, elaborate orchestrations, etc., the less reliable will be the memory and recall of a piece of music. This is why the listener of a highly avante garde contemporary composition finds it difficult to track and scan for sense and syntax. The melodic line of such a composition often contains widely spaced, high/low, seemingly non-sequential, unrelated intervals of notes, with many spaces in between, in a melodic contour that appears jagged or non-existent (again, *Gestalt*). Detection of sound *patterns* in a melodic flow is what the brain likes best. Simple melodies, using fewer gaps in tone spacings, and more scale-wise movement, offer simpler patterns, more easily discernable in a scanning and tracking process. (Refer back to the discussion in Chapter 4 of the *Gestalt* laws of sensory perception.) In contemporary music, often the detection of patterns becomes a rather obscure, forbidding, difficult task, requiring many hearings to decode.

Here again, as with pitch processing discussed above, it cannot be assumed that an individual's auditory scanning process is functioning adequately enough to derive and deliver accurately the *essence* (*Gestalt* law number 5) of the information being heard. In addition to the possibility that the earlier-described anatomical hearing architecture might be inappropriately entraining and transducing pitch frequencies, thus issuing erroneous signals for transport to the brain, there is also the question of whether the auditory *tracking* of a melodic flow and contour is taking place correctly (Berger 2002).

## Auditory tracking

Coupled with general auditory focus, auditory scanning, pitch identification, appropriate transduction, and perception, is the essential factor of *tracking* precisely the temporal acoustic information *as it is being transmitted*. The manner by which one sequentially tracks sound often determines the sense one ultimately derives from a linear (melodic) music configuration and/or a spoken sentence. Listening to a melody or piece of music is exactly like tracking a spoken language: it is a *cumulative process* in which the brain scans, tracks, tags (for spatial and temporal identification), re-creates, and determines relationships among the sounds received (Berger 2002; Berger and Schneck 2003; Schneck 1997, 2003a; Schneck and Schneck 1996). In effect, the brain of the music listener is actually *re*-composing a composition that the auditory system (and complementary sensory systems, e.g. touch) and brain have essentially *de*-composed into component parts (frequencies and amplitudes of vibrations, etc.).

When one eats a meal, the food is first broken down (digested) into component parts: proteins into amino acids; fats into fatty acids; carbohydrates into simple sugars. The products of digestion are then absorbed (assimilated) and transported via the cardiovascular system (heart and blood vessels) to their respective destinations (cells), where they are stored, to be reassembled as needed into usable life-supporting produce. One may envision the processing of sensory information in exactly the same way.

- Incoming information ("food") such as sound, or any other type of adequate stimulus (energy), is first reduced to its component elements ("digested" into corresponding frequency, amplitude, etc.).

- It is then "absorbed" by transduction into electrochemical action potentials.

- It is then dispatched, via the afferent pathways of the peripheral nervous system (analogous to the cardiovascular system for food), to the central nervous system, where it is tagged (encoded) in subcortical regions of the brain, and eventually stored in various cortical locations (nerve "cells").

- Cortical nerve cells further encode, fine-tune, and file (store) the information *in the exact sequence in which it was received*, for eventual use, comparison, decoding, and so on.

- As necessary, these stored components are then reassembled ("recomposed," as it relates to music), not unlike how cells make produce from digested raw materials, or how the visual system reconstructs a scene or picture (Ornstein and Thompson 1984). This reproduces exactly the input that was originally transmitted to the auditory sense.

In effect, then, hearing a piece of music is literally a "virtual reality" experience in which the listener is co-composing the music, exactly as the creator intended, within a few milliseconds of having heard it.

The hippocampus in the paleoencephalon (the subcortical "old" brain; see Chapter 4) is believed to have the primary responsibility for sequentially tagging (encoding) each piece of auditory input. Such tagging gives the information the aforementioned spatial and temporal significance, like a coat-check person who tags each item in the exact sequence in which it is received (and also uses the tag to identify the person to whom the coat belonged). The coded information is then dispatched to *information-specific* sites (neocortical "mailboxes," if you will) that are also sensory-modality and space-and-time specific, so that the brain can subsequently identify the sensory significance of a piece of information both from its corresponding tag and from its cortical location.

The brain further discriminates among sounds to distinguish language from other auditory inputs, such as bird calls or music, recognizing that music is *a continuous looping of sounds*, as opposed to the transitory stops and starts of speech. Of course, it takes only nanoseconds (hundred millionths of a second) for all of this to transpire, but the complexities are so vast that it is altogether amazing that any accuracy in hearing is obtainable. Here, once again, as was the case with pitch discrimination and perception, it cannot be assumed that auditory tracking is functioning as expected, and that the hearing apparatus is sequentially and accurately entraining and firing meaningful action potentials to the brain (any malfunction in this process would result in the nervous system's equivalent of "indigestion"!). This is a factor that is especially important to consider when providing treatment for persons with language difficulties.

## Melody in therapy

The presumption that the presentation of "familiar" music to a listener will be perceived as such is a major leap of faith on the part of the music therapist. The anatomical, physiological, and morphological complexities of the auditory system are vast, and audiological/neuroscientific research into human auditory function is still in its infancy. Certainly, there are technological limitations: the instrumentation necessary to measure what it is that the ear actually perceives or discriminates is sophisticated, assuming scientists even know *what* to measure. Indeed, investigators are not really sure what it is they are looking for. Thus, they rely mainly on a form of subjective self-reporting, which can be inaccurate at best, and to a lesser degree, on some theoretical computer simulations that are based on implicit assumptions that are as yet not totally verified.

Neuroscientists have been researching brain processing of music in persons with such auditory maladies as amusia, and the possible existence of a kind of auditory dyslexia. Amusia refers to an inability to process sound as "music" (Brust 2001; Peretz 2001; Peretz, Champod, and Hyde 2003). Auditory dyslexia refers to a condition in which sounds are inverted, perceived non-sequentially or out of context (even backwards), or bypassed altogether (Berger 2002). This condition would be similar to visual dyslexia in which words are turned upside down, inverted, or otherwise misread. Inefficient auditory tracking might also be due to the possibility that the speed (tempo) of the presented melodic or spoken information is incongruous with the speed of information-processing in the auditory system and brain of the recipient (discussed in Chapter 4; see also Magne, Schon, and Besson 2003; Overy 2003; Schneck 2003a). This is especially relevant in diagnosed populations with brain trauma, various neurophysiological disorders, and language development deficits.

Language development relies heavily on the brain's ability to hear, track, accurately process, and loop frequency variations together, *in sequence*, as heard in the prosodic tempo. If the auditory input is inaccurately processed, for example, because the incoming information was delivered at a speed faster than the ear and brain can "hear," adequately encode, and accurately decode it, then drop-outs (see Chapter 4) can jeopardize speech attainment, regardless of oral motor facility. Auditory scanning and tracking of sound, including tracking at the verbatim *tempo of the incoming stimuli*, are major variables in language development. This is why it is important to slow down the pace of music therapy and language inputs. Assessment of an individual's information-processing rate, both sensory and cerebral, is consequential to the goal of a sensory intervention.

By now it should be understood that human physiological function is highly individual-specific (Schneck 2001a), and that audition is as extremely complex a sensory activity as is any other in the human body. It includes a multitude of cascading variables, any one of which can malfunction at any time, and at any point in the process – and not necessarily always in the same way. So how can *melody* be effective in aiding human physiological function to reach a desirable level of adaptation? A myriad of techniques and approaches are described in the music therapy literature (e.g., Adamek *et al.* 2000; Standley 2000; Standley and Prickett 1994). But the key to addressing any behavioral responses lies with the clinician. He or she, armed with a knowledge of physiology, must have the ability to account for possible contributing causes of responses, in order to construct and develop interventions with the potential to address both the cause and the symptoms. Since music therapy is primarily an acoustic/tactile/visual intervention, its effectiveness will immediately be contingent predominantly on the recipient's *hearing process,* and to a somewhat lesser degree on his or her *tactile and visual competence.*

Taking all of this into account can be an ominous task; all the more reason for practitioners to study and understand physiological function as it relates specifically to the processing of musical stimuli. Assessment of a client begins with knowing what questions to ask when taking a clinical history. Certainly, in some cases there may be limited opportunities to alter homeostasis. Much more research, asking the right questions, and developing protocols for answering them, is needed in order to actually keep track of what is changing physiologically, how it is changing, and (most importantly) in what dose–response sense (how much, how often, for how long, etc.).

A soothing, pleasant melodic line, such as that found in a lullaby or favorite song, has the ability to calm fear spirals (see Chapter 5). Since the brain has difficulty simultaneously handling too many different stimuli, inputs have to be prioritized, and choices made accordingly. Often, the right kind of music will take priority in enticing the brain's attention away from troubling thoughts. As the brain scans and tracks music information, it becomes more preoccupied and interested in listening for all the tonal relationships than in continuing to worry about other problems; this process is called *thought redirection.* And when a melody is especially entreating, varying in contours, tonalities, rhythms, phrases, spaces, and timbres, or when it is a familiar reference to one's key life events (childhood, homeland, or special persons), the brain will remain attentive and sometimes become so relaxed as to give way to sleep.

On the other hand, if a melody is demanding, employs many interval leaps from high to low, and is a bit more challenging to scan and track, the physiological organism becomes animated. Listening will be at higher levels of alertness because the sound could be perceived to be dangerous or threatening, and an increased flow of epinephrine (adrenaline) and various stress hormones might ensue. As stated above, the accuracy of auditory scanning, tracking, and processing is contingent upon the body's ability to *entrain* the presented flow of pitch/prosody information. A lack of direct one-to-one correlation between the presentation of acoustic information and the recipient's ability to *process* that information accurately creates homeostatic disturbances. This factor alone is precisely why the presentation of *melodic* information serves as an ideal intervention for developing auditory tracking, rhythmic (prosodic) integration, and expressive language. Preferably, melody should be presented in a single horizontal line, which is to say, without harmony and multi-instrumental orchestration, and it should contain varying or modified rhythmic tempos.

A common use of melody as a clinical intervention is that of treating Alzheimer's patients and aging populations that exhibit memory and movement deficits. Concetta Tomaino (2000), Director of Music Therapy at the Institute for Music and Neurologic Foundation, Beth Israel Hospital, Bronx, New York, describes how her work using familiar tunes, which she plays on an accordion, helps instantly to revive (at least temporarily) both movement and memories in many hospitalized victims with various forms of dementia, Alzheimer's, and immobility (see also Aldridge 2000, Pachetti *et al.* 1998, and Prickett 2000). However, as has been reported in some published research (Prickett 2000), inaccuracy in processing of pitch, prosody, and phrase in aging populations becomes in many cases a contending element in effectively deriving positive therapy results through music.

Although temporary memory retrieval that results from hearing familiar melodies is comforting, what does it mean in the longer term? Beside the purely auditory considerations, much more research is needed in order to establish specific dose–response levels, in order to assess realistically whether homeostasis can, in fact, be altered over the long term by music interventions; and specifically whether or not such interventions are effective in addressing memory deficiencies, pitch discrimination issues, and auditory tracking problems in aging and related populations. Perhaps a slower-paced presentation of the music might be required, along with increased melodic cues, to aid effective detection on the part of the listener – akin to ear-training exercises and similar interventions used by musicians. Although the factor of "reminiscence" in the aging population receiving music therapy is comforting, and can alter certain fear behaviors in the moment, the catalytic use of music, applied as a *continuous disturbance* (forcing function) to stimulate functional adaptation mechanisms, is also still in its developmental stages.

The same can be said for the use of melody to address auditory problems of populations exhibiting language delays and various other diagnoses. (For an overview of music therapy literature and interventions in speech delays, see Loewy 2004 and Berger 2002.) One assumes that simply the presentation of melody is sufficient to address change. It is often conjectured that music and language may be two sides of the same coin, and that perhaps right hemispheric function of certain music elements, such as melody, can influence left hemispheric language areas involving the rhythm of speech. A recent intervention called *Melodic intonation therapy* (Kraus and Galloway 1982; Roper 2003) is being applied to treat aphasia (defined in Chapter 7), speech apraxia, and accompanying language deficits. In speech apraxia, the individual knows intellectually what words he or she wants to say, but is unable to articulate those words, perhaps owing to a partial or complete paralysis of the muscles of speech (dysarthria). In a sense, "the spirit is willing but the flesh is weak." Both apraxia and dysarthria are *non-symbolic* disorders of speech, as opposed to aphasia, which *is* a problem involving symbolic processing; but it is not uncommon for apraxia and dysarthria to accompany aphasia.

Melodic intonation therapy (MIT) involves speaking in a melodic manner, and is said to be making positive contributions to language development. However, basic auditory problems are not being considered when evaluating and diagnosing deficits, including the possible inability of the patient to track and link sounds together accurately, as in aphasia. Unless music therapy is directed at the *aural* situation along with *oral* motor elements, language attainment could very well remain limited. The published literature on melodic intonation therapy indicated above is unclear about why positive results have *not* been more widely encountered, leading one to wonder whether the right questions are being asked.

Deficiencies in perception, synesthesia (cross-sensory processing), hearing impairments, and subtle auditory processing issues are often underdiagnosed. Relevant information required to make a proper diagnosis is usually not provided by basic audiology tests and treatments. For example, consider the case of Robert, the 14-year-old introduced in Chapter 5, diagnosed with Asperger's syndrome. According to standard audiology tests, Robert is found to have no auditory problems. Yet he cannot accurately reproduce a pitch tone. Although he seems to recognize his favorite melodies when he hears them (tracking), it is not entirely clear exactly what he is actually hearing and perceiving, nor what his identification strategy is for such recognition. It could be that he is not tracking the melodic line at all, but perhaps "feeling" the tune, in the same way as Evelyn Glennie. Alternatively, he might be identifying the tune from the lyrics, or the rhythm patterns, or any other element, including orchestration, dynamics, and even the performer of a song on a CD. This is where a music therapist might consider eliminating some of the elements (especially the lyrics) when presenting a melody, as a way of determining how the tracking and recognition abilities are manifested.

The fact remains that Robert is basically "tone deaf," unable to actually reconstruct and render the melodic pitches and intervallic contour of a familiar song with any degree of accuracy. For instance, Robert cannot accurately determine whether the melody is moving upward or downward. Given that he is also deficient in clear speech articulation, the possibility could be that he does not fully *hear* the linked frequencies of a word, and therefore he reproduces them according to the same garble in which he hears them. Thus, in addition to slowing Robert's speech rhythm (described in Chapter 7), his treatment plan includes music intervention exercises that involve slow-paced tunes, preferably with brief phrases of melodic motifs in scale-wise motion with limited intervallic leaps. He appears able to intone these more comfortably and accurately, although inconsistently. Robert is also spoken to, and is requested by the therapist to speak, in exaggerated inflection (slower, more tonally inflected, similar to the aims of MIT). This appears to be of some value in aiding the breath control and tempo of his speech. As of this writing, it can be reported that progress in the accuracy of pitch discrimination and imitation is becoming noticeable.

In order to eliminate complications that result from problems with oral motor or larynx abilities (dysarthria) in the rendering of accurate pitches, Robert is often asked to find the pitches presented by playing these on a xylophone or keyboard rather than through vocalization. Included in these exercises is an effort to assess Robert's ability to discriminate low from high registers. Thus far, he displays a better ability to match registers than to match pitch; he can better detect high or low, than *what*.

However, something must be changing, because Robert's improvisations on the keyboard, when he uses just the black keys (his choice, which happens to be equivalent to the five-tone scale), is yielding some interesting insight about his auditory tracking abilities. His playing is less random, as if he may actually be hearing consecutive pitch sequences in his head and attempting to develop a melodic contour rather than playing random, unassociated sounds. He plays five notes consecutively, up and down, with few repetitions or interval skips. This could indicate some inhibition in sound exploration, similar to his underemployment of large instruments in the session. What Robert *does* sense quite accurately is rhythmic pulse, pattern, and pace; he can beat a drum in pulse with his favorite melody, and sustain a given or self-created rhythmic pattern over the pulse. This could indicate that he tracks rhythm well, perhaps by feeling it in his body, but cannot process both rhythm *and* melody concurrently.

## Cross-sensory processing of pitch and melody: clinical considerations

Of the five cases presented in Chapter 5, the one of particular interest regarding auditory processing is that of 5-year-old Rhea, diagnosed as autistic. Recall that she loves music, especially the drum. Although her pitch discrimination appears to demonstrate "perfect pitch" tendencies, Rhea becomes extremely agitated when songs are played (or accompanied) on any type of instrument other than the drum. Having eliminated fear responses that might result from unfamiliarity with the setting, the therapist, or the music, and having eliminated the element of music *dynamics* (louds and softs) as possible contributors to her agitated behavior, the therapist could surmise that among several other problems that might explain such behavior could be:

- the possibility that her "absolute pitch" is disturbed by out-of-tune instruments
- that some timbres are difficult for her to process and/or modulate (i.e., comfortably accept changing timbres)
- that some as yet unknown sensory processing aspects are involved here
- all of the above.

The element of timbre (considered further in Chapter 9), combined with perfect pitch, would also impede language attainment, in which Rhea is delayed. Despite the possibility that some aspects of timbre and pitch processing seem viable candidates for contributing to Rhea's responses, the specific cause(s) of her agitated arousals is still unclear.

Of peculiar interest, however, is Rhea's continual need to *cover her ears* and simultaneously *narrow her eyes* when music is present. More and more,

according to her parents, the child resorts to this behavior of seemingly diffusing simultaneous visual and auditory inputs by covering her ears and
squinting her eyes. While music interventions have been addressing her fear
responses of anxiety, agitation, and avoidance, treatment is now also focused
on investigating whether Rhea might be diffusing these sensory inputs for
reasons beyond tolerance. Could she be displaying symptoms of synesthesia?
Is it possible that the child *sees* sounds in a multisensory processing manner,
which could be confusing, distracting, disturbing, and somehow disabling
her, thus exacerbating her fear responses? Does she *see* colors or shapes
simultaneous to *hearing* certain pitches and melodies? Rhea absolutely
cannot tolerate the tune "Twinkle, twinkle little star," in any form, and all her
therapists have been asked to refrain from using this melody. Rhea screams
and agitates at the sound of the melody, whether it is sung, played on various
instruments, delivered via a recording, on TV, or other manner.

There could, of course, be a number of reasons for this situation, not the
least of which would be that she simply does not like the tune. But because of
her current habit of holding her ears while squinting, it is also conceivable
that Rhea has parallel or cross-sensory processing, and may be processing
acoustic information in an entirely different manner, with other sensory
organs. Although it is difficult to diagnose the problem fully (since she
cannot self-report or give a history), the idea of multisensory interpretation
of stimulus (e.g., pitch or melody) cannot be discarded, especially considering Rhea's diagnosis of autism which often exhibits issues of sensory integration. An interesting case related to this is a recent study conducted at the
University of Zurich (Beeli, Esslen, and Jaencke 2005) that investigated a
professional musician who experiences particular tastes, as well as colors,
when hearing different musical tone intervals. The musician apparently
makes use of those synesthetic sensations when undertaking the identification of tone intervals. Tests of her ability to identify pitch intervals according
to how they taste to her proved her identifications to be quite accurate,
according to the researchers.

In Rhea's case, music therapy efforts are under way to determine the
problem, and to design interventions that can further assess and address
them. Among these is the presentation of the melodic sequence (the
"Twinkle" tune) in several different keys, meters, and prosodic progressions.
For instance, in one session the tune, devoid of lyrics, was disguised by being
played on the piano (as usual) in three-quarter (waltz) time instead of the
original 4/4 (four beats to a measure), and in the key of F-sharp major, with

exaggerated, varied elongations of notes, so that it became rather a variation of the original melody. Rhea relaxed and found the "tune" to be quite acceptable in this altered format. Whether or not she recognized the song is unknown.

For the remaining cases previously introduced along with Robert and Rhea, melody has been the key to reducing fear anxieties. The presentation of improvised melodies, in addition to some familiar tunes, delivered with minimal accompaniment styles and limited use of dense chordal structures, tends to facilitate *auditory linear tracking*. But here again, melody does not operate alone and it is important to keep in mind that many of the points made regarding the scanning and tracking of melody apply equally well to the element of *rhythm* already discussed, and for that matter to *all* of the elements of music. Indeed, beside combining with and contributing to rhythmic structures, melody's effectiveness in therapy and out of therapy depends greatly on the instrument(s) or voice(s) that are used in its presentation – which brings us to the third basic element of music, *timbre*. The quality of a sound, its texture, must be considered when discussing the effect of music on physiological function. It is this specific element that differentiates danger from safety in acoustic information, and, above all, it is this *quality* of music that further supports the emotional syntax of melody. Moreover, timbre, along with a fourth element of music, *harmony*, derive from physically related concepts, so they can be examined together, along with an additional and important fifth element – *dynamics*.

Chapter 9

# Timbre, Harmony, and Dynamics: Adding Richness and Depth to Rhythm and Melody

I know that the twelve notes in each octave and the varieties of rhythm offer me opportunities that all of human genius will never exhaust.

Igor Stravinsky, *Poetics of Music*

## Introduction

Why are we considering timbre and harmony under the same umbrella? Good question! The simple answer is that both timbre (sound *quality*, which distinguishes a pure "tone" from a compound "note") and harmony (*polyphony*; literally "many sounds"), generated by a vertical arrangement and progression of notes that are expressed simultaneously (creating "chords"), derive from the same physical principles; namely, those that govern what happens when two or more pitches are sounded together. On the one hand, *timbre* is associated with a *single* note, within which is embedded an inherent *overtone and undertone frequency spectrum* (many tones) that envelops a single fundamental frequency ("pure" dominant tone; see Chapters 3 and 4). The fundamental frequency, then, establishes the so-called *tonality* of the sound (or, as it relates to concepts in harmony, the equivalent *root* of a chord). The associated frequency spectrum establishes the timbre of the sound (or, equivalently, *sonority*, when speaking about chords and chord progressions).

It is the unique blend of specific frequencies that allows one to distinguish a violin from a flute, a flute from a trombone, a trombone from a trumpet (or any other instrument, for that matter); your mother's voice from your grandmother's, your teacher's voice from your brother's or sister's (or any other voice); somebody scratching their nails on a chalk-board from someone rubbing the palm of their hand on that same chalk-board; various bird calls – or, in general, any one sound from another, even though, in each case, the fundamental sound frequency ("pitch") and basic sound amplitude ("loudness") might be identical. What one "hears" is different.

*Harmony*, on the other hand, is associated with *several* notes, each having a different fundamental frequency, superimposed on one another, vertically, to create a *chord* (as opposed to linked together horizontally to create a *melody*). When sequences of musical pitches are stacked vertically over one another and sounded together, they support and synergize with the emotional content of melody, adding color, richness, and depth to the sound. This richness, fullness, and depth is referred to as sonority, which is to the element of harmony what timbre is to the element of pitch. Both result in a more impressive sound, for the same physical reason – the superposition of more than one frequency. Harmony gives music three dimensions: vertical architecture (i.e., pitches stacked one on top of another); horizontal flow (chord progressions); and depth (implied front and back, experienced as sonority). It gives *body* to flatness, *thickness* to thinness, *substance* to shallow-ness. Harmony can influence, and even disguise, an instrument's timbre to the point of often creating an illusion of a totally different, unrelated sound quality. For instance, the harmonic combination of a flute and a clarinet playing together can provide a totally new timbre, a sound that does not have the quality of either a flute *or* a clarinet, but a new, integrated combination of both.

As mentioned, despite their being separated into two distinct elements of music, both timbre and harmony, as concepts, actually derive from the same physical principles – what happens when different sound frequencies are superimposed upon one another. In the case of timbre, the sound frequencies are enveloped within the frequency spectrum surrounding a single fundamental tone. In the case of harmony, the sound frequencies are enveloped within chords comprised of three or more pitches sounded simultaneously (or in a variety of flowing accompaniment styles), each pitch contributing its own timbre, as well. Thus, the principles underlying the concepts of timbre and sonority are essentially the same, and that's why timbre and harmony live under the same roof.

## Timbre: the texture of a note

The quality or texture of sound that one experiences is a natural consequence of the following facts:

1.  imperfect sound generators do not vibrate uniformly throughout

2.  imperfections in the media through which sound waves travel, and the physics of wave dispersion (discussed below), cause these waves to change as they are transmitted through space

3.  a less-than-perfect auditory apparatus does not necessarily transduce and translate (i.e., perceive) the signal received as a faithful, exact replica of that generated.

These features are examined in the following sections.

### Sound production: timbre generated

As discussed in Chapters 3 and 4, there is a dominant *fundamental frequency* (labeled $f_0$ and called the "fundamental tone" or *center frequency*) associated with the natural frequency of vibration of a sound generator. However, because nothing in life or nature is perfect, including how things vibrate, the composite nature of materials that generate sounds makes it virtually impossible to secure from them a perfectly pure tone. Rather, most sound-producing bodies vibrate in segments at the same time that they vibrate as a whole, such that different portions of a sound source vibrate at different frequencies centered around $f_0$. Thus, superimposed on the "tone" are:

- integral multiples (2, 3, 4, 5…), called *harmonics*, of the center frequency

- fractional multiples ($\frac{1}{2}, \frac{1}{3}, \frac{1}{4}, \frac{1}{5}…$), called *sub-harmonics* of the natural frequency.

Collectively, these over- and undertones produce a "note" which includes the fundamental tone, superimposed upon which are the *partial* tones (harmonics and sub-harmonics) that correspond to the separately vibrating segments of the imperfect sound generator. This family of frequencies, called the *frequency spectrum* of the note, meld together to give the generated sound a distinct, material-specific quality or texture, uniquely associated with the sound source (instrument, voice, bird, chalk-board, nails, etc.). The span from lowest frequency in the spectrum to highest is called the *bandwidth* of the spectrum. The narrower the bandwidth (the "tighter" the over- and undertones are clustered around the fundamental), the more "perfect" the material. Moreover, there is usually a type of symmetry around $f_0$, such that the undertone series is essentially a mirror image of the overtone series; when this is the case, the frequency spectrum is said to be *normally* distributed. This means that the discussion of timbre can be limited to talking about overtones, and the reader can thus easily extrapolate from that discussion to what goes on in the undertone series.

The first overtone (by convention, generally called the *second harmonic*, because the fundamental tone is defined to be the first harmonic, $f_0$) is called the *octave*. The octave has a frequency equal to twice the fundamental; i.e., $2f_0$. The second overtone (third harmonic) has a frequency equal to three times the fundamental; i.e., $3f_0$; and so on. But notice the following: the *ratio* of the first overtone frequency (second harmonic) to that of the fundamental tone (first harmonic) is $2:1 = 2$; the frequency ratio between the second overtone and the first is $3:2 = 1.5$; the third overtone to the second is $4:3 = 1.33$; the fourth overtone to the third is $5:4 = 1.25$. As one moves progressively up the overtone series, the *interval* between any given harmonic and the next one up the line keeps getting smaller. That is to say, there is a progressive decrease in frequency ratio between the upper overtone and the lower one as one moves up the harmonic ladder. There is a significant consequence to this decreasing interval structure.

## The phenomenon of "beats"

In order to understand the consequences of a decreasing frequency ratio, consider first the simple physical situation wherein one strikes a tuning fork. This consists of two steel tines or prongs, juxtaposed on a common handle, each vibrating back and forth at the same fundamental frequency $f_0$, when the simple instrument is struck against another surface. As it vibrates, each tine sends out alternating waves that have peaks and valleys associated with the tines moving cyclically away from (generating peaks) and towards (generating valleys) each other. This is exactly analogous to what one sees if a cork is dropped into a pool of still water (or, in the case corresponding to the tuning fork, two corks dropped into the water at the same time, very close to one other). One can see the wave propagating away from the cork as it bobs up (peaks) and down (valleys); and because there are two such corks, generating *sets* of waves, the waves will interact with one another as they travel through space.

Likewise, as the sound waves propagate outward, away from the tuning fork tines, there will be specific locations where some of the wave peaks generated by one tine will add to the peaks generated by the other. This type of wave reinforcement is called *constructive wave interference*, and it acts to amplify the sound generated separately by each tine, since in the constructive case the waves simply add together. Conversely, there will be other spatial locations where some of the wave peaks generated by one tine will collide with and add to the valleys generated by the other, so that the waves generated separately by each tine will actually subtract from one another at these locations, forming what are called "dead zones." This type of wave sub-version is called *destructive wave interference* because at those points in space the waves will cancel each other out, leading to "zones of silence." It is rather easy to demonstrate these phenomena: simply strike a tuning fork and, as it vibrates, hold it by its handle close to one ear and rotate it around its vertical axis. One can hear a distinctive, undulating "wah-wah" sound as alternating constructive/destructive interference patterns strike the eardrum.

Now, in the case of the tuning fork (or our two corks), constructive and destructive wave interference patterns resulted from two tines that were vibrating at the *same* fundamental frequency, $f_0$ (i.e., both corks were bobbing up and down at the same rate); and the only consequence was the generation of simple (that's the operative word here), on-off-type, discrete, alternating zones of silence with zones of reinforcement – nothing particularly offensive to the perception of the sound involved. The observer merely notices the sound getting louder and softer as the ear intercepts these various zones.

On the other hand, the interference patterns that are generated when two *different* frequencies are sounded together leads to a much more compli-cated phenomenon known as *beats*, which can be offensive to the ear. "Beats" refers to specific, continuous (as opposed to discrete), periodic variations in amplitude that result from the *complex* interference patterns created by the superposition of two oscillating waves of slightly different frequencies. In fact, the number of beats (cyclic "moans") delivered with rising and falling inflections ("wobbles") heard per second is exactly equal to the arithmetic *difference* between the fundamental frequencies of the two interfering pitches. Piano tuners actually rely on the phenomenon of beats to determine when the two or three parallel strings that comprise each note in the middle and upper registers of the piano keyboard are in tune with one another. That is to say, they listen for beats when the strings are struck, and adjust the tuning pegs until the beats are extinguished and a synchronized, uniform sound is produced, devoid of disturbing beats ("wah-wahs"). That is when the note is considered to be "in tune." A similar technique is used for the single strings, because in order to be "in tune" they must resonate without beats relative to the octave and fifth above them (i.e., one must get a so-called "open sound").

## The phenomenon of sound "concordance"

The phenomenon of beats leads to the corresponding concept of sound concordance, better known as *dissonance* and *consonance*. The former refers to frequency intervals that are displeasing to the ear (peaking at around 23 or 24 beats per second). "Displeasing to the ear" might not be the best way to describe dissonance, because "displeasing" is a subjective concept. Perhaps a better way to think of dissonance is in terms of intervals that are *unstable*, in the sense of bearing an inherent tension that seeks resolution. Dissonant intervals create a certain sense of movement and rhythmic energy – they have a drive to go somewhere, to resolve; they are in search of a destination. Composers often exploit this resolution-seeking attribute, toying with a listener's sense of expectation, creating a sense of drama and suspense, often leading to unexpected results. Without the suspense of dissonance in search of resolution, music might drift aimlessly and endlessly in a stagnant sea of stability, which is consonance.

Consonance is the destination of suspended dissonance, the "ah, at last" moment of resolution. It connotes sound frequencies that are separated far enough apart from one another such that, if they are sounded together, disagreeable beats are *not* produced, and the combination of the two sounds generates a pleasing, stable musical interval (although, speaking scientifically, it is still not known what the physiological basis for "pleasing" is). It may be that what is sensed as "pleasing" corresponds to the physiological sensation one experiences when the human system *entrains* vibrations that resonate synchronously and comfortably with the natural frequencies of body tissues and organs, a kind of constructive interference pattern, if you will, between the music and the body. If that is the case, then what is "displeasing" might correspond to an incongruity between a given body and the resonating frequencies of the incident sounds, a kind of destructive interference pattern that causes a physiological "wobble."

Alternatively, certain types of sound quality, note textures, and/or harmonies might recruit specific neural networks and processing mechanisms that "code" for pleasant/unpleasant emotional states. That is to say, *harmonic entrainment* may involve a network-specific protocol wherein consonant intervals are processed more favorably (and thus perceived to be more "pleasant") than are dissonant intervals (with their associated beats, strident tone clusters, and harmonic "disorder"). The bottom line, though, is that, as it relates to consonance and dissonance, *we know it when we hear it, but we do not know why.*

Therefore, a therapist must understand that, depending on specific anatomical and physiological variables, certain clients might be experiencing the discomfort of beats, and perceiving dissonant tone clusters that, to any other individual, might be totally consonant and harmless. Once again, *nothing can be taken for granted!*

Getting back, then, to the discussion of timbre, it was mentioned earlier in this chapter that as one ascends the overtone ladder, the difference between any given harmonic and the next one up decreases. Eventually, a point is reached at which two harmonics get close enough to one another such that beats start to become a problem. Indeed, this occurs by the time the seventh harmonic (sixth overtone) is reached, where the frequency ratio is 7:6. It is certainly the situation that prevails for the ninth harmonic (9:8 frequency ratio of the major second, or whole step in the musical scale), and, for physical reasons, all higher *odd-numbered* harmonics. That is why, on the piano, the hammer is placed to strike the string at a point approximately one-eighth of its length from the end, to ensure that the seventh, ninth, and higher odd-numbered harmonics will be weak enough not to be noticed and hence disagreeable. That is the good news: higher harmonics have relatively high frequencies, and high frequencies dissipate quickly, over very short distances (see Chapter 8). Higher harmonics are also generally weak in amplitude and die out (attenuate) rapidly. Thus, timbre is not usually greatly affected by these higher harmonics in "typically functioning" people, under "commonly encountered" circumstances.

The therapist must realize, however, that he or she is not always working with typically functioning individuals, under commonly encountered circumstances. So, again, *nothing can be taken for granted!*

The fundamental and all harmonics up to the sixth, when sounding together, produce a harmonious note. Studies of musical tones (Helmholtz 1954; Jeans 1968) reveal that *overtones* and/or pitches sounded simultaneously will be "pleasing" if the frequencies involved have the simple ratios:

- 2:1 – the octave, which adds clearness and brilliance to the center frequency
- 3:2 – the perfect fifth, which thickens the tone

- 4:3 – the perfect fourth, two octaves above the fundamental, which adds even more brilliance, perhaps even some "shrillness" to the sound

- 5:4 – the major third, which, too, adds brilliance and richness to the tone

- 6:5 – the minor third, which adds a "delicate shrillness of nasal quality" to the sound.

(Jeans 1968, p.87)

To these may be added the frequency ratios 5:3, the major sixth; and 8:5, the minor sixth, which rounds out the most compatible combinations. These are in *decreasing* order of compatibility; i.e., the intervals are less and less pleasing as the ratio of frequencies gradually includes larger and larger numbers. That is to say, the *smaller* the individual numbers are in the frequency ratio, the better the consonance, and vice versa. Thus, the diminished fifth (at 64:45) and/or augmented fourth (at 45:32) produce beats that are so *displeasing* that these intervals are often used in the sirens of emergency vehicles to warn of alarming situations. Next, in decreasing order of large combinations of numbers, come the *semitone* (at 16:15), the minor seventh (at 16:9), the major seventh (at 15:8), the minor tone (at 10:9), the major tone (at 9:8), the minor seventh (at 9:5), and the harmonic minor seventh (at 7:4). Consonance between two sounds is more marked the greater they share a common number of close harmonics or coincident overtones (Buser and Imbert 1992).

## Sound propagation: timbre transmitted

The transmission of sound from its source to a receiver is rather a complicated process, for several reasons. First, there are the imperfections of the transmission medium itself. These include (but are not limited to):

- a variation of material properties according to where one is located in space, known technically as *spatial non-* or *inhomogeneity*

- a variation of material properties *at a given point in space*, depending on which *direction* those properties are measured (top to bottom, side to side, etc.), known technically as *concurrent anisotropy*

- material behavior that is *not directly proportional* to the intensity of the propagating wave that is disturbing it, known technically as *non-linear* behavior

- non-uniform mass density and other material properties

- varying mechanical "stiffness"

- non-constant (with respect to time, as opposed to space) thermodynamic and physical properties.

All of these considerations are collected into a single parameter called the *acoustic impedance* of the transmission medium. The acoustic impedance of the medium through which sound waves travel can fail to allow propogation of the waves in a manner that enables them to remain true to their source. Furthermore, superimposed on the traveling waves are additional physical considerations that significantly alter them as they propagate through space. Among these, generically referred to as *wave attenuation*, are the following.

- *Wave dispersion* refers to a progressive skewing of the acoustic frequency spectrum towards the lower frequencies as the sound moves further and further away from its source, because the higher-frequency components die out along the way, as described in more detail later.

- *Sound absorption* refers to a progressive weakening of the sound intensity as its energy is gradually converted into heat along its path.

- *Wave reflections* result from waves bouncing off generally smooth objects in their path, and interacting with surrounding waves, thus contributing to constructive and destructive interference patterns, as described in the earlier section on "beats."

- *Diffraction* refers to an uneven spreading of the waves as they negotiate their way *around* (as opposed to bouncing off) obstacles in their path.

- *Refraction* refers to a turning or bending of waves as they pass through non-uniform, non-homogeneous, anisotropic media.

- *Wave scattering* refers to a random bouncing-around of sound waves that come into contact with *rough* surfaces in their path.

To discuss each of these in detail is far beyond the scope of this book, but a few of them deserve further attention because of their specific effect on sound *timbre*. In particular, try this simple experiment. Place your hands in palm-to-palm contact with one another, and begin rubbing them back and forth *slowly* ("low frequency"). You might feel some warmth developing, but not much. Now, gradually begin increasing the frequency of the back-and-forth movement and notice how much more heat is generated. Indeed, the faster you go, the hotter it gets. In fact, most people do this instinctively when trying to warm up after having been out in the cold; they rub their hands together very rapidly.

What you have just demonstrated is why higher-frequency forms of energy (in particular, sound) do not travel as far as do lower-frequency forms of energy. The higher-frequency energy "burns up" faster than does the lower-frequency energy. That is to say, the former, in the case of sound, becomes quickly converted from acoustic energy into heat energy, and so one hears only the low-frequency bass notes propagating through a wall, not the higher-frequency treble notes, which burn up before they can penetrate the wall.

Now, think back to the frequency *spectrum* (timbre) generated by an imperfect sound source. Based on the above reasoning, it follows that the higher-frequency overtone components progressively burn up as the sound propagates through space. Thus, the further one gets from the sound source, the more of these high-frequency harmonics disappear from the spectrum, skewing it more and more towards the fundamental and its sub-harmonics, destroying its symmetry around $f_0$. *This phenomenon is known as wave dispersion.*

Owing to wave dispersion, sound moving away from its source progressively loses more and more overtones, dramatically changing its timbre. So, do people who are way in the back of an auditorium hear a sound quality different from people in the very front of an auditorium? Absolutely! Moreover, because of this same process whereby *acoustic* energy is converted into *heat* energy, *all* of the components in the frequency spectrum also weaken (attenuate) as they move through space, in a process called *sound absorption*, or *damping.*

Damping causes the amplitude of the sound waves to diminish as they propagate away from the sound source; so, not only do persons in the back of an auditorium hear a sound of different *timbre*, they also hear a fainter sound than do those seated nearer to the sound source. The increasing faintness with distance causes all of the sound to eventually die out completely.

Standard physics textbooks and/or the literature on wave motion in general, and sound transmission in particular, will give you further information on wave reflection (and its effects on beats), diffraction (and its effects on attenuation), refraction (and its effects on wave *trajectory*), and scattering (and its effects on all of the above) – and also the Doppler effect (Giancoli 1989), which addresses alterations in the pitch of a sound when there is relative movement between the sound source and the sound receiver. Suffice it to say here that the acoustic energy arriving at the ear of the listener contains information that is quite different from that contained in the sound waves that were generated at the source. The situation becomes even further complicated when one is required to *interpret* what one hears.

## Timbre and the voice

The physics of timbre has implications on speech development in delayed and brain-incident populations. Voice production includes all of the above considerations regarding overtones, undertones, the material properties and anatomical architecture of the vocal cords, and so on. The vocal timbre of the person transmitting a sound, whether sung or spoken, includes aspects of high- and low-frequency vibrations and dispersion that often add to the problem of expressive and receptive language attainment. High-frequency alphabet letters, such as "f," "t," "d," "k," "b," "p," and others that do not include intoning (as do vowels, and letters such as "r" or "g") can be extremely difficult to detect in a compromised auditory system. In addition, the vocal timbre of a male bass or tenor voice resonates differently from that of the female soprano or coloratura voice. It can be the case that someone speaking the word "far" will be heard by the receiver as saying "ar," where the first high-frequency "f" is missed (a classic drop-out effect). If the same word is spoken by a male, timbre distortion could make the sound appear as "or," succumbing to the long, low tone, or "oh" rather than being processed as "ah," the sound energy of which will tend to dissipate sooner. And, if the higher-frequency letter is in the middle or at the end of the word (e.g., "after" or "laugh") the high-frequency "f" sound may not be detected at all.

Keeping the above in mind, the introduction of music presented (live) on instruments of parallel timbres can play a major role in helping to address auditory and language difficulties. An electric keyboard is useful in presenting an array of timbres not readily available otherwise, such as a tuba, various brass (horns, trumpets) and reed (saxophones, clarinets) instruments, organs, and even sounds unrelated to any instrumental timbres (wind, water, telephone rings, etc.). Three of the case studies presented in Chapter 5 – Robert, Rhea, and Bucky – tend to display specific auditory and timbre-related expressive and receptive language difficulties. Each individual requests or prefers specific instrumental timbres during music therapy sessions.

Robert, as we indicated, speaks very quickly and inarticulately, suggesting that he perhaps *hears* language the same way that he *speaks* it. He prefers to play either very high-frequency instruments such as maracas (which produce what is called "white sound") or the tuba or French horn on the electric keyboard. When he hears these, explores those sounds on his own, or requests a song to be played using the sound of either of those timbres, he relaxes, smiles, and automatically tends to slow his spoken responses. On the other hand, he often agitates at the sound of the metal-keyed xylophone (metallophone), preferring instead the wood xylophone, if any, and is absolutely intolerant of either blowing into, or listening to, the soprano recorder. He appears to accept the alto recorder timbre more comfortably. Of interest is the fact that his mother's voice tends to be of a rather shrill, high-pitched timbre, and Robert seems to struggle to process her speaking. His "nanny," on the other hand, speaking the exact same sentence and emotion, but in an alto, smooth-timbre voice quality, seems to be better understood by Robert, judging from his more immediate responses to her. His father, as well as his male teacher, both exhibit similarly resonant, baritone-like vocal timbre qualities akin to French horn-like timbres. Over the several years of exposure to music therapy treatment, Robert has been able to adjust to a wider variety of timbres of higher frequency, and the tenor metal xylophone is serving to assist with pitch and register recognition. One wonders how Robert's auditory system processes his own vocal timbre. Does he hear himself speak in loud "brassy" timbres? Does he hear the inarticulation of his words compared to the words of others? Is he "self-dispersive" or "self-attenuating"? These questions are as yet unanswerable.

Bucky, on the other hand, detests any tonal instrument, and abhors the sound of acoustic piano. A piano has 88 keys, most of which contain at least two or three parallel strings. Each string provides its individual timbre and overtone series as earlier discussed, creating beats if even *slightly* out of tune with its neighbor. Moreover, even if the two or three strings that define any given one of the 88 notes are in tune relative to *each other*, that set of strings creates beats of dissonance with the set closest to it, a minor half-step away. In addition, there is an overwhelming resonance of timbre/overtones/volume that reverberates in echo around the music room, superimposing further chaotic auditory information on a possibly already stressed auditory system.

Could it be that the 24,000 "strings" of Bucky's basilar membrane might, anatomically, be "out of tune"? Unfortunately, unlike the strings of a piano or other stringed instrument, those of one's basilar membrane cannot be "tuned." An individual is stuck for life with the anatomical configuration of his or her basilar membrane – the tension, thickness, length, and mechanical properties of that anatomical architecture. Techniques of clinical intervention must be sensitive to this possibility, and structured accordingly.

Recall that Bucky is a very slow, very low-muscle-tone boy who is legally blind. Therefore, his auditory system is perhaps over-compensating for his lack of vision in ways that are not clearly defined. It is conceivable that Bucky may hear uniformly the entire frequency spectrum that defines the timbre of the sound, and all of the beats created by sound interactions, such that he cannot discriminate that spectrum from the actual "pure" tone (the fundamental) around which the timbre resonates.

Bucky does not like to sing, nor does he like to extend his voice in elongated sounds of song. His language is similar. He uses abrupt or short sentences, elongating very few words. Bucky does not whine, for instance, when issuing a complaint, he simply increases volume and agitates in abrupt shouts. Is it possible that Bucky hears his vocal overtones as he intones sounds, and finds these to be disturbing? When the therapist sings along while playing an instrument, Bucky asks that the singing cease. Does he hear too many unpleasant beats as suggested earlier? The music most acceptable and comfortable for Bucky during therapy sessions is the rhythmic renditions of various percussion instrumental sequences pre-programmed on the electric keyboard. He does not enjoy a melody being played over the rhythms. His choice of instruments for his own playing consist of two small clave-like rhythm sticks with barely audible sound.

Bucky's language development has been very slow; but ever since his encounters with music therapy, and the presentation of a variety of timbres, dynamics, and rhythms, he has come to enjoy imitating the percussion timbres, and odd sounds of clicks, clacks, buzzes, hisses, pops, and the like – predominantly sounds that have no associated pitch, per se. When (and if) Bucky undertakes to "sing," it sounds more like jazz "skatting" – clicks, hisses, pops, and limited elongations, such as "boo-boing," "beeeee-grrrr," and so on. For Bucky, the employment of the kazoo, which vibrates and requires the use of the voice to hum into the instrument, helped make his vocalizing more tolerable for him. The kazoo, of course, adds an entirely new timbre to his own humming voice, and also projects his voice outward. Without the kazoo, Bucky will rarely use his voice in a song-like manner. Other than particular timbres on the keyboard, the recorder – a single line instrument with somewhat purer tones (at least, less noticeable overtones) – is used often in treatment to help Bucky with auditory tracking of elongated sounds which he is asked to imitate from time to time.

Rhea will tolerate the timbre of the piano only when *she* plays it, and she plays only triads (chords) consisting of the *interval of thirds*. Recall, Rhea is the child suspected of displaying symptoms of synesthesia, implicating multisensory overlapping sensory processing. She finds any chord other than those using thirds to be totally unacceptable. When playing on the piano, Rhea does not simply bang and pound at it, but meticulously seeks to find the intervals of thirds, sometimes just the two notes and sometimes three (e.g., A–C–E, or C–E–G, etc.). In searching for the cause of her agitation with the tune "Twinkle, twinkle, little star" – which she accepted in the key of F-sharp major, in 3/4 time (see Chapter 8) – it has since been presented in a melodic-line-only format, with no accompaniment other than a block triad (F#–A#–C#) held while the melody unfolded over it. This was acceptable to her. However, she preferred hearing it played on the electric keyboard, in the timbre of a harpsichord, which offers less resonance than does the acoustic piano.

Rhea's language development is suspected of exhibiting timbre-processing implications. When her mother speaks in her very high-pitched, whiney, elongated manner, Rhea holds her ears and squints her eyes. When the therapist, whose vocal timbre is lower, in the middle vocal range, repeats the same information, Rhea listens without holding her ears or squinting. When Rhea was observed in her school setting, similar occurrences were noted with different teachers (ear-blocking, eye-squinting, etc.). Again, one must wonder what, exactly, Rhea hears when she herself speaks or emits vocal sounds. She does sing to herself, but very quietly. The possibility that *timbre* and *overtone processing* are playing a role in Rhea's tolerance of sound, and her inability to process language, cannot be overlooked. It has been noted, however, that with the slow and careful presentation of varying timbres (on the keyboard as well as acoustic instruments such as recorder, guitar, harmonica, kazoo, violin, etc.), Rhea is becoming more curious to stop and listen, and – upon repeated presentation of these interventions – more tolerant of the varying timbre sounds. Her motivation to evoke language

204	THE MUSIC EFFECT

sounds has improved as well, and she provides missing lyrics to songs, and omitted words to sentences spoken by the music therapist.

## Sound perceived: timbre interpreted

Embedded in our discussion of Robert, Rhea, and Bucky is a common denominator that identifies all human beings: that of the *imperfect listener*. Regardless of whether or not the listener is typical, anatomically, he or she experiences not only the same *physical* constraints addressed thus far – which is to say, the anisotropy, non-homogeneity, non-linearity, non-uniformity, etc., of tissues and organs, that affect the production and propagation of the sound itself – but much more. The listener is also constrained *physiologically*, by factors related to such things as:

1.  *Gestalt* laws of perception (Chapter 4)
2.  cerebral information-processing rates and pathways (*ibid.*)
3.  homeostatic (perhaps gone-awry) operating set-points (Chapters 4 and 5)
4.  the fear spiral (*ibid.*)
5.  typical (or atypical) responses of chemical messenger systems (Chapter 6)
6.  mechanisms of entrainment (*ibid.*)
7.  auditory system processing (Chapter 8)

and many other factors, some of which have been detailed in this and earlier chapters.

For example, recall from our discussion in Chapter 8 of the architecture of hearing (and Figure 8.1) that various portions of the basilar membrane respond to different sound frequencies. It follows that, from a strictly *structural* point of view, the timbre perceived by any given listener will *first* be a function of the anatomical configuration of that individual's basilar membrane (as we suggested earlier in our discussion of Bucky). In turn, that anatomy will determine the range of frequencies included within the spectrum of sound energy received to which that individual's basilar membrane will be responsive; i.e., the timbre which that listener will be at least *capable* of uniquely experiencing. Thus, related to these considerations, the situations one may encounter include the following:

- It might very well be the case that, in certain diagnosed populations such as the three cases mentioned above, the anatomy of the basilar membrane (and/or the cilia in contact with it, and/or the nerve fibers attached to these cilia, etc.) may lead to certain drop-outs of specific frequency components in the spectrum. These drop-outs will significantly modulate what the listener is *capable* of hearing versus what the outer ear *actually* receives.

- In others, the membrane might be particularly sensitive to the higher harmonics that do not typically excite this tissue, so that these individuals might perceive as being "harsh" timbres that others would consider totally acceptable.

- Some listeners might hear dissonant harmonies that others would consider consonant. That is, their basilar membrane, as suggested earlier, might be "out of tune".

These are just three examples. Thus, a careful evaluation of the anatomy of the hearing architecture, from its input site at the outer ear, all the way through to its cerebral site of perception, is crucial to the proper diagnosis and treatment of any given affliction that might include auditory complications. Such evaluation would include, for example, clinically assessing to what "pure" tones an individual is most responsive, and how. If it turns out that the basilar membrane and its associated anatomical architecture is functioning as it should, the next issue to be addressed would be an evaluation of the input/output characteristics (as quantified by the *transfer function*) of the hearing apparatus; i.e., its *physiological response* as opposed to its anatomical configuration. Here, in addition to transfer functions, one must also consider several of the other functions already discussed in earlier chapters, such as auditory scanning and tracking, operating (reference) set-points, feedback feedforward control loops, neural networks, synesthesia, and so on.

There are many more aspects to such auditory function than can be covered in detail in a monograph such as this, but an important one deserves special mention, especially as it relates to the timbre of sound presented at high, listener-specific threshold intensities. This consideration relates to the sound *distortion* that results from the non-linear input/output characteristics of the auditory system (Buser and Imbert 1992). That is to say, if an experimental subject is exposed to an isolated, single *pure* tone – a fundamental frequency $f_0$ devoid of any harmonic content – then, beyond a certain subject-dependent threshold *intensity* or "loudness," the subject hears harmonics anyway! In other words, a timbre is *subjectively* experienced where there was none in the auditory signal presented. This "ear-created" phenomenon is thus referred to as *aural harmonics*, whereby a pure *incident* sound wave has been converted into a compound multi-frequency *perceived* sound wave. Could it be, then, that Rhea – who tends to shut her hearing down with her hands over her ears – is "hearing" *phantom harmonics*?

Much is still to be learned about aural harmonics. Suffice it to say here that it is attributed to a failure of the ear to respond in a one-to-one, faithful-reproduction sense (i.e., directly proportional, *linear* fashion) to the signal received, if that signal is too loud – "loud" being a subjective term that depends on the specific listener. This non-linear, dynamics-dependent behavior distorts the purity of the imposed signal (a pure oscillating sine wave), thus introducing frequency components (timbre) into the wave that were not there at the outset. These components are entirely ear-generated artifacts. There are several other such distortions, some of which may be involved in specific diagnosed populations. Such populations could benefit from having their hearing processes evaluated with these issues in mind.

When speaking about perceived sound timbre, one must also consider the anatomy and function of the auditory central nervous system, all of those issues that have been addressed in earlier chapters. These include entrainment, transmission, information-processing networks, and adaptations related to the satisfaction of basic human needs. An individual perceives sound quality in terms of personal threat, learning to discriminate between the sound of a lion roaring and a mother's calming voice, an impending thunderstorm and leaves rustling in the breeze, brakes screeching and the hum of a well-oiled engine, the piercing sound of ambulance sirens squealing versus the sweet singing of the "Sirens" that are the group of mesmerizing nymphs portrayed in Greek and Roman legend, and so on.

The use of varying timbres for the purposes of music therapy interventions plays a key role in helping to develop auditory discrimination. Varying timbres, applied by music therapists as *continuous disturbances* (persistent forcing functions), can eventually drive the ear/brain to develop strategies for discriminating sounds, ultimately aiding in the auditory integration of the frequency spectra embedded in these sounds, and impacting upon language development, sound tolerance, auditory focus, fear abatement, sense of self, and more.

One final thought relative to processing of timbre is the sound quality associated with an individual's environment. Large gatherings and places such as shopping malls, supermarkets, concert halls, and the like, have a characteristic timbre all their own. Many people (both "typical" and diagnosed) complain that the noise and volume of such environments are stressful ("threatening"). It has been found, in music therapy sessions with persons of sensitive hearing, that volume (i.e., loudness) is not necessarily the cause of agitation and stress in these environments, since, in the music therapy studio, loudness is not a problem. Instead, the source of the discomfort may derive from the overlapping of frequency spectra embedded in the sounds, timbres, overtones (especially if music is playing in the background), and the general sea of indistinguishable sounds which a sensitive auditory system has difficulty processing. In other words, "loudness" may not be the problem, but rather "quality" – the timbre of accumulating, superimposed sounds. For diagnosed populations, the music therapist has the best resources for testing this auditory issue, and treating it with timbre/ harmony/volume infusions that could redirect auditory processing toward more *functional adaptation.*

## Harmony: general considerations

In the discussion of melody in Chapter 8, it was stated that the understanding of pitches as "melody" depends on the sequencing relationship among notes, the frequency and prosody in which those notes are rendered, and the profile (contour, soundscape) of highs/lows and intervallic flow, as all of these evolve in the horizontal, forward flow of sounds across time and space. It is understood, too, that the frequency spectra of the sounds (sonority; timbre), their tonality (key; fundamental frequency), and the modality (pitch intervals; frequency ratios; scales) used in presenting or inventing a "melody" derive from, and directly reflect, the emotional states of its creator. Furthermore, considerations of auditory processing, tracking, pitch discrimination, and perception all contribute to the listener's understanding of sequential tones as being "a melody."

A major element in the listener's perception of tones as melody is that of the *implied* harmonic environment within which a series of notes evolves. In an extensive research study of a listener's perception of *pitches,* as they relate to one another to evolve into what one considers to be a melody within an implied series of keys and sequential chord progressions, Povel and Jansen (2002) suggest that "the formation of a harmonic interpretation is of

paramount importance in the processing of tonal music, and largely determines the goodness...of these sequences" (p.81). In other words, when
hearing a series of pitches, generally consisting of combinations of
scale-wise notes and various interval leaps, the listener's brain will *implicitly*
seek to relate the flow of notes to some correlating harmonies from which
the notes are derived, thus establishing a basic *key center* around which
harmonic progressions seek to reach resolution (*Gestalt* laws of perception
revisited; see Chapter 4). According to the study, these instinctive factors of
music processing are innate, regardless of cultural influences, because of the
harmonic implications of a given flow of tones – suspensions that seem to
lead toward resolution.

Recall, for example, that the frequency ratios of the intervals in the
overtone series described earlier (see pages 193–194) are such that the
octave (2:1 frequency ratio, upper note to lower note), third (5:4), fifth (3:2),
fourth (4:3), and sixth (5:3) are the basic consonant or "pleasant" ones. It
follows, therefore, that one seeks to *resolve* into such consonance those
harmonic sequences that contain, either directly or implicitly, uncomfortable
frequency ratios, such as the seventh (15:8), second (9:8), and various aug-
mentations and diminutions of these. Thus, a common practice in music
composition is to have the seventh note lead into the eighth, the octave (2:1);
or the second note leading back to the first (the "unison," 1:1) or third (5:4);
and so on. Apparently, according to the study cited, such tendency does not
particularly depend on the kind of scale or key center employed (e.g., as
developed in Pythagorean, Western tonal music theory). It is apparently a
function only of whether or not the predominance of pitches *seem* to lead
toward some "home" pitch, about which others circulate. As such, the impli-
cation of harmonic structure, implicitly embedded within a melodic line,
plays a major role in clinical applications for auditory tracking issues (accurately tracking, note-for-note, a melodic line to conclusion).

Consider a case in point. Rhea often appears not to be attending during
the presentation by the therapist of a musical tune, until that tune is
presented with certain notes omitted. At that point she will instinctively and
correctly sing the possibly missing next note. This phenomenon occurs
regardless of whether the song happens to be familiar, or improvised by the
therapist. Then, Rhea's attention remains steady during the rest of the song's
evolution (no lyrics are used). She seems to know what pitch would logically
be next, as if she understands implied harmonic progressions at the age of 5
years. Many other young clients of varying ages have also been able to

partake of this type of "melodic construction" based on suspended pitches driving towards resolution; i.e., leading to relaxation in the form of implied consonance. This is a further example of the body's instinctive need to process information in a *purposeful* manner, to resolve issues that are perceived to be in need of settlement (*Gestalt* law number 5).

Indeed, this aspect of harmonic tension (suspension) and relaxation (resolution) has been used effectively as a music therapy intervention in the cases of Robert, Laura, Bucky, and Rachel, to induce similar muscular extension and flexion, breath control, attention and anticipation states, etc. With the release of muscular tension comes the release of emotional stress. Therefore, the body's *entrainment* (see Chapter 6) of pitch suspensions waiting to be resolved provides an effective clinical tool for mobilizing the subject's anticipation of psychological release, that release coming when the implied harmonic progressions are resolved and the melody reaches its resting point. Melodic phrases can be as brief or as lengthy as would be deemed effective under various circumstances.[1]

## Harmony: changing moods and changing colors

As previously defined, the element of music called *harmony* often connotes the simultaneous sounding together of three or more pitches, to create a polyphonic ("many sounds"), vertically "stacked" arrangement of sound called a *chord*. This architectural sound structure is organized to flow in space and time, in what is termed a harmonic or chord *progression*. Each chord is configured (i.e., built around a fundamental pitch called the *root* of the chord, above which, when the chord is in *root position*, are two or more other notes, usually separated by the interval of a major or minor third (e.g., C–E–G; F–A–C). The root may be positioned as the lowest note of the three, or the chord may be reconfigured so that the root is located in the middle, between the other two notes, or at the top. If it is not configured with its root in the base position, the chord is said to be "inverted," with the degree of inversion depending on exactly where, in the vertical structure of the chord configuration, the root is located.

---

1     Incidentally, the pentatonic (five-tone) scale, Balinese (four-tone) scale, and even the Oriental quarter-step tones, harmonically drive towards a "home" pitch, based generally on the corresponding overtone series. Even the five-tone scale can derive intervals of thirds, fourths, fifths, and seconds that seek resolution.

Various levels of inversion can result in different *harmonic intervals* being embedded within the chord structure. Recall that "intervals" refers to the differences in pitch, or vertical spacing, between any two notes of the chord which are sounded together. Some of these intervals might be dissonant, wherein the difference in fundamental frequency between the two pitches is of such a ratio as to produce disagreeable beats. One can actually discriminate (specifically identify or "hear") beat frequencies up to about 6 or 7 Hz (cycles per second), beyond which all one perceives is subjective dissonance, being most disagreeable at a beat frequency of around 23–24 Hz.

On the other hand, certain intervals are consonant, wherein a pleasing resonance is experienced, as described earlier in this chapter. The term *modality* (and its relatives, in the form of derived musical *scales*) is used to describe specific frequency ratios that characterize corresponding pitch intervals within the frequency spectrum of any given tone or chord. Recall that *tonality* has to do with the fundamental frequency of any given pitch; or, in the case of chords, the root of the chord and the associated key to which it resolves. Also recall that sonority has to do with the frequency spectrum itself, surrounding the fundamental frequency of a given pitch; or, in the case of chords, the frequency spectra of the various intervals embedded within the chord structure.

It therefore seems plausible to suggest that the modality, tonality, and sonority of individual chords, their inversions, their progressions, and the ways in which the body *entrains* them, could have clear clinical implications, as observed with Rhea and others. These aspects of harmony might even "strike a chord," so to speak, with the very personality type of the individual involved. For example, the idea was alluded to in Chapter 6 that there may be specific A-major, B-minor, F-major, etc., personality types that resonate with specific harmonies and key signatures. Rhea, for example, accepts music in the keys of F#, A and B (major or minor) more readily than she enjoys the same songs played in other keys. The range and register of these three particular chord roots are often more amenable to the singing voice of young children than are songs pitched in the keys of C, D, or others.

Taking the above reasoning one step further, the possibility exists that carefully designed and controlled clinical studies could show several effects.

- *Tonic modes* (e.g., the key of C major and the chords, chord progressions, and harmonies that define this key), because of their inherent *stability* and "grounding" (they are, indeed, the strongest tonal factor in music), can be quite effective in controlling either highly aggressive behavior or its opposite, timidity and shyness. Prophet and Spadaro (2000) suggest that the body organs and systems most responsive to tonic modes are the heart and blood vessels (i.e., the cardiovascular system) and the thymus gland. The latter is a small, ductless endocrine gland located near the base of the neck and responsible, especially in youngsters, for the normal development of immunological function. The authors also suggest that the most effective instrument for expressing these modes is the harp.

- *Super-tonic modes* (e.g., the key of D major), which tend to become absorbed into sub-dominant modes (see below), might have some as yet ill-defined relationship to the human drive for sexual fulfillment. So, quite logically, they are most associated with the organs and systems of reproduction, and their cousins, those of elimination, including the kidneys. The woodwind family of instruments are apparently, according to Prophet and Spadaro (2000), very effective in expressing super-tonic moods.

- *Mediant modes* (e.g., E major), because of their moody and "sobering" nature, can be a beneficial intervention when dealing with the need to balance either an egotistical sense of superiority or its opposite, inferiority. These modes tend also to be very cerebral, so the body's nervous system, cerebral cortex, and pineal gland *entrain* mediant modes the best, as expressed most effectively by the entire family of stringed instruments. (The pineal gland is a "pine-shaped" endocrine structure located in the brain which secretes, among other biochemicals, the hormone melatonin.)

- *Sub-dominant modes* (e.g., F major), by virtue of their inherent sense of balance and equilibrium, can induce feelings of joy and expansiveness not unlike those derived from sexual fulfillment. These modes tend to evoke a positive image of one's self and, as such, are also associated with certain portions of the brain and the master (pituitary) gland. The musculoskeletal system, too, is recruited for issues related to proprioception, balance, and equilibrium. The piano seems to be the instrument of choice for expressing these modes (Prophet and Spadaro 2000).

- *Dominant modes* (e.g., G major), as a balancing complement to mediant modes, and in support of tonic modes, have a centering effect on physiological function, driving the body towards a better sense of balance, equilibrium, stability, and calmness. The brass family of instruments seem to express this mode the best, and are reflective of its association with the lungs and respiratory system, the throat, and the thyroid and parathyroid glands located in this anatomical region. Here, again, *entrainment* through the musculoskeletal system can also address issues of balance and equilibrium.

- *Sub-mediant modes* (e.g., A major), as a complement to super-tonic modes, but with much less influence on tonality, can be an effective intervention in managing sleep/wake activity because of their ability to invoke feelings of peace and tranquility. Interestingly, the system of the body with which these modes are most associated is the digestive system and its complementary organs, including the liver and pancreas; and the instrument of choice for expressing these modes is the organ.

- *Leading-tone modes* (e.g., B major), as a complement to tonic modes, because of their drive towards the tonic, can contribute to one's sense of satisfaction that is derived from *resolution* (the same physiological/physical principles that are related to seeking closure of dissonant harmonies into consonant ones). The brain, autonomic nervous, and endocrine systems play a role here, especially the adrenal glands. Percussion instruments (drums, tabla) seem best suited to express these modes, perhaps because of their endogenous drive.

All of the above, at this stage of our understanding, is of course speculative and merely suggestive (based on anecdotal evidence). But the concepts, examined within the framework of the material presented in this book, are intriguing to the extent that, if research could verify them, in both principle and fact, then corresponding *dose-dependent* clinical protocols could be developed in practice. The results could prove to be quite significant for the use of music in the treatment and management of diagnosed populations.

It is of interest, when speaking about harmony, to point out further that the basic *major triad* (such as the first–third–fifth notes of a scale, among others) has a pleasing combination of intervals that are in the ratio of 4:5:6, with the root of the chord being at the very bottom. The second (middle) note up from the root establishes the consonant interval of a *major* third in relation to the root (i.e., a frequency ratio equal to 5:4, as previously defined); and the third (top) note up establishes the consonant interval of a *minor* third in relation to the second note (i.e., the frequency ratio 6:5), and a consonant *perfect fifth* up, in relation to the root (frequency ratio 6:4 = 3:2). In the *minor triad* (three-note chord), the position of the major and minor thirds are exactly reversed. That is to say, in this chord, which has a frequency ratio of 10:12:15, the *minor* third, at a frequency ratio of 12:10 = 6:5, exists between the bottom notes, and the *major* third, at a frequency ratio of 15:12 = 5:4, exists between the middle and top notes, but the relationship spacing (interval) between the top notes and the bottom note is still at the frequency ratio of a *perfect fifth*; i.e., 15:10 = 3:2.

In keeping with the *Gestalt* law of proximity (see Chapter 4), the body prefers to be exposed to chords that progress in small steps (as is also the case when it comes to the perception of melodic contours), and that contain "tight," close, consonant intervals, as opposed to leaping and distant movements. According to the *Gestalt* law of directionality, the human organism also prefers continuity over discontinuous changes in pitch/harmony; and, adhering to the Law of Pragnanz, the ultimate objective is to seek stability, consistency, and resolution.

By way of summary, then, *chord progressions* – especially those involving dissonant harmonies resolving to consonant ones – add mood and "color" to the environment of sound, creating auditory illusions. They can appease or excite the body's energies and moods, as suggested above; they can be irritating or pacifying, intoxicating or sobering, stimulating or inhibiting, mesmerizing or distracting.

Rachel's schizophrenic disposition, for example, prefers to dwell within the minor keys and harmonies. She often requests music interventions flowing with arpeggiated, sorrowful-sounding harmonic progressions (chords the individual pitches of which are played one after the other resembling a melody, rather than in block sonorities), within a minor, rather than major, tonality. This is the acoustic environment in which Rachel is most comfortable, enabling and supporting her need to wallow in her fear-driven, aggravated plight. Thus, the music therapist provides "sad," flowing harmonic progressions modulating through various minor modes, for the first portion of her session, as a reassurance tactic of support.

However, as Rachel's mood *entrains* with the minor modalities, the therapist begins to introduce some major chord harmonies while maintaining the same flow of arpeggios and tempos. These subtle harmonic changes to major harmonies tend to lift Rachel's spirit towards seeing the "brighter" side of things. Rachel's entire music therapy treatment consists of providing an enveloping music environment, basically non-verbal, in order to allow the flowing elements of timbre, harmony, and dynamics to influence her responses. It has not failed to bring about a "refreshed" feeling, according to Rachel, at the end of the sessions. Although Rachel does not know why this happens, the clinician knows that as the music ultimately finds its way from minor modalities to only major harmonic progressions, and concludes on a resonant major chord, Rachel's fear sensations dissipate, giving way to changes in her outlook and attitude.

## Harmony: dimensional hearing and auditory figure–ground

Melody is generally a single line moving in a horizontal manner, a soundscape containing scale and leap sequences, and highs and lows. As such, it is *two*-dimensional, requiring accurate auditory tracking and scanning to make musical sense of the pitch relationships flowing in a horizontal line. The linear flow of melody also contributes to one's auditory spatial perception. One detects if the sounds are going "up" (which is also associated with increasing pitch frequency), or "down" (which is associated with decreasing pitch frequency), or are high frequency or low frequency, and are "moving forward" (a *spatial* interpretation of a linear, *temporal* sequence).

Harmony adds the third dimension to vertical and horizontal movement: *depth*. Because of their multi-pitch nature, chords and chord progressions provide listeners with an auditory illusion of "back" and "front," inner and outer sounds (depth) within the experienced thickness of sound textures. Some sounds appear to be more forward (i.e., closer to the ear and/or at the perceptual foreground of the hearing architecture) while others appear to be further back (i.e., more distant from the ear and/or at the perceptual background of the hearing architecture). Since one's ears undertake the auditory scanning process discussed in Chapter 8, the harmonic and chordal materials are constantly scanned in three dimensions, resting on different sounds all the time. This is referred to as dimensional hearing – the need to scan musical sound structures from several "sides," to hear them as projected in different directions, in order to reconstruct and interpret their *intent*, and to further understand spatial pitch relationships as being "music" rather than random noise, or "sound" organized for some other purpose (language, ambulance sirens, thunder, etc.).

When harmony supports a melody, the tendency is to track primarily the melody (the "figure" or "foreground"), and basically place much of the accompanying harmony in the background of awareness. This is similar to the element of *figure–ground* in photography, wherein the subject of the snapshot is in the foreground and other images are somewhat blurred into the background. Auditory figure–ground and dimensional hearing are among the auditory processing factors that are most often problematic in many diagnosed and delayed populations, especially in autism spectrum disorders, language delays, and geriatric populations. For these populations, incidental acoustic energy takes on the characteristic of being a "wall of sound," and the listener loses the ability either to detect or to focus on the important acoustic information (auditory focus) while committing to background the less important information. This can be a dangerous, highly disturbing experience, since not being able to tell the difference between important and benign auditory information could be detrimental to one's survival. In addition, if every and all sounds are taken to be equally important, the physiological system will remain in a constant state of fear stress, not knowing what is safe sound, and what is dangerous.

Music therapy interventions can help develop auditory focus, figure–ground discrimination, and dimensional hearing skills, by employing tasks similar to those used for ear training of musicians at schools of music. When a participant is forced to "hear" certain musical elements, by teaching him or her to be especially on the lookout for certain predetermined musical cues such as a trill or a familiar tune, and furthermore, if that individual is conditioned to respond in certain ways each time those cues are presented and detected, then he or she will eventually learn to *listen for* certain elements and to discriminate them from among the rest of the musical information presented.

Laura, for example, the adult diagnosed autistic introduced earlier, has major auditory figure–ground issues. She has no language, perhaps partially owing to her inability to focus her hearing on the voice of the speaker when there are other sounds surrounding her which she cannot tune out. Her receptive language is acceptable as long as she can look directly at the speaker, and there is little or no other background sound simultaneously present. Otherwise, she can be extremely distracted, and often lacks focus on the music if there is any extraneous sound about the music therapy room. However, despite this, Laura can sustain a rhythmic beat (pulse), and responds best (by relaxing) when the music contains harmonic flowing arpeggio accompaniment with limited sonic density or a need to track long melodic lines. Her music therapy treatment includes figure–ground auditory training, consisting of cue/response tasks, for 20 of the 45 minutes of each meeting. Since beginning these interventions, Laura's ability to remain focused on specific music material has increased, and she can now negotiate cue/response tasks of increased difficulty, to her advantage. She also appears to be somewhat less distracted by background sounds and noises, and can concentrate on the task at hand – which is the making of music with the therapist.

Music therapy has the most efficacious resources for the treatment of dimensional hearing and auditory figure–ground difficulties, when applied clinically with these specific goals in mind. Many persons, whether among the diagnosed or the "typical" populations, exhibit figure–ground problems, often in undetected, subtle ways. For example, at a party, when someone says "I can't hear you, the background chatter is too noisy," it suggests an inability of the auditory system to focus on differentiating the *figure* from the *background* without distraction.

## Dynamics: expression of attitudes and emotions

In general, harmonic progressions in musical works have the ability to elicit the entire spectrum of human emotional and physiological responses. Harmony encapsulates the entire body in a "sea of sound" which the body cannot ignore, good or bad. And, of course, seas have associated with them waves of varying amplitude, which, in music, brings us to the element of dynamics.

Loudness and softness (more commonly, sound "volume") speaks to the emotional *intent* of a communication. One shouts when frightened, angry, ecstatic, excited, commanding, or otherwise driven to extremes of emotional expression. One tends to whisper (i.e., speak without vibrating the vocal cords) when subdued, embarrassed, telling secrets, perhaps expressing hostility, malice or gossip, planning a conspiracy, or being respectful of another's privacy. People tend to be quiet when being pensive, sad, or otherwise driven to emotional lows. Indeed, embedded in the amplitude, power, and intensity of sound energy is the corresponding intensity of the emotion being expressed. Body language connotes the same types of expressions. One stomps the feet, bangs on tables, slams doors shut, moves "loudly" and quickly, becomes physically intense and energized, and makes noise while jumping up and down, when one is angry, disappointed, excited, hurried, or otherwise harried. These activities are accompanied by increased muscle tension and blood pressure as the body mobilizes for action.

Conversely, people tend to move softly and lithely when sad, confused, insecure, tired, or aware of others who are resting. In music, these variations of energy and intensity are subsumed under the term "dynamics" – an element of music briefly introduced in Chapter 2, more rigorously defined and quantified in terms of *decibels* in Chapter 3, and alluded to more generally throughout the book thus far. In the realm of body movement, dynamics refers to the distribution of weight, reconfiguration of body and limb centers of gravity (kinematics), and muscular energy (kinetics) that is expended in the way that the movement is executed, and for what purpose (Schneck 1990, 1992). A person diagnosed with low muscle tone displays "soft" movements when walking, tends to play musical instruments more quietly (owing to limited dynamic energy of arm movements), and generally is rather dynamically inflexible, unable to modulate easily between strong and less forceful movements.

What one's auditory system perceives as dynamics in music derives, in the language of physics, from the *amplitude* of a sound wave, the extremes of its vibration trajectory around its neutral position (i.e., how "high" the cork bobs up and down in the water, referring back to the example presented earlier in this chapter). Thinking back to the basketball player of Chapter 3, and the height above the ground to which the ball travels with each dribble and rebound, it is intuitively apparent that the higher the ball goes (the greater the amplitude of its trajectory) the greater the energy with which the ball is endowed. It takes a greater effort to get the ball to bounce higher. Thus, amplitude of sound vibration, in turn, derives from the energy contained in the sound waves: the greater the energy imparted to the sound wave (by a musical instrument, the human voice, the vibrating source "dribbling" the air molecules around it, the blast of thunder, etc.), the greater the amplitude of vibration. And the greater the amplitude of vibration, the louder the perceived sound. That is to say, the amplitude of vibration of the sound waves incident on a human eardrum, in turn, determines the corresponding vibration trajectory of the basilar membrane of the inner ear. The basilar membrane's amplitude of vibration is thus faithfully proportional to the power of the incident sound. (You might wish to refer back to the discussion of the auditory system in Chapter 8.)

When the amplitudes of vibration of the outer eardrum, the inner eardrum, and the basilar membrane become excessive, tiny oscillations of these delicate physiological tissues turn into wild undulations. They begin to tug at their supports, and the tugging soon becomes painful. At its extreme, such tugging can seriously damage the hearing apparatus, as is inevitable if the ear is subjected to persistent loud sounds (high-decibel rock concerts, high-volume boom boxes and car radios, loud earphone listening, etc.).

Thus, to summarize briefly, from a physiological point of view:

- Lower decibel levels (*dynamic* entrainment) of less than 60 dB "soft" music are generally preferred over higher ones (60–120 dB "hard" rock and techno-music).

- Lower-register frequencies (*pitch* entrainment), in the 32–2048 Hz range, are preferred over higher ones (2048–8192 Hz).

- Corresponding sound qualities (*timbre* entrainment) that are less shrill are preferred over those that squeal and grate on one's nerves.

In treating diagnosed populations, however, once again the clinician is reminded that *it cannot be assumed that the loudness perceived by the therapist is at the same level as what the client hears.* Suppose, for example, that the tissues in the patient's ear are thinner, less compliant, and significantly more responsive to sound vibrations than what is considered to be typical. If that is the case, then what to the therapist might seem to be a perfectly acceptable conversation level of 50–60 decibels might, to the client, perhaps with auditory issues, be perceived to be 140 dB. Soon that individual is plugging his or her ears with the hands, reacting violently to what others think of as being perfectly acceptable conversation levels, and the reasons for this behavior may not be evident.

Conversely, if the tissues of the inner ear are thicker, stiffer, and less responsive to the amplitude of sound vibrations, the client might be hearing 50–60 dB conversation levels as a mere whisper (or not at all), and thus appear to be having difficulty in comprehending and responding to a command, when in fact he or she might not be *hearing it* well enough to react. Moreover, if the client does not know enough to say "I can't hear you," and/or if the diagnostic evaluation is not thorough enough to pick up that subtlety in sound perception, what may wind up being *labeled* as a type of learning disability or attention deficit disorder (ADD) might in reality be nothing more than a deficiency in the perception of sound *dynamics*. So, sensitivity to, and awareness of, the anatomy/physiology/morphology and *perception* aspects of sound dynamics is significant to the evaluation of where and how music might be most effective as a clinical intervention.

The element of dynamics, combined with harmony, timbre, and rhythm, has served Bucky's diagnosed needs extremely well. Bucky has extremely low muscle tone, is extremely slow, and is consumed with fear and stress predominantly resulting from his severe lack of vision, which inhibits his exploratory instincts. Music therapy interventions address his low muscle tone and his cautious, fearful demeanor by providing a densely thick, energetic, rather resonant, loud music environment. This serves as a sound structure enabling Bucky to perceive a kind of auditory boundary to the room. What's more, the voluminous vibrations emanating around the room and reflecting off the walls can be felt by Bucky's body, providing indirect proprioceptive information to his brain about where his body is in this space. In addition, this massive dose of vibration animates Bucky into *moving* more dynamically, playing the drums loudly to keep up with the dynamic volume of the music, or marching around the room by pounding his legs into the floor. Taking into account the subjectivity of what constitutes "loud," the therapist solicits Bucky's opinion, and observes a demeanor that would indicate "too loud." Such demeanor would take the form of covering his ears, or perhaps a sudden discontinuing of task accomplishment on Bucky's part, and so on. Adjustment is made to a volume level *just below* his threshold of discomfort, but still within a "tolerably loud" level.

Rhea, on the other hand, does not enjoy listening to loud music; yet, when she plays the drum, she strikes it with loud dynamics, and sudden accents on certain beats. She employs similarly erratic dynamics when playing the xylophone, suddenly accenting a pitch after playing it several times in a more delicate manner. Rhea's body movements contain the same erratic dynamics, with an inability to modulate easily from forceful movements to less energetic ones. In her case, the music therapy application of dynamics and harmony in the interventions involves a wide variety of graduated louds and softs, unpleasant chord clusters alternating with pleasant-sounding (consonant) chords, as a way of helping Rhea's system to learn how to easily modulate more gradually between force and release, comfort and discomfort, dissonance and consonance. Although Rhea tends to hold her ears and squint often, this behavior as a response to the element of dynamics and harmony is rather inconsistent, and it is still difficult to determine the reason for the behavior.

We next consider the final basic element of music – form. Form relates the *structure* of music (rhythm, pitch, melody, timbre, harmony, dynamics, etc.) to the *function* of music – the *music effect*. What is it that one hopes to communicate and/or attain through music, and what form will best achieve those goals? The answer to this question is considered in the next chapter.

# Chapter 10

# Form: Creating Aesthetic Wholeness

A system of tonal or polar centers is given to us solely for the
purpose of achieving a certain order, that is to say more definitively,
form, the form in which the creative effort culminates.

Igor Stravinsky, *Poetics of Music*

## Introduction

Relationship among sonorities forms the basis for the transformation of
what at first appear to be random sounds into what the brain will recognize
as systematically organized "music," a cohesive, sonic, aesthetic form replicating human emotion and physiological behavior. The word *aesthetic*
derives from the Greek word for sensation. Out of curiosity, we checked a
thesaurus for synonyms of "aesthetic." The first ten associated words, listed
in alphabetical order, were: artistic, critical, cultivated, cultured, discriminating, elegant, exquisite, graceful, refined, urbane. These suggest that, in
common usage, aesthetic connotes more than just objective sensation, but
sensation of a specific subjective kind, associated with one's perception of
beauty and pleasant impressions.

On the other hand, the only three antonyms provided for "aesthetic"
were: gauche, insensitive, worldly. The last word was, in turn, listed as being
synonymous with: hedonistic, materialistic, mundane (among others which
included greedy). Thus, something that is not aesthetic seems to be allied
with some subjective type of negative sensation or attitude. Interestingly,
however, both synonyms and antonyms for "aesthetic" included allusions to
*urbane* (which, in a positive sense, implies a cosmopolitan, worldly-wise
outlook on things), and *worldly* (which, in a negative sense, connotes a type
of self-centered worldly-wise attitude about things). One is led to speculate,
then, that something aesthetic includes both positive *and* negative sensations, and that perhaps human sensations – emotions and aesthetic experi-

ences "of this world" – defy clear, tangible verbal definition. Incidentally, among the synonyms given for "sensation" were: emotion, feel, feeling; which supports our earlier discussion that emotions (sub-cognitive) precede feelings (cognitive), even in alphabetical order!

Several years ago, at a university seminar on aesthetics, one of the speakers suggested that aesthetics is about "about-ness" – it is what it is, as it is, and as one perceives (subjectively) *it* to be. A composer colleague of ours was once asked by a listener of one of his works, "What is this piece about?", to which the composer retorted, with great animation, "What is it about? It's about B-flat and C-sharp and trumpets and horns and scales and glissandos and…if I could tell you in words, I wouldn't need to compose it in music!" Perhaps the seminar speaker made a valid point about "about-ness." Music is about *itself*, as our composer friend bellowed; it's an aesthetic expression originating *from* human beings, *for* human beings, and containing the entire spectrum of human emotional energies, from the most negative to the most positive, in the most "worldly" sense. This composer, himself, is about B-flats and trumpets and horns and screaming glissandos (soundscapes sliding downward or upward) and fear and terror, and sudden dynamic jolts. All these elements of his own life's experiences take form in his music. Music is about itself, just as a mirror is about itself, becoming dynamic according to how one views one's self in its reflection. Human emotions are *about* human emotional energies, and these often defy formal definitions that are limited by words.

*Form* in music is synonymous with the form of what humanity is as emotional creatures. Human beings, in turn, *con*form to – *entrain* – the music. That is to say, the human mind seeks *structure* (the elements themselves) in music, *order* (purposeful combinations of these structural elements), and *relations* (sensory integration) among the inputs, from which it *synthesizes* a perceived reality; see the discussion of the *Gestalt* laws in Chapter 4, and Schneck (2001b). Thus, the physiological entrainment of form allows the individual elements of music to be experienced in terms of their intended *function*. In a sense, form becomes the morphology of music, expressing music's function through the integrated sum of its parts, but accomplishing much more than each part could, acting independently of the others, or even added simply to the others. The elements of music, through the vehicle of form, combine to send a message, communicate an emotion, elicit a response, create or reference an experience. Indeed, we human beings *are* our music;

and music is who we human beings are. It is a give-and-take exchange in the truest symbiotic sense.

Moreover, because human beings sense, they listen for aesthetic satisfaction, that is, sensory stimulation of the mind and body, whether pleasant or unpleasant, in anticipation of positive resolutions. The person and personalities, the "humanness," is within the music that is perceived, created, and expressed; the music with which one resonates and becomes attached; the music to which one's physiological system cannot help but respond. Indeed, it is *the music effect!* Mere words fail to explain emotions effectively. Emotional energies must be experienced, *felt.* These most basic of all human experiences and physiological functions could very well explain why and how music evolved in the first place.

The vibrational energies of music, manifested within rhythm, melody, harmony, timbre, and dynamics, take form as an overall aesthetic, each musical work having a life of its own, with a past–present–future – including positive and negative sensations that encompass its history in time and space as it replicates and influences human behavior. Musical form evolved in tandem with, and as a reflection of, the corresponding evolution of increasingly complex societies; and music became progressively more sophisticated (and complicated) as did the human experience.

## Making the whole greater than its parts

To this point in the book, we have identified the key ingredients (major elements of music) contained in the recipes for "making music." As is the case with any recipe (e.g., like that for baking a cake), different quantities and combinations of the same ingredients will produce different products (e.g., cakes) for different purposes, and they will taste different to different people. Furthermore, once assembled and baked, the original ingredients will bear little or no resemblance to the final product that comes "out of the oven" – in this case, the musical composition. So it is that if one assembles rhythm, melody, harmony, timbre, dynamics, etc. one way, the product may come out in the form of jazz; assemble the ingredients another way and the product is a sonata allegro form, or a round, or a symphony, or a theme and variations, or a rondo. It is not the intent of this book to examine all forms of music, but rather to emphasize that, although a listener might not be able, in a verbal and technical sense, to explain *why* (or how) his or her reactions to music occur, the listener still experiences and reacts in some way to musical form, cognitively and/or sub-cognitively. In other words, again, one *knows* it when one *experiences* it, even if one cannot strictly *define* it.

Relationships in a musical stream take form within the space and flow of time. Such relationships are evolutionary and temporal (i.e., non-static, moving and developing in time). Generally, a musical event begins with the introduction of an idea, an experience, or an emotional need that seeks expression. The idea is then developed through a middle section, wherein it undertakes a journey in search of a satisfying destination. Finally, it reaches an ultimate resting point, and *resolves*. (Although there are "stream of con-sciousness" musical forms that do *not* end as such, but rather appear to continue indefinitely and infinitely as they fade into the future.) The past, present, and future of a musical life occurs sequentially and temporally: a first event leading to a second, and a next, and so forth, within a time span. Music tells its creator's story, and does so by relying on sequential relation-ships that are organized by its creator(s). The relationships may be notated (i.e., written down in an archival sense for others and future generations to repeat); or they may be improvised and dissipated, thereby capturing only the impulses and immediacy (the instantaneous needs of the creator) at the moment of their expression. In this respect, some jazz musicians claim that writing anything down is contrary to the very essence of improvisation, which is all about the *moment* of creation. In addition, jazz musicians dislike to record anything (electronically or in writing) – such as, for example, capturing a session on tape – because the musician claims that he or she might not feel the same way the next time the same piece is played, and therefore does not want to be associated with only one (the recorded) version of a musical rendition. Obviously, there are pros and cons to this issue.

Musical phrases generally begin with simple motifs and fragmentary ideas, from which, eventually, sequences begin to surface, forming mini-sequential segments. These segments, called *phrases*, then compound into larger bodies, such as whole movements of a piece, large sections, a theme and variations, rondos, fugues, jazz riffs, etc. The final result is an overall big-picture framework, a symphony, concerto, opera, sonata, song, and so on. Simple tunes, for instance, contain sequential melodic and harmonic relationships that define and lead toward various segments within an overall form. This might be manifest, for example, as an alternation between the song's verse and its chorus, or, in jazz, may appear as improvised alternating jazz riffs ("turn-taking" segments among players, referred to as "taking fours" or "eights", etc.) that embellish harmonic, melodic, and rhythmic elements.

Form, in music, as in anything else, derives from: (1) the organization, by impulses and concepts, of (2) specific elements (referred to as an underlying structure), that are (3) instinctively and purposefully combined and put into some identifiable order by the composer, to (4) intentionally assume characteristics that will define the creator's essence in the music, the final synthesis. As the music evolves over time and space, its emotional quality, its shape, tonal mass, dimensions, possibilities of multiple auditory "views," and the overall parameters of the piece, proclaim the creator's intent. Simply put, musical form embodies those sequences in which events will take place to derive an overall, completed piece.

## Eight specific attributes of form

There are at least eight specific attributes that characterize the musical element of form.

### MOVEMENT

The work is leading somewhere, moving forward to a destination. It can proceed quickly to its conclusion, or move more slowly – sometimes even so statically, with recurring repetition, that to the listener the music appears not to be moving at all, as in the compositional forms of minimalism and some rock music.

### PATTERN

There is a planned determination of how elements will be presented, whether by pre-composed organizational choice notated by its composer, such as in composed songs, or by random (aleatoric) happenstance assigned to occur at designated moments, such as in improvised music, late twentieth-century contemporary works, and jazz, in which patterns alternate between pre-composed and improvised segments (riffs). Overall, *form pattern* refers to the manner in which the individual parts of the music are "pieced together" to form the overall work: whether or not sections will be repeated, and, if so, how, when, and how often (such as in rondo, canon, and round forms); whether the piece will have several different movements (as in symphonies, sonatas, and concertos); if several sections will be embedded within one movement (as in the sonata allegro form); and so on.

EMPHASIS

This connotes the determination of what the composer intends for the listener to hear, specifically; the selectivity and priority order of musical events for the purpose of drawing the listener's attention to particular nuances, qualities, and quantities of information. The emphatic form of music underscoring horror films, for example, employs harsh dynamics, shrill timbre, dissonant harmonies, quick recurring rhythmic pulsations (replicating the fast heartbeat and panting associated with fear and suspense), and augmented intervals (usually causing dissonances), in a format that often begins with lesser intensities building to thicker, fuller, sudden loud sounds supporting the anticipation of "horror."

CONTRAST

This attribute, in musical form, supports all of the above, further illustrating the mood, disposition, emotional energies, and communicative intent of its creator. Contrast contributes to a listener's interest and attention span. Contrasting speeds, dynamics, harmonies, and timbres (especially in orchestrations that combine various, widely differing instruments) not only elicit the listener's instinctive recognition, association, and entrainment with the music's emotional content, but also *emphasize* that content in a driving way.

RHYTHM

In its role of uniting divergent elements, rhythm not only provides the basic *unifying* pulse of a work, over which are superimposed various rhythmic patterns; it establishes too a *time span* to the sequences in which various events within a piece take place. It is in this controlled pace, within which events take shape in an overall piece of music, that its form is finalized. Energetic sections of the music may be followed by periods of silence, which in turn might be followed by calm sections that increase to yet more energetic segments. One portion of a piece may be longer than another. Since music is a *temporal aesthetic* (indeed, it exists only in time), time plays a critical role in its discernment: how, and how soon, the creator, improviser, and/or producer of music chooses to present musical material establishes the corresponding form through which the expression will be perceived. Once again, the listener's attention and anticipation of events is manipulated by the rhythmic form in which sequences of material are presented, providing still another dimension to the ones discussed in Chapter 7 for the role of rhythm in music.

BALANCE

Although music is an aesthetic phenomenon perceived internally within the mind and body, it's form bestows a sense of implied balance between dissonance and consonance, and long and short sections; also implied are illusions of contrasting *weight* in sounds (some sounds seeming to be big, thick, and heavy, others as small, thin, and light), and sound *quality* (i.e., timbres of various instruments), and the manner of interplay among those aspects. These attributes yield a sense of dimensional balance in a piece of music, adding to the listener's levels of comfort versus discomfort, equilibrium versus unsteadiness, stability versus uncertainty, and poise (or security) versus insecurity.

SPACE

Music not only takes up time, but also space in the listener's inner imagination. The spatial form in which music elements occur appears to consume space (see the discussion of dimensional hearing in Chapter 9). Again, we have illusions of high and low, depth of inner/outer, near or far-away sounding note sequences, long and short lines of movement, filled or empty spaces, and more. While the attribute of space is more implied than actual in music (whereas in the visual arts space is actually consumed), music does contain a sense of dimension relative to space consumption.

UNITY

The ultimate order out of chaos "in which the creative element culminates" (Stravinsky) is unity. Unity in music consolidates the divergent, disjointed, incongruous, into a form validating its creator's personality, physiology, and creative impulses in an integrated, functionally effective, compositional body. The evolution of unity through form brings about that cohesive quality that makes a work feel complete and finished, with a sense that all the parts absolutely belong together exactly in the combination and sequence presented (the "cake" is complete).

## Some examples

Form connotes the sum total organization of individual parts, combined and integrated to support and sustain the life of a piece of music – a composition that describes its creator's thoughts, feelings, attitudes, physical intensities, and general disposition (even his or her health and personal situation at the time of writing). Form delineates the "lifestyle" of a musical work, consistent with its expressive intent and the reactions that it elicits from the listener. For example, the "lifestyle" of a piece of music by the French impressionist composer Claude Debussy (1862–1918) takes on the form of misty, evanescent sound qualities. These are brought about by Debussy's use of quiet string and wind instrumental combinations, which generate calm, unagitated streams of melodic and harmonic lines, flowing over pulses and paces that are nearly undetectable by the listener. (Recall from Chapter 9 that woodwind and string instruments are also particularly effective in super-tonic and mediant modes that elicit "sobering" responses.) Debussy's music most often excludes loud drums, which elicit "driving" emotions in leading-tone modes, deep bass brass instruments, which elicit feelings of "joy and expansiveness" in dominant modes, stringed instruments playing fortissimos (Italian musical term for "loud"), crashing cymbals, and screaming trumpets and horns. The quality of Debussy's music is rather subdued and ethereal, calling to mind the colors soft blue (perhaps some violet), gray, yellow (perhaps some gold), and white, and shapes that have indefinite, ill-defined borders – all tending to manipulate the listener's synesthesia-like inter-sensory processes. Debussy's music contains very limited contrasts. If his work were a concrete, touchable or viewable object, Debussy's music might be soft, velvety to the eye and touch. *Nuages* (clouds), from his suite *The Nocturnes*, illustrates this point; its effect on the listener is calming and stress-reducing, leading to an increased meditative demeanor, perhaps even lulling the listener into a sleep state.

In contrast, the "lifestyle" of the music of the German-born classical composer Ludwig van Beethoven (1770–1827) is more energetic and intensely emotional, with full use of orchestral timbres that provide very rich colors and textures. Beethoven's music makes use of clear and often quicker pulses and rhythmic patterns, with much contrast. He employs the full gamut of dynamics and tempos, from slow, ultra quiet, to fast, ultra loud, and he effectively uses sudden, shocking emphasis (sforzandos and accents, in musical terms) to punctuate the mood between quiet streams. The turbulence and urgency in Beethoven's own life (personal situations), and the frustrations of his deafness (state of health), are clearly represented in all of his works, whether they be sonatas for various instruments, symphonies, chamber music, or his only opera, *Fidelio*. The reader is encouraged to listen to the final movement of Beethoven's Symphony No. 9, the Choral Movement, to experience the intense musical lifestyle that generally permeates the form of Beethoven's works. The impact of Beethoven's music on the listener is highly emotional, exciting, intense, even *inducing* stress and agitation in many cases, as contrasted with the music of Debussy. But, almost always, Beethoven's music resolves, leads to a release by the time the work concludes. In Beethoven's music, the listener's attention is maintained at a high state of anticipation, awaiting the resolution of *suspensions* of dissonances and dynamics. As a point of interest, the harmonic structures that seemed most gratifying to Beethoven, and in which he often composed (or toward which he directed his compositions), were the keys of E♭ major and its relative, C minor. Since keyboard instruments of his day were not as "tempered" as those of today (i.e., regulated to sound the same in all registers), it was often the case that a scale structure actually sounded different, depending on the location of its notes. (Therefore, E♭ would provide a different timbre quality and sensation than, for instance, E major.)

## Music elements in form and therapy

We have a duty towards music, namely, to invent it.

Igor Stravinsky, *Poetics of Music*

The eight attributes appearing in form, examined above, are inherent in many (if not all) musical forms. Their uses are contingent upon the conscientious effort of the composer to employ the elements of music to *effectively* communicate detailed information to the listener. Furthermore, the composer ensures that one note follows another, inevitably and exactly, to impart a specific message and to elicit distinct responses from the listener. In the end, music, an aesthetic art form, represents a complete integration of sub-cognitive instinct and emotion with cognitive attention, intellect, purpose, and understanding.

However, musical endeavors undertaken by many diagnosed populations exhibit the exact *opposite*; i.e., a *lack* of organized sound relationships and form, and a deficiency in coordination and integration between emotion (impulse) and cognition. Therefore, the musical results very often appear disjointed, unconnected, unrelated, formless. This is not due to a lack of musical knowledge, per se. Many non-musically trained individuals, when playing around with music, instinctively strive to combine certain instruments, notes, and rhythms; or, they seek to pick out familiar tunes. Even when formal music training is absent, most people will generally organize their aural curiosities into some *form* of sound relationships. Thus, through a music-making activity with a client, the executive mental function that gives one the ability to recognize and organize his or her impulses within a given music environment can immediately inform a music therapist about: (1) an individual's *mental* capacities for spontaneous planning, selection of options, and organization of task and environment; and (2) the participant's *physical* states (and abilities) for executing an organized event.

In diagnosed populations, most often the person discharges random sounds, devoid of particular relationships, continuity, or form, unless the leader/therapist designs specific form-producing elements such as tuning a xylophone to the four- or five-tone scale, suggesting rhythmic patterns for drumming, assigning instruments, and so forth. True, many "in the moment" improvisations, even from musically aware individuals, do not *always* yield detectable musical relationships and forms, with identifiable beginning–middle–end flows. Nevertheless, in most cases of music-making, note-to-note relationships and form do emerge and evolve within improvised impulses, and these can often be analyzed according to whether they were variations on a theme, who led and who followed, and what purposeful melodic configurations, repetitions, contrasting dynamics, rhythms, etc., surfaced to show a clear pattern. (The Nordoff and Robbins (1977) music therapy protocol is to retain on video, and actually to transcribe, the "in-the-moment" improvised music of the client on to music notation paper for further reference.)

In music therapy sessions, the existence, or lack thereof, of musical form emanating from a participant's undertaking provides useful clues about the functional and mental status of the diagnosed participant. Does (or can) he or she develop or attend to patterns? Does (or can) he or she combine different sounds and instruments in an organized manner? Does (or can) he or she "orchestrate" (purposefully combine) a sequence of instruments to designate what, when, and *how* each instrument will play which sounds? What tempos and dynamics would best accommodate the efficiency or effectiveness of which instruments? By observing the manner in which a person participates in music-making sessions, and by diagnosing possible causes of effective or ineffective undertakings, clinical goals can be derived to address the person's instincts, emotional states, cognitive awareness (and abilities), personality, and level of physiological function. Which physical abilities appear to be "intact"? Which of these are in need of some attention and possible intervention? Is the auditory system tracking the way it should, according to "typical" function? Can the brain think/do simultaneously; i.e., can it multi-task? Is there even a thought process taking place? Can one musical experience be generalized to another musical (or non-musical) situation? For example, having heard a familiar song on a CD, radio, cartoon, etc., can the participant transfer that recognition to a new environment in which the same song is now represented, but in a different way, on a different instrument, or even in a different key? Does the individual exhibit an awareness of: (1) patterns; (2) repeated sounds; (3) stops/starts; (4) notes moving upward or downward (melodic contours); (5) high and low registers; (6) loud and soft dynamics; (7) fast and slow tempos; (8) thick or thin textures; (9) "same" and "different"; and much more?

## Rhythm as form in therapy

In addition to rhythmic pulse (periodicity), pattern, and pace (tempo), there is an *integrated rhythm* that transcribes these attributes into the basic format of a piece of music. Integrated rhythm determines the rate at which events occur within an overall structure, a rate that bespeaks of the creator's own internal rhythmic processes, and elicits certain levels of anticipation and reactions from the listener. In evidence within the rhythmic form of a piece of music are corresponding body rhythms, the rhythms inherent in information-processing networks, the rhythms associated with reactions to events and experiences, and general personality characteristics, such as those that define fast, energetic, dynamic persons, or slower, deliberate responders. As illustrated in the music of Debussy and Beethoven, the length of time that transpires as one processes what one experiences tends to be uniquely correlated with the manner in which events take shape in that person's music-making. This correlation lends further credence to the fact that a person's music is completely reflective of his or her own persona and rhythm of life.

The rhythmic form of Bucky's music, as one might guess from previous descriptions of him, is always extremely slow and deliberate. This is evident in more than just his preferred musical pulse and rhythmic patterns. The length of time it takes for Bucky to move (modulate) from one musical idea to the next is quite expansive, which is reflective of the corresponding time it takes for him to move from one life event to the next. His overall musical rhythm format is so widely spaced as to obliterate any evidence of possible relationships among musical events; such relationships appear to be non-existent. Furthermore, his improvisations are very brief and extremely fragmentary. Bucky's musical understanding – his awareness of how and why the sounds he hears on a radio or in the therapy room are "music" – is quite astute, and he has the ability to describe music information as being fast or slow, loud or soft, high or low (in registers), and so on. At times, he also conveys that he detects certain patterns in the form; for instance, he identifies the repetition of the verse section following the chorus, and detects when the song is reaching its conclusion. Yet, when Bucky undertakes to make music, which he usually prefers *not* to do (but just to listen), his awareness seems not to influence his own music-making. He does not copy or imitate what he hears; nor does he create his own responses in a relational format. In this situation, his visual constraints are not the main cause, since his tactile sense seems to compensate by being keen, and he recognizes the tactile and sound qualities (timbres) of the various drums, sticks, claves, etc. Still, Bucky selects the smallest claves, and plays them for no longer than 10 seconds, considering his "music" completed (a full one minute would seem like an eternity to him). He never attempts to pick out (on the xylophone or keyboard) a song he knows, nor copy a rhythmic pattern played by the therapist if it happens to be longer than four counts.

On the other hand, Bucky's extremely slow personality demeanor seems to *contradict* his inability to remain patient through a lengthier occurrence. One would think that his slow comportment would bring with it a sense of "patience to endure." But this is not the case. Staying on task for several minutes is beyond the realm of Bucky's operating body rhythm. This has led the therapist to conjecture that perhaps, in addition to the presence of a fear spiral (Chapter 5) manifested in his slowness, there might also exist an information-processing–rate problem such that his sense of the *actual* passing of time is distorted (Schneck 1990, 2003a; Schneck and Schneck 1996). Once the information is actually processed (which, in real time, may be quite lengthy), Bucky's patience to await a task completion, or to repeat one, runs out very quickly and he seeks to leave the scene or the task. Repetitions and silences may actually increase his sense of fear. In all, he seems to display a behavior of "wait, walk slowly, stop and listen, evaluate…then run away"! All of Bucky's music-making activities depict this personality characteristic, as if, once he has established that there is no imminent threat, he sees no need to hang around waiting to see what is going to happen. This behavior pervades his academic arena, as well as the music therapy sessions, and many other undertakings. Bucky's sense of completion is at odds with the corresponding time requirements of a given situation. In fact, this "listen–run" rhythm characteristic is also manifest in his incessant need to be moving about the room, as if the pacing and changing of locations will somehow protect him from some unknown. It also suggests that his erratic energy emissions might require constant movement outlets.

These observations of Bucky have imposed the use of the aspect of form into some of his music therapy goals, which already include a host of rhythmic interventions discussed in Chapter 7 on rhythm. Changes of pace and "stick-to-it" tasks have increased Bucky's willingness to grin and bear it, along with yielding some interesting format ideas. He had progressed to tasks that require the development of purposeful, repeatable rhythmic patterns – in any manner he chooses, but having a definite relation to one another – involving at least three different instruments of his choosing, for a duration of a minimum two recapitulations. After the first several months of such undertaking, the recapitulation requirements increased to three, and are now up to four. These now include the insertion of additional elements, such as change of speed (tempos and time spans), dynamics, patterns, and/or formats of his choosing, *per* recapitulation.

When such tasks were first introduced, Bucky was very unhappy, impatient, complaining, asking to go to the bathroom, and at times resorting to tearful escape tactics. Despite the discomfort (to Bucky) of the intervention (children also cry when shoes are put on their feet for the first time!), the therapist concluded that "discomfort" and "disease" are not synonyms, and that the uneasiness of the treatment was small compared with the need to expand Bucky's levels of attention, tolerance, and negotiation skills, and that the discomfort would eventually dissipate (which it has). Bucky's level of attention and patience required expansion, not only in the best interest of his physiological and emotional functions, but also for his achieving success in the cognitive, academic arena. And indeed, this approach has observably contributed to the timing of his attention, thought processes, and *motor planning*, and was adopted in his school setting (where he was asked to repeat an exercise several times because he got it right, and not because of errors). Bucky now seems to tolerate discomfort with a more positive attitude that enables him to "flow with the moment," rather than battle with objections. Contributing to Bucky's having become less fearful and more functionally adaptive are, among other elements, the alleviation of the anxieties that resulted in "fight-or-flight" behaviors, combined with an increase in body and movement dynamics, verbal skills, confidence in his auditory ability and tactile skills to assess the environment on behalf of his vision, and awareness of his body in space (proprioception).

234

For Laura, whose fear responses kept her from following her instinctive personality rhythms lest she be admonished for doing so, the rhythmic format of musical events also served to perpetuate functional adaptation. Now Laura is much less erratic in her compulsions, can remain focused on one idea, and enjoys "her music," which in turn helps her remain calm and confident.

Rhea, exposed to similar interventions to Bucky, is learning to await her turn. That is to say, the rhythmic aspects of turn-taking involve tolerating and enduring the body rhythm of the "other" by temporarily adjusting one's own, and thereby developing the patience needed for controlling impulses. An overall rhythmic form (at what time something occurs) also develops one's ability to stick to a single task for several repetitions, and helps in the quest to generally organize one's self and the environment.

Rachel's improvisations, usually performed on the xylophone, tend to perseverate on many recapitulations of one idea, upon which she obsesses (in music as in life). Her music therapy sessions involve subtle interjections by the therapist, of faster rhythm patterns, major (as opposed to minor) tonalities, and expansion of Rachel's musical motifs, all of which often nudge her toward reconfiguring (snapping out of) her "broken record" routine, and thus moving her ideas forward. The therapist's intention is to help Rachel move forward, away from an obsessive-compulsive state of function.

Robert has the greatest difficulty inventing rhythmic patterns and determining the time span that his ideas could take on various instruments. Just like Bucky's, Robert's system resists being organized into new time-span forms. His erratic, fear-ridden behavior often displays compulsivity and task-evasion characteristics similar to Bucky's, Rhea's, and others with various diagnoses. Sudden changes in task interests, and the many attention-deficit expressions of his behavior, keep Robert stuck in one routine. When he was exposed to similar interventions to Bucky, Robert spent close to two years in music therapy attempting to satisfy the terms of the intervention without battle. Rejection of task came by way of his attempting to negotiate undertaking another task, promising that he would later return to the task at hand (which, of course, would never happen). By now in his therapy, Robert has become so interested in his own ability to "invent" continuously related musical ideas, spaced in unique forms, that he is also attempting to imitate some formats that he experiences in his favorite CD tunes.

Generally speaking, most human beings are not particularly conscious of the passing of time, unless a person is in emotional extremes: bored, racing to meet somebody when running late, in pain, anxious to hear about the outcome of an event, etc. Nor are persons necessarily aware of how the time span among musical events contributes to one's responses, attention span (rate of anticipation), or even how the composer manipulates the listener's sense of time and responses. For the fun of it, the next time you listen to, play, or sing music, you might note your own attention and patience levels in response to the rhythmical form in which the musical events are unfolding – the *timing* of the music. It will reveal some interesting information.

## Melody, timbre, harmony, and dynamics in form and therapy

Without the existence of some kind of form in music, the relationships (if any) among the various elements and attributes of music are inane. Even the aleatoric (improvised) works of the iconoclastic composer John Cage (1912–1992) contained an intentional start, continuation, conclusion, even when these were brought forth by his merely sitting at a piano, motionless, in absolute silence, for some two-plus minutes. Cage's "music," which so often seemed formless, still contained a *sense* of form that was true to the composer's intent, however unconventional. This composer still delivered his message by controlling *when* the listener will listen (anticipation), if not necessarily *what* he or she will hear and interpret (perception). *Intentionality* is the main objective of form. Without the composer's intent to make a particular statement at a certain point through music, to express something that could not be elaborated by any other form of human interaction, communication through music would be basically uninformative. Form is the manner through which the elements and attributes of music express intent: elements that are assembled in ways that deliver a message; and, as mentioned previously, that message is at least partially reflective of the corresponding state of the human experience. Hence the different forms associated with different eras in music history.

Musical form, in essence, is the sum total of all the information that preceded this chapter. In a sense one can think of music as a *medium*, through which the basic *physics* of energy, vibrating in the 20–20,000 cycles-per-second range, which is called *sound*, is exploited to uniquely express human emotions, in organized ways. It is *organized sound*. The physics is experienced through the basic sound attributes of pitch (vibration frequency), dynamics (vibration amplitude), timbre (vibration frequency spectrum, harmonics, sub-harmonics, etc.), and register (pitch location in the range of human hearing). Human emotions are expressed by assembling these sound attributes into the music elements of melody (pitches following sequentially, one after the other, arranged into phrases), harmony (combinations of pitches sounded simultaneously, which introduces additional physical principles related to vibration phase, beats, constructive and destructive interference patterns, consonance, dissonance, frequency ratios, etc.), and rhythm (pulse, pace, pattern, perseveration). The *organization*, then, is expressed through the music element of form, which puts all of this together for the purpose of delivering a message and eliciting a response. In most of the music one experiences, perhaps excluding the "experimental" avante-garde composers such as Cage and others, it is the following aspects of this medium, combined into an overall form, within which musical communication becomes manifest:

- the *timed* movement and changes of music's linear phrases

- the specific moments when highs, lows, upward and downward movements, etc. occur (again, timing)

- the selection of instruments that best exemplify the "meaning" (using the word figuratively) of melodic motifs (timbre; register)

- the harmonies and scale modes from which the notes of a melody are taken, and which evolve to underscore the emotional context of the melody

- the dynamic energy levels that are commensurate with a particular musical expression.

*Melody*, discussed in Chapter 8, contains the basic behavioral characteristics and emotions of its creator. Its contour moves sequentially within phrases and rest points, and almost always leads toward some conclusion, even if it is just a simple fade-out. The impact that a melody will have upon the listener is directly related to the *timbre* of the instrument(s) or voice(s) that its creator chooses to precisely express the emotion contained within its statements. The form in which the element of timbre is embedded is manifest within the corresponding use and orchestration(s) of instruments; that is to say, which instrument(s) are selected to play which phrases, how, and when, in a work for a group of instruments. Timbre used in the form of a work is also inherent in the specific solo instrument(s) selected to express the mood and feelings of the creator, and about whom much can be learned through his or her music. (The expression "You can't hide yourself in music" is very appropriate here.)

Johannes Brahms, for instance, favored the French horns in his orchestrations (his father was a French hornist); Brahms also used strings, especially violins, to impart his romantic passions. Frederic Chopin and Franz Liszt, both incredibly gifted pianists, wrote predominantly for the piano, although Chopin has some solo works for cello. Mozart, himself, was said to be afraid of the sound of the trumpet when he was a child, and he expressed a hatred for the flute. Nevertheless, by the time he became an adult, he employed these instruments in both solo and ensemble music (Marshall 1991). Although composers are prone to writing for various instruments, and many (like Schubert, Rossini, and Verdi among others) for voice, the choice of timbre and form in which these are used elicits intended responses from the listener, as discussed in earlier chapters.

*Harmony* and *dynamics* provide conclusive evidence of the emotional moods, energies, and personality types of their employers. Harmony is formatted to present sequences of suspension and resolution to dissonant and consonant experiences. The length of time it takes for a suspension or dissonance to resolve not only plays on the *listener's* nervous system, by affecting his or her attention and anticipation, but also provides information about the *creator's* nervous system, his or her emotional needs, and sense of time and space. In support of harmonic intent, dynamics further alerts the listener to what is in store, as exemplified by the music of "horror" films, for instance. Dynamics can drive the music, determine where it is heading, and thus contribute to the overall form of the work. Increases and decreases in volume, supported by certain instrumental timbres, evokes entrained responses from the listener. Where, when, and how accented notes are used for sudden changes in dynamics combine with timbre to contribute further response possibilities.

With reference once again to the final movement of Ludwig van Beethoven's Symphony No. 9, it is an example of an entire orchestra frantically thundering the opening of the movement, with very loud, fast-moving compilations of sonorities. This serves as a *fanfare*, announcing the upcoming entrance of the solo basses, which contemplate the melodic theme that is ultimately to be sung by a solo vocal baritone. By the time the poem by Friederich von Schiller (1759–1805) about human brotherhood, "Ode to Joy", is actually sung in the final movement of the symphony, the listener is at full attention in anticipation of the event. Through the judicious use of dynamics, timbre, orchestration, and musical form, Beethoven has prepared the listener to receive his and Schiller's message.

This use of musical form is not accidental. Rock music's incessant use of high-volume electric keyboards, guitar, and strings, along with vocalists screaming into a microphone, singing and playing in constant fortissisimos (i.e., beyond loud, at decibel levels approaching the threshold of pain) that boom around a room not only creates a high level of animation in the listener, but also depicts the urgency of the message: *Listen! And hear what I need, and to which you must respond – NOW!*

Listeners also derive information from the form which these elements and attributes take in the music of diagnosed populations, as discussed throughout this book. A possible exception is *harmony,* which usually appears only as either dissonant tonal clusters, or consonant ones, but without the client's actual harmonic "awareness" (unless the person happens to be trained or knowledgable in music). Harmony, per se, is more apt to be within the form of music presented by the therapist. But for the other elements, much can be observed.

Robert's and Rhea's need for loud dynamics and the use of mostly percussive timbres bespeaks, among many other possible causes, of their inability to easily or comfortably modulate muscular and personality intensities. It puts into question their auditory function, motor planning capabilities, individual fear levels, possible inability to fully reference their bodies in space, and more.

Laura, Bucky, and Rachel, on the other hand, display the recurring need to play slower, quiet sounds, mostly (with the exception of Bucky) sought after on tonal instruments, although "melodies" are not actually played or created. Bucky prefers to play two sticks, and if he is at the piano will play only the highest or lowest notes on the keyboard, perhaps owing to his lack of visual orientation. These two keyboard locations are easiest to detect (he becomes agitated when asked to try playing in the middle registers). With various other populations, the manner in which the music elements unite (or do not) into some "form" of expression provides information that can be translated into clinical music therapy goals as well. For example, the therapist can ask "Do musical passages conclude? Do they ramble? Are several timbres combined, and how? Can he/she/they repeat (imitate) something?" and so on.

This final element of music, form, unites all that transpires within music, within a music therapy situation, and within life, bringing all the individual elements into one aesthetic, integrated whole which is much more than just the sum of its parts. The form of a session, the form of a musical undertaking, the form of music interaction between therapist and participant(s), the forms of human fears, and above all, the form of physical, physiological, mental, and emotional human function, will culminate within the music of the human being.

This brings our discussion of the "music effect" full circle, from the original considerations of what it means to be human to, in the final analysis, how nature and nurture interact to *influence* human behavior. That is to say, as it relates to the fundamental physiological processes of entrainment and accommodation, we now ask: How does one's *experience* with music affect one's inherent responses to musical stimulation? How does one *adapt* in the presence of music, not only in terms of what is genetically inherited, but also in terms of what is genetically and/or experientially *expressed* as a result of gender, exposure, conditioning, formal training, age, and so on? In the next chapter, we examine some aspects of the effects of *nurture* on *nature*, as we summarize and recapitulate, in order to bring the subject of this book to some logical point of focus – *the music effect.*

Chapter 11

# Nature Expressed Through Nurture

Music makes me forget myself, my actual position; it transports me
into another state, not my natural one; under the influence of music
it seems to me that I feel what I do not really feel, I understand what
I do not really understand, that I can do what I can't do.

Leo Tolstoy, *The Kreutzer Sonata*

## Introduction

Throughout this book, we have endeavored to confirm the observation
expressed by Leo Tolstoy, quoted above. We have repeatedly stressed the
importance of understanding that there is a direct symbiotic relationship
between music and human physiological function – the *music effect* on human
behavior. We have also emphasized that underlying this interrelationship are
human emotions, and the fear cycle that is operative in many of the
diagnosed populations for which clinical interventions are necessary.
*Entrainment* was described as being an innate physiological phenomenon that
plays a major role in stimulating *adaptive response mechanisms* that account, in
part, for the emotional human organism's ability to survive. We have also
indicated that, while music is always *therapeutic*, when carefully applied as
*therapy*, it exploits these very aspects of physiological function to intervene
clinically for the purpose of eliciting more desirable response options over
the long term. That is to say, the focused application of music elements, in
part or in total, on a continuous basis, helps to establish new operating
set-points for homeostatic processes.

The elements of music as expressions of both the physics of sound and
the structure and function of the human body, especially its basic emotional
nature, can *drive* the human organism to respond in ways that derive directly
from this form of focused sensory stimulation. Many of those responses can

be attributed to the inherent *nature* of the organism, which, in addition to the physiology and anatomy discussed thus far, also includes:

- *gender* – response variability between males and females
- *genotype* – genetic heritage and affinities (does a "music gene" exist?)
- *phenotype* (anatomical architecture) – the visible result of the interaction between a genotype and its environment
- *enneatype* – nine basic personality types: artistic (the creator), doubting (the skeptic), Epicurean (the sensuous), giving (the gratuitous), pacesetting (the leader), passive (the observer), conciliatory (the peacemaker), extroverted (the performer), and idealistic (the perfectionist), attributes that also influence an individual's music expectations and preferences
- *race* – kindred lineage, ancestry, history (perhaps language, as well)
- *state of health* (of mind and body) – a key role in determining both receptiveness and responsiveness to the music environment.

There are various other interweaving variables.

## General relationships of the human being to music

Taking all of the above into consideration, we note further that the ability of the human body to entrain, respond, and adapt to its environment is a *generic* property not unique only to musical stimulation. Indeed, it is the result of a more fundamental ability that the human organism has to learn and change, through nurture, at any level of function. This includes education and learning at both the sub-cognitive, instinctive level (which derives from nature), and the cognitive, analytical level (which derives through conscious learning). The mechanisms we have been discussing include, among others:

- exposure to a *continuous disturbance* (forcing function, which in this case is embedded in the elements of music, but in general could be any other form of sensory stimulation)
- *physiological entrainment*
- *accommodation responses*

- establishment of new *operating set-points*

- *functional adaptation.*

By these mechanisms, nurture plays a key role in affecting whether or not, and how, one will respond to specific types of musical stimulation. Interestingly, the word "nurture" derives from an old French word, *nourture*, which originally meant "adaptation." Music is, literally, a nurturing type of stimulation of the senses, reflecting and supporting human emotions while simultaneously influencing particular innate physiological behavior to yield both immediate change and new, long-term adaptive alterations – to learn new response options.

Exposure to distinct musical stimuli can nurture various types of responses in particular age groups, beginning as early as *in utero*, and extending through adolescence, adulthood, even into senescence. In fact, age-related responses to music are more the rule than the exception. For example, most mothers seem to know instinctively that: (1) infants prefer lullabies to any other form of music; (2) they would rather hear a female voice than a male's, or any particular instrument; and (3) they react more favorably to live music presentations than to recorded ones. This knowledge is supported by recent investigations such as those of Coleman *et al.* (1997) and Trehub (2000).

Among the physiological parameters that are most responsive to these infant musical preferences are heart rate, hemoglobin oxygen saturation in red blood cells (increases with musical exposure), caloric intake, respiration rate (number of breaths per minute), and weight gain following birth (greater daily gain when exposed to musical stimulation, in both male and female, premature and full-term babies). Not enough has yet been determined concerning: (1) which types of music, (2) in what settings, (3) under what types of conditions, (4) for how long, and (5) how often, will produce what kinds of results (i.e., increased heart rate versus decrease, etc.). In other words, there do not yet exist specifics that can be used to formulate and quantify *dose–response relationships*. Preliminary findings do pique the interest and imagination of researchers who observe evidence that the effectiveness of musical stimulation is certainly undeniable and worthy of further investigation.

Furthermore, though much still remains to be learned, it appears from early experimental results that fetuses and newborn infants quickly learn to discriminate between two different pitches, low ones eliciting more effective responses than high ones. This makes sense *in utero*, when one considers that low-frequency sound waves can penetrate the womb and travel much more deeply into the tissue than can high-frequency sounds, which dissipate rapidly. The fetus has probably been exposed to many more low pitches than high ones, and this type of soothing *nurturing* undoubtedly carries over into the baby's earliest exposures to the external environment.

Neonates and infants tend, too, to prefer the *timbre* of lower-pitched instruments (such as that of a bassoon) to higher-pitched ones (like the piccolo). The timbre aspect of this preference seems less obvious than the pitch aspect, especially when one considers the previous observation that these developing forms of life prefer to hear female voices, which tend to have a higher pitch, and a totally different timbre from that of males, or bassoons. Perhaps, again, an infant is simply more conditioned to hearing its mother's voice (nurture), having developed an intimate relationship with it for the past nine months or so; but the answers may be more complex than that and require further investigation.

Moving into the adolescent years, one comes across an interesting study by Gerra *et al.* (1998). These researchers investigated how high-school male and female subjects (median age 18.6 years), none of whom had any specific previous training in music, responded to two different types of music: classical (Beethoven's Symphony No. 6) and fast-paced technomusic generated on electronic instruments, processed through a computer, and characterized by high-frequency beats and strident tone clusters. The responses were quantified in terms of variations in the circulating levels of both neurotransmitters (beta-endorphins and norepinephrine) and stress hormones (adrenocorticotropic hormone, ACTH, and growth hormone, GH); increases in these are associated with activation of the hypothalamic–pituitary–adrenal (HPA) axis, and correspond to a stressful condition not unlike the anxiety that characterizes the fear response.

Using these parameters to gauge the emotional state of the students, it was evident that Beethoven's symphony "quieted" the HPA axis, while the technomusic excited it to a stressful level; and the more the subjects disliked the music, the greater was this disquieting effect. These observations may be reflective of the relationship between nature and nurture. For example, in previous chapters we discussed the fact that, by nature, the body does not react well to dissonance, beats, and strident tone clusters, and it also prefers the timbre of nature's sounds to those generated by a computer. This may very well be because the body finds the sounds to be unpleasant because it has not yet been exposed enough (nurtured) to such sounds to consider them acceptable. Perhaps a hundred years from now the results of experiments such as those of Gerra *et al.* might turn out quite differently, because by then exposure to technomusic might have become the norm. This is exactly analogous, for example, to what has happened with the music of Hungarian composer Béla Bartók (1881–1945), which originally was perceived to be dissonant and quite unacceptable to the untrained ear in the early twentieth century, compared with how it is received and perceived now.

Music therapy work with geriatric persons who may or may not have diagnostic issues attests to the ability of music to stimulate physiological and psycho-emotional aspects of function for older generations (e.g., Aldridge 2000; Miller *et al.* 1996; Prickett 2000; Tomaino 2002). Tastes, preferences, musical styles, and music generally relevant to personal histories have been observed to evoke at least short-term betterment in behavioral conditions, and in some cases have helped arrest further deterioration of function. Areas of function addressed by music therapy for older populations include memory gain, cognitive alertness, movement strength and gait organization, attention span, speech rehabilitation, energy animation, and other debilitating conditions associated with the aging process and commensurate diagnoses.

In general, the relationship of a person (of any age and ability) to a particular music event, and the response to such an event, are based on:

1.  the nature of the person's physiological function

2.  the personality characteristics with which he or she has been endowed

3.  the nurturing elements of the musical stimulus

4.  the administering clinician

5.  the acoustic environment to which the person is exposed.

In other words, the actual expression of a human system's function results from a combination of exposure and experience.

## The nature/nurture relationship in clinical settings

Earlier chapters have elaborated on the fact that it is the relationships music elements have *to one another* that organizes them in such a way as to make sound recognizable to the human being as "music." Similarly, it is the relationship that nurture has to nature that underlies *the music effect* on physiological function. In this respect, several additional aspects of this relationship need to be considered.

One of these derives from the fundamental interactions that take place between the music therapist and the recipient(s) of the therapy services; that is to say, the essence of the creative and humane clinical interactions between clinician and client. It is this musical relationship that ultimately unites *instinct* with *awareness*, creating a unique, in-the-moment musical *form*. This relationship among the participants, affecting therapist and client alike, completes the integration of nature (emotion, instinct, anatomy, physiology, etc.) with nurture (cognition, reason, psychology, entrainment, expression, etc.) and yields *adaptation*. In the clinical music therapy setting there are at least two human beings involved. Each contributes to the session his or her own psycho-emotional state, individual physiological function, personality characteristics, tastes and preferences, and innate and learned knowledge; and each performs a distinct role embedded within the hierarchical setting (i.e., the therapist/client roles).

In addition to two separate and unique individuals uniting to "make music" together as one, this relationship sets the tone and form of the music and the music therapy setting. It expresses nature through nurture, and integrates emotion, physiology, and cognition, to influence the music, the music-making process, and its eventual outcome. Moreover, contributing to this relationship are:

1. The relationship of musical elements to each other (the kind of musical configurations employed by each participant).

2. The relationship of each individual's own musical configuration to that of the other(s) (blending of minds and natural instincts).

3. The relationship of musical elements to one's current emotional/physiological state (who am I and how do I feel at this moment?).

4. The relationship between the music undertaking in the moment, and the therapy goals to induce physiological/psycho-emotional adaptation in the long run.

The relationship between the musical undertaking and the therapy goal – which is to "nurture" *natural* change – has been tracked in various chapters throughout this book, using several descriptive indicators from five case examples and their uniquely diagnosed nature of function. Physiological and clinical knowledge are key factors contributing to the development of nurturing goals that can be achieved effectively by exploiting the nature of changes that result from functional adaptation. The music therapy clinician can effectively ascertain the nature of a behavior and its possible cause(s) based on the musical interaction. He or she is also able to prioritize the symptoms and causes of a behavior that require immediate attention through music interventions. These considerations will generally establish the relationship between designed musical intervention and the goal: the nature of the problem and the nurturing required to re-educate physiological function. The primary nature/nuture relationship between therapist and service recipient is basically established in the very first meeting and musical interaction.

The importance of this type of relationship has been alluded to throughout this book, and is understood to play an important role in leading the recipient toward functional adaptation (self-nurture). The element of trust, of course, is of primary importance in any relationship, but especially in the music therapy clinical setting. Mutual trust and respect between the music therapist and participant breeds confidence, safety, reduced fear, increased motivation to participate and interact, enjoyment, and potential for effective changes. (Confidentiality in the therapy is, of course, self-explanatory and a given.)

After that first therapy meeting, the ensuing important elements of a nature/nurture relationship are the clinician's thorough understanding of not only the recipient's physical and emotional circumstances, but his or her own, as well. "How do I feel about myself today?" "How do I feel about the other person(s)?" "Am I tense, uncomfortable, fearful, insecure, knowledgeable, focused, goal-oriented, energetic, tired, hungry, impatient?" "What are my expectations of this session?" "Why am I asking for this particular task? What do I hope to achieve?" These and other self-investigative questions can bring about answers that may impact on the therapy relationship in the moment, as well as the music generated, the general mood of the session, and its outcome.

In the process of making music, all parties involved are equalized into one event. Diagnosis tends to dissipate in the process of making or hearing music. There is no right or wrong, only better and best. The learning that takes place within the therapy relationship, among all parties involved, increases the potential for attaining better results. Certainly the goal is to eventually alter physiological function; but first, the intent is to better the effect of the *music*, which in turn will better the emotion and physiology thereby opening up the lines of communication that can make change possible. Pride, completion of task, enjoyment of product, and so on, all transpire as a result of relationships that develop from the music that is being created by everyone working together towards a common goal.

In summary, the magic of the concept of *relationships* lies not only within the music itself, and not only between the music and human physiology, but also within the relationship of the music of the therapist with the music of the therapy recipient. This relationship is that which ultimately creates a higher form of its own, a joint statement of being. This relationship among therapist, recipient, and music presented (or produced) transforms into a relationship between *nature* (everything that is anatomically, physiologically, and emotionally inherent in human function) and *nurture* (everything that is ultimately expressed as human function). In the end, it is through the music that the nature of the human being is effectively nurtured.

## Putting it all together: some final thoughts

It is our belief that by integrating knowledge of:

- human anatomy and physiology
- the physics of sound vibrations and their interactions with living systems
- personality characteristics
- information-processing networks in the brain and sensory systems

with knowledge of how these are expressed through and affected by the elements of music, the scientific and music therapy communities can more efficiently and effectively address clinical issues of physiological, psycho-emotional, social, and cognitive *functional adaptation*. After all is said and done, one returns to the basic fact that humans are, first and foremost, emotional creatures whose brains and physiological function are primarily preoccupied with survival.

Throughout this book we have sought to develop the paradigm that music, as it is and has been created by human beings, is a direct reflection of this inherently emotional being. The elements of music function precisely as do the corresponding elements of physics and chemistry, as these are expressed in human anatomy and physiology. Indeed, the elements of music *derive* from the same elements of human physiology – they are exactly what humans are. As was stated right at the outset, in the very first sentence of the

Prelude to this book, *nature*, as expressed through the fundamental laws of physics, works exactly the same way, whether it is operating inside or outside the human body. Consisting of complex orders of emotion and behavior, music reflects human physiology in every way. It must. It was invented by humans; and in the forms in which human beings experience it, music can only bear characteristics familiar to humans.

The human brain has an inclination to track and link sounds because that information is critical to safety and survival. Thus, music evolves through linkages of complex sound patterns. Human beings also have a need to communicate feelings; we are social creatures. Thus, music is the receptacle into which one's feelings are placed in order that one may reveal one's self *to* one's self, as well as to others. Human beings must move – evolve, resolve. Thus, music is temporal; it exists in time, is moving, driving, evolving, evanescing, dissipating, resolving. A person's affinity to "visualize" allows him or her not only to hear sounds inside the head, through a complex system of auditory perception, but also to attach visual significance to that perception; i.e., to "see" what one hears. After all, music perception exists *only* inside the spaces of the mind. It takes the form of an auditory virtual reality.

Why did humans invent this particular form of emotional expression? Perhaps it was because, in fulfilling the need to emote, to expel, convey, and share emotional energies with others everywhere, a universal language was necessary, one that everyone could understand and to which one could instinctively relate. Music is that language. It speaks to everyone in all tongues, and requires no semantic or cognitive interpretation. No formal training is required, just the innate instinct to respond to music. There need be no how-to rule books, no regulations, no right or wrong, no hiding places, no insinuations – just flowing in the moment of feelings. Music is all about just being – human.

There are many questions yet to be answered, and there are many opportunities for carrying out meaningful research. Some studies, for example, are needed to formalize and verify the stipulation that, as a medical intervention for changing *homeostatic set-points*, there is indeed a significant role to be played by the clinical use of music. This role needs to be specifically, rigorously defined and quantified in a dose–response sense. Researchers have endeavored to prove this, and several representative samples and references to their work has been provided throughout this book.

We have taken the reader on a journey through the human body, and have demonstrated how music reflects human function and can impact behavior. This is not an accident. Music exists because life exists, and because human beings need music to exist. Humans need music in order to reach their highest potentials, and to satisfy their innermost needs – physiologically, psychologically, intellectually, and, most important of all, emotionally. By recognizing and understanding that humans are, first and foremost, emotional creatures, the relationship between nature and nurture can be better discerned in terms of that very emotion (instinct), and the physiological function that results from a sense of danger derived from what are perceived to be threats to survival (stress, fear, etc.). Humans are, after all, about human physiology driven by the fundamental, emotional instinct to survive – to be "safe."

*The music effect* is not about a particular composer, musical style, geographic location, language, or performance group. It is, at once, about *all* of these. It is about the attributes of scientific reality (physics) as embedded into music's six interwoven elements. It is about how these elements define emotion, evoke responses, alter physiological and mental function, and more. It is about the manner in which these elements can be combined to effect profound emotional sensations and responses that words fail to describe. The music effect is about music's ability to truncate the fear spiral, and to evoke emotional and intellectual connections both with oneself, and with the creator and any listeners or other participants. Why? Because music has a profound effect on human behavior; because it can resonate with basic physiological function to "transport me into another state," in the words of Leo Tolstoy that opened this chapter. Everyone – from composer, to performer, to service provider, to listener/recipient – is changed in the presence of music. Some are changed immediately and temporarily, others are perhaps delayed, but certainly more permanently over the long term.

After all is said, we recognize that humanity created distinct forms of music as a mirror image of the human animal. And, like a mirror's reflection, music consistently and accurately returns to humanity its own image. There is probably no other human invention that has such an intensely profound and penetrating effect on human behavior as has this aesthetic form of expression. Music may very well be the single most brilliant creation of humankind.

Chapter 12

# Coda: Where Are They Now?

The five music therapy participants who have been used as case examples throughout this book have made positive progress in the areas of needs discussed, and that progress can be attributed in great part to the music therapy interventions that were administered over several years. There has also been progress made in many other areas of physiological, psycho-emotional, and cognitive aspects of interventions that have been designed to induce homeostatic changes in these cases. Although many other goals have not been addressed in depth in this text, it is important to realize that *sensory integration*, by its very definition, means that the brain considers *all* physical sources that are available to it for obtaining information about, and respond-ing to, the internal and external environments of the body. Integration processes are also driven by sensory systems that include, in addition to those already considered, the coordination of:

- vestibular and visual systems

- the proprioceptive system

- the tactile system.

The *vestibular and visual systems* involve mechanisms that organize senses of balance and equilibrium, locomotion of parts or all of the human body, steadiness, and spatial information (up, down, far, near, etc.). From these derive the muscle tone development that allows for efficient movement, pro-pulsion, mid-line orientation, orientation of the body in space, and more (Berger 2002; Schneck 1992). One's ability to see must correlate correctly with what one *perceives* when seeing. Visual perception contributes to sense of space and balance, allowing the brain to confirm dimensional attributes.

The *proprioceptive system* (coordinated with the vestibular and visual systems) involves internal monitoring mechanisms (interoception) that provide information transmitted from muscles, joints, and internal organ receptors. This supports information of the vestibular and visual systems to indicate where one's body is in space, the position of the arms, legs, torso, head, and so forth (Berger 2002; Schneck 1990, 1992). Furthermore, if the brain is not receiving accurate assessments, behavioral responses will be correspondingly askew. How much knee bend is required to step up on a stair? How far does the arm need to stretch in order to reach an item?

The *tactile system* (coordinated with vestibular, visual, and proprioceptive systems) involves taste, touch, tongue movements, and organ messages that are transmitted through the nerve fibers of these systems (Schneck 1990; Tortora and Grabowski 1993). How we touch, and/or how we sense something or someone's touch upon us, contributes to our behavioral responses to stimuli (Berger 2002).

These three major sensory systems need to be coordinated and integrated fully with all of the other physical systems in order for anyone to receive and process information relevant to self-identity. Disparity within these sensory systems has as much to do with perpetuating the fear response as any incoming external event. When the brain perceives an imbalance, it will call for immediate corrective responses ("control signals"). For some people this could mean quick actions, constant movement, quick or extremely slow movement, fast or slow eye movements, and so on. These sensory systems have been taken into consideration when treating the five participants whom we have been tracking in this book (starting with Chapter 5). Many interventions were designed to address these contributors to the fear responses. With this in mind, it seems appropriate, as a postscript, to review the achievements to date of our five participants.

Of all the cases, two have made the most remarkable progress. Their positive transformations can be attributed not only to their actual *exposure* to music therapy, but in great part to the length of time that each has been exposed to music therapy interventions. These two persons are Bucky and Robert.

## BUCKY

Bucky began music therapy when he was 6 years old. He suffered several strokes *in utero*, has developmental/cognitive and sensory delays, and is considered to be legally blind. At 8 years of age, he still displayed considerable fear responses, extremely slow reactions to directive(s), slow speech and cautious movement, and general distrust of his environment. He refused to sing, vocalize, or hum in pitch. He would question each activity requested, and generally remained in a "fight-or-flight" demeanor. *Rhythm* and *volume* (dynamics) were implemented to energize Bucky. Many instruments were offered for his enjoyment, and interventions seeking to stretch his ability to sustain an activity were among the approaches. In addition, much work was done with specially designed music activities to engage his vestibular, tactile, visual, and proprioceptive systems, in efforts to help his system integrate sensory information better.

Bucky has now turned 10 years of age, and in the past two years has made the most incredible progress. Not only is he now fear*less* in his general personality, but he has also developed functional strategies with which to navigate comfortably through the environment and negotiate his interests. His creative imagination is astounding. He has become extremely interested in learning to play the piano, and has even developed a manner by which his vision can be accommodated in order for him to play familiar songs. Large musical alphabet letters, A to G, are placed on a magnetic board, in the pitch sequences of familiar tunes (C–C–G–G–A–A–G, for instance, for "Twinkle, twinkle little star"). He touches these with one hand, locates the pitches with the other, and plays them. Furthermore, he has undertaken to scramble the letters, and make up his own songs! (Totally his idea.) He is so pleased with himself that his parents have had to procure a piano for their home. He prefers the extreme registers of very high and very low, perhaps in large part owing to the fact that his vision inhibits his comfort level with the middle registers, which he cannot "perceive/see" very well. He can feel the extreme ends of the keyboard. (Eventually, the assistance of Braille piano books and key stickers will become part of Bucky's music exploration.)

As for other things to do in the music therapy session, Bucky *absolutely* prefers to design his own musical activities, now combining a wide variety of instruments, where previously he played only the smallest of claves. The louder, the merrier! The faster and more energetic the music, the faster are his movements (much faster than before). His balance and gait are more secure; his upper/lower body coordination (e.g., marching and playing tambourine simultaneously; jumping on the trampoline while simultaneously clapping the cymbals in rhythm to his jumps) is no longer problematic. His grasp of heavier drum sticks (upper-body motor planning and proprioception) is no longer an issue. He enters the music room with such high energy that it often takes a few breathing/recorder-blowing exercises to "calm" his system a bit.

Bucky's academic work is at its highest level, and his teachers are amazed at the changes in this person. It is tempting to attribute all of these advances solely to music therapy, but of course we know that it is due to a *combination* of therapy interventions, although perhaps the most influential has been the music. As part of a larger therapy "team," music has influenced many allied interventions, while also absorbing the efforts of other clinicians into the music environment. The main point is that these music therapy interventions, based predominantly on the physiological perspective throughout his four years of consistent weekly sessions (excluding vacations), have enabled Bucky's systems to change. His physiological systems and central processing units (brain and spinal cord) have been taught new options (subcortical), and lo and behold, the executive (cortical) brain now trusts the undertaking of both instinctive and cognitively organized activities. This is integration of the highest form.

## ROBERT

Diagnosed with Asperger's syndrome comorbid with some obsessive-compulsive and oppositional-defiance disorders, Robert was 11 years old when he first began music therapy treatment. We introduced you to him at the age of 14, three years into his therapy. At that time he still displayed a great deal of oppositional fear-response defiant behaviors. His body and language rhythm were super-fast and unintelligible; his eyes darted everywhere; he was unable to comply with requests, but instead tried to divert our attention. He had great difficulty organizing the environment and staying on task. There was much rejection of undertaking activities, suggestions, conversation, and like behaviors. He tended to be quick-tempered, and always in a "fight-or-flight" response. (Note that, here, "fight" precedes "flight." In Bucky's case, this order would have been reversed to "flight-or-fight," because he typically preferred to "flee" the scene rather than stop to "fight.")

Robert is now 17 years old. He is now being home-schooled by several educators, and has several different therapy interventions, including speech. Robert also is exposed to several socialization activities, and continues his music therapy sessions, which now include more psychodynamic interventions. One of his major adaptations involves the areas of his body and speech rhythmic pacing. Physiologically, Robert is now slower and better paced; he is not "ahead of himself," as he could be described in the past. His speech is slower and much more articulate, as are his listening skills. He generally has more patience and willingness to flow with the moment. His taste in music has changed from the very fast, loud songs he preferred in the past, to more "third-stream" groups (slower, ethereal, gentle flowing sounds) with clear articulation of lyrics. Robert is better able to recognize his feelings and sensations, and is eager and willing to share these both in music (songwriting) and in conversation. In short, he no longer seeks to "flee" the environment or interaction but rather enters the environment in a well-paced manner.

Robert's creative abilities have increased as well. In his improvisations, he now clearly seeks to create a form, a shape to his music, using musical rhythmic and pitch relationships. He plays notes on the piano that he selects specifically so that they follow one another in particular sequential relationships, which he can repeat. He also indicates clear endings to his "piece," whereas previously he would simply stop short of closure. Robert organizes percussion instruments according to how, when, and what patterns he wants to play on each, or wants others to play, and he designs the sequences in which rhythmic events will take place. Visually, his eyes no longer dart about the room, either in the music therapy environment or, according to reports from his allied clinicians and educators, in other situations. In his vision, ocular motor movements have become much more stabilized. He can sustain visual and auditory focus for significant lengths of time, observing his own playing activity; that is, he looks at his hands and arms when seeking particular notes on the xylophone or piano. In fact, he can *stare*, which is something altogether new. His physical coordination, muscle tone, and general movements are gaining adaptive mannerisms, and his ability to alter his body dynamics (from the constant rigidity to a softer, graduated flow) is flexible and much more fluid. He can beat the drum very quietly, and *gradually* increase to very loud (crescendos and diminuendos), whereas before it was all extremes.

There are many other indicators of Robert's progress, too lengthy to describe at this point, and involving many treatments concentrating on his vestibular, tactile, visual, auditory, and proprioceptive coordination. Suffice it to say here that it has taken almost six years to bring Robert to this point of functional adaptation: one 45 minute session per week, which, when he reached 16 years of age, was increased to 60 minutes per week. This is a clear indication of how important is the development of rigorous *dose–response research* to the music therapy treatment professional. If Robert had had music therapy for 45 minutes daily during all those years (instead of weekly), would his progress have occurred sooner? Are age development and maturity part of the equation? If so, how? Nevertheless, we are delighted with the adaptive progress Robert has achieved, largely resulting from music therapy, since music provided him with the opportunity to combine, redirect, and integrate so many facets of his fear cycle and sensory processing.

Robert continues music therapy (as does Bucky). Now that we have helped to reorganize much of his physiology away from the fear and oppositional responses of "fight-or-flight," and helped him become more comfortable in his own body, we are moving further into psychodynamic and family music therapy treatments. For Robert, at his age and level of understanding of himself, it is essential to help him understand himself *psychologically*, his role in the family and among friends, and various social interaction issues. To date, these interventions, and his ability to discuss his feelings, both through music and verbal communication, are progressing quite comfortably, with minimal resistance.

## LAURA

Laura (38 years old, diagnosed autistic) has been receiving music therapy treatment for only approximately 10 months, with weekly 45-minute treatments. She is now just beginning to demonstrate some physiological and emotional functional adaptation. She is much less fearful, and no longer enters a session in anticipation of some punitive response. She has become increasingly independent in the environment, selecting and indicating her instrumental preferences, and hand-signaling what she would like the therapist to play (usually pointing to the keyboard or piano).

Laura's vocal sounds are increasing, as are her attempts to articulate words. Cognitively, she can now indicate various colors, letters, and numbers, primarily because she enjoys playing the various colored, lettered, and numbered hand bells. Laura's social workers and home counselors (she lives in a group home) have attested to the fact that she seems to be "different." For us, it is a bit early to assess progress. In less than a year of exposure to music therapy treatment, and at Laura's age, the dose–response issue remains undetermined. It is positive, however, to observe clear changes in responses that are moving away from Laura's usual fear demeanor. In many ways, she has become more assertive, indicating food and clothing preferences to her aides, preferences for certain plants at her day job in the plant nursery, and several other self-aware self-expressions. Laura's aides are of the opinion that music therapy has been *the* major contributor to her personality progress, since she has no other interventions (and has never had other therapists, not even speech pathologists). Realizing that this is not a scientific observation, we would prefer to believe that it is at least suggestive of music therapy's role in Laura's functional adaptations, and that further research would confirm that this is, indeed, so.

## RACHEL

Rachel (31 years old, diagnosed schizophrenic) has been difficult to track. At the time of her music therapy treatments she had been receiving music therapy treatment for 6 months, receiving one 45-minute session weekly. From the time of her admission into the psychiatric ward, to the time of her "liberation," as Rachel called it, her psychological problems appeared somewhat quelled. However, after her release she has not been available for further assessment or treatment. One can only surmise and hope that, as a result of her music therapy encounters (moving from defeatism to optimism, depression to hope, etc.), Rachel has adopted ways of using music to her advantage, whether listening to positive material, or playing music on an instrument. At the time of her discharge she had expressed an interest in calming herself and her fear response by taking piano lessons. We hope that Rachel has been successful in doing so, and that her music therapy encounters have left some lasting changes in attitude and demeanor.

## RHEA

Rhea (age 5, diagnosed with Down syndrome/autistic characteristics) has not continued with music therapy treatments. She is the most recent recipient of music therapy, and remained in this treatment for the shortest amount of time. Five months in private sessions of 45 minutes once a week was insufficient to determine accurately her massive sensory integration problems, her auditory issues, or her possible synesthesia indications (recall that she hated one particular song, but could tolerate it when disguised into certain keys and rhythms). Rhea's case is a perfect example of the errors often made by parents and others when opting for "cognitive" learning over reorganization of physiological malfunctions. Rhea has since relocated, and has been placed in a school with a special *behavioral* educational program extending into after-school home time. There is no music activity of any kind in her program. This is regrettable because her musicality and her inner creativity have been quashed in favor of automatic reading/writing/arithmetic. This is an example of exactly what was discussed in our opening chapters; that there is a tendency to "barter away" the development of instincts in favor of cognition. We believe that a well-balanced developmental dose of each (rather than an either/or situation) could provide a more effective opportunity to pursue functional adaptation. (When the body is comfortable, learning capacity increases.)

In the final analysis, Rhea will survive largely because of her *instincts and intuitions*, and not because she was required to sit still and endure numbers and letters for periods of time. The window of opportunity for retraining her sensory functions early, in order to allow for "education" to fill the spaces, is *now*, at her ripe age of 5 years. Rhea's fear responses will only be further embedded by fear of reprisals for not following instructions or doing as she is told.

We conclude with an observation: "Our ignorance of the laws and processes that govern our universe, in general, and the operation of our multi-faceted, multi-dimensional human organism, in particular, can mislead us into expending enormous and unnecessary volumes of energy functioning in conflict with those very processes we are trying to understand!" (Daniel J. Schneck, from a lecture on fundamental physiological function). There really are only two types of people: those who have been diagnosed, and those who have not *yet* been diagnosed. Any one of us can become a diagnosed person; as the saying goes, "There, but for the will of God, go I." This makes it even more important to *nurture* human instinct and intuition, for those survival instincts will be left to us when cognition and all else fails.

We hope that progress will continue for the five case studies presented, and a whole host of others. We also look forward to a growing literature supported by further research into questions and issues presented throughout this book, that will yield a broader understanding of the role of music therapy as a clinically prescribed treatment, and of *the music effect* – the role of music in human adaptation.

# References

Adamek, M.S., Gervin, A.P., and Shiraishi, I.M. (2000) "Music Therapy and Speech Rehabilitation With Brain-injured Patients: Research, Intervention Models, and Assessment." In C. Furman and E. Charles (eds): *Effectiveness of Music Therapy Procedures: Documentation of Research and Clinical Practice*, 3rd edn. Silver Spring, MD: American Music Therapy Association.

Aiello, R. and Sloboda, J.A. (eds) (1994) *Musical Perceptions*. New York: Oxford University Press.

Aldridge, D. (2000) *Music Therapy in Dementia Care*. London: Jessica Kingsley Publishers.

Alexjander, S. and Deamer, D. (1999) "The Infrared Frequencies of DNA Bases: Science and Art." *IEEE Engineering in Medicine and Biology 18*, 2, 74–79.

Andreasen, N.C. (1997) "Linking Mind and Brain in the Study of Mental Illnesses: A Project for a Scientific Psychopathology." *Science 275*, 1586–1593.

Bartlett, D.L. (1996) "Physiological Responses to Music and Sound Stimuli." In: D.H. Hodges (ed) *Handbook of Music Psychology*, 2nd edn. San Antonio, TX: IMR Press.

Beck, R. and Cesario, T. (2001) *A Song A Day Keeps The Doctor Away?* University of California at Irvine, www.uci.edu.

Beeli, G., Esslen, M., and Jaencke, L. (2005) "Synaesthesia: When Coloured Sounds Taste Sweet." *Nature 434*, 38.

Békésy, G. von (1960) *Experiments in Hearing*. New York: McGraw-Hill.

Békésy, G. von and Rosenblith, W. (1951) "The Mechanical Properties of the Ear." In: S. Stevens (ed.) *Handbook of Experimental Psychology*. New York: John Wiley.

Berger, D.S. (1999) *Toward the Zen of Performance: Music Improvisation Therapy for the Development of Self-confidence in the Performer*. St Louis, MO: MMB Music.

Berger, D.S. (2002) *Music Therapy, Sensory Integration and the Autistic Child*. London: Jessica Kingsley Publishers.

Berger, D.S. and Schneck, D.J. (2003) "The Use of Music Therapy as a Clinical Intervention for Physiologic Functional Adaptation." *Journal of Scientific Exploration 17*, 4, 687–703.

Bittman, B., Berk, L., Shannon, M., Sharaf, M., Westengard, J., Guegler, K.J., and Ruff, D.W. (2005) "Recreational Music-making Modulates The Human Stress Response: A Preliminary Individualized Gene Expression Strategy." *Medical Science Monitor 11*, 2, BR31–40.

Bregman, A.S. (1999) *Auditory Scene Analysis: The Perceptual Organization of Sound*. Cambridge, MA: MIT Press.

Brown, S. (2001) "The 'Musilanguage' Model of Music Evolution." In: N.L. Wallin, B. Merker, and S. Brown (eds) *The Origins of Music*. Cambridge, MA: MIT Press.

Brown, T.S. and Wallace, P.M. (1980) "Audition." In: *Physiological Psychology*. New York: Academic Press.

Brust, J.C.M. (2001) "Music and the Neurologist: A Historical Perspective." In: R.J. Zatorre and I. Peretz (eds) *The Biological Foundations of Music*. New York: Annals of the NY Academy of Sciences.

Buser, P. and Imbert, M. (1992) *Audition*. Cambridge, MA: MIT Press.

Coleman, J.M., Rebollo-Pratt, R., Stoddard, R.A., Gerstmann, D.R., and Abel, H.H. (1997) "The Effects of the Male and Female Singing and Speaking Voices on Selected Physiological and Behavioural Measures of Premature Infants in the Intensive Care Unit." *International Journal of Arts & Medicine 5*, 2, 4–11.

Coren, S. and Ward, L.M. (1989) *Sensation and Perception*, 3rd edn. San Diego: Harcourt Brace Jovanovich.

Cossu, G., Faienza, C., and Capone, C. (1994) *Infants' Hemispheric Computation of Music and Speech*. In: C. Faienza (ed.) *Music, Speech and the Developing Brain*. Milan: Guerrini e Associati.

Cowley, G. (2003) "Our Bodies, Our Fears." *Newsweek*, 24 February, p.42.

Cytowic, R.E. (1999) *The Man Who Tasted Shapes*. Cambridge, MA: MIT Press.

Cytowic, R.E. (2002) *Synesthesia: A Union of the Senses*. Cambridge, MA: MIT Press.

Dallos, P. (1986) "The Search for the Mechanisms of Hearing." Online reprint, April 2001. Available at www.worldandi.com/specialreport/1986/june/sal1064.htm

Damasio, A.R. (1994) *Descartes' Error: Emotion, Reason, and the Human Brain.* New York: Grosset/Putnam Books.

Damasio, A.R. (1999) *The Feeling of What Happens: Body and Emotion in the Making of Consciousness.* New York: Harcourt Brace.

Damasio, A.R. (2001) "Emotion and the Brain." In: A.R. Damasio, A. Harrington, J. Kagan, B.S. McEwen, H. Moss, and R. Shaikh (eds) *Unity of Knowledge: The Convergence of Natural and Human Science.* New York: Annals of the NY Academy of Sciences.

Damasio, A.R. (2003) *Looking for Spinoza: Joy, Sorrow, and the Feeling Brain.* New York: Harcourt Brace.

Damasio, A.R. and Moss, H. (2001) "Emotion, Cognition, and the Human Brain." In: A.R. Damasio, A. Harrington, J. Kagan, B.S. McEwen, H. Moss, and R. Shaikh (eds) *Unity of Knowledge: The Convergence of Natural and Human Science.* New York: Annals of the NY Academy of Sciences.

Darwin, C. (1998) *The Expression of the Emotions in Man and Animals. 3rd edn. (First published 1872). New York: Oxford University Press.*

D'Attellis, C.E. (2001) "The Tempered Scale as an Optimization Process: From Pythagoras to J.S. Bach." In: C.E. D'Attellis, V.V. Kluev, and N.E. Mastorakis (eds) *Mathematics and Simulation with Biological, Economical and Musicoacoustical Applications.* Athens: WSES Press.

Deacon, T.W. (1997) *The Symbolic Species: The Co-evolution of Language and the Brain.* New York: W.W. Norton and Co.

Deliege, I. and Sloboda, J. (eds) (1997) *Perception and Cognition of Music.* East Sussex: Psychology Press.

Diallo, Y. and Hall, M. (1989) *The Healing Drum: African Wisdom Teachings.* Rochester, VT: Healing Books.

Dolan, R.J. (2002) "Emotion, Cognition, and Behavior." *Science 298,* 1190–1194.

Faienza, C. (ed.) (1994) *Music, Speech, and the Developing Brain.* Milan: Guerrini e Associati.

Friedman, M. and Rosenman, R.H. (1974) *Type A Behavior and Your Heart.* London: Wildwood House.

Fries, P., Reynolds, J.H., Rorie, A.E., and Desimone, R. (2001) "Modulation of Oscillatory Neuronal Synchronization by Selective Visual Attention." *Science 291,* 1560–1563.

Gardner, M. (1992) *Fractal Music, Hypercards and More: Mathematical Recreations from* Scientific American Magazine. New York: W.H. Freeman & Co.

Gerber, R. (1996) *Vibrational Medicine: New Choices for Healing Ourselves.* Santa Fe, NM: Bear & Co.

Gerber, R. (2001) *Vibrational Medicine: The #1 Handbook of Subtle-energy Therapies,* 3rd edn. Rochester, VT: Bear & Co.

Gerra, G., Zaimovic, A., Franchini, D., Palladino, M., Giucastro, G., Reali, N., Maestri, D., Caccavari, R., Delsignore, R., and Brambilla, F. (1998) "Neuroendocrine Responses of Healthy Volunteers to 'Techno-Music': Relationships with Personality Traits and Emotional State." *Journal of Psychophysiology 28,* 99–111.

Giancoli, D.C. (1989) *Physics for Scientists and Engineers, with Modern Physics,* 2nd edn. Englewood Cliffs, NJ: Prentice-Hall.

Goldberger, A.L. (1996a) "Fractals and the Birth of Gothic: Reflections on the Biologic Basis of Creativity". *Molecular Psychiatry 1,* 99–104.

Goldberger, A.L. (1996b) "Non-linear Dynamics for Clinicians: Chaos Theory, Fractals, and Complexity at the Bedside." *Lancet 347,* 1312–1314.

Goldberger, A.L., Amaral, L.A.N., Glass, L., Hausdorff, J.M., Ivanov, P.Ch., Mark, R.G., Mietus, J.E., Moody, G.B., Peng, C.-K., and Stanley, H.E. (2000) "PhysioBank, PhysioToolkit, & PhysioNet: Components of a New Research Resource for Complex Physiologic Signals." *Circulation 101,* e215–e220.

Goldberger, A.L., Amaral, L.A.N., Hausdorff, J.M., Ivanov, P.Ch., Peng, C.-K., and Stanley, H.E. (2002a) "Fractal Dynamics in Physiology: Alterations with Disease and Aging." *Proceedings of the National Academy of Science USA 99* (Suppl. 1), 2466–2472.

Goldberger, A.L., Peng, C.-K., and Lipsitz, L.A. (2002b) "What is Physiologic Complexity and How Does It Change with Aging and Disease?" *Neurobiology of Aging 23,* 23–26.

Goldman, D. (1996) "High Anxiety." *Science 274,* 1483–1490.

Goldstein, A. (1980) "Thrills in Response to Music and Other Stimuli." *Physiological Psychology 8,* 126–129.

Hargreaves, D.J. (1986) *The Developmental Psychology of Music.* Cambridge: Cambridge University Press.

Helmholtz, H. (1954) *On the Sensations of Tone.* New York: Dover Publications.

Hildebrandt, G. (1976) "Die Koordination Rhythmischer Funktionene Beim Menschen." *Verhandlmgen Der Deutschen Gesellschaft Fur Innere Medizin 73,* 922–941.

Hildebrandt, G. (1986) "Zur Physiologie Des Rhythmischen Systems." *Beitrage Zu Einer Enweiterung Der Heilkunst 39*, 8–30.

Hildebrandt, G. (1987) "The Autonomous Time Structure and Its Reactive Modifications In The Human Organism." In: L. Rensing , U. Mackey, and M.C. Heiden (eds) *Temporal Disorder in Human Oscillatory Systems*, Proceedings of an International Symposium, University of Bremen, 8–13 September 1986. Heidelberg: Springer-Verlag.

Hodges, D.H. (1996a) "Neuromusical Research: A Review of the Literature." In: D.H. Hodges (ed) *Handbook of Music Psychology*, 2nd edn. San Antonio, TX: IMR Press.

Hodges, D.H. (1996b) (ed.) *Handbook of Music Psychology*, 2nd edn. San Antonio, TX: IMR Press.

Holden, C. (2003) "Deconstructing Schizophrenia." *Science 299*, 333–335.

Hsu, K.J. and Hsu, A. (1990) "Fractal Geometry of Music." *Proceedings of the National Academy of Science USA 87*, 938–941.

Hudspeth, A.J. (1997) "The Science of Sound: How Hearing Happens." Webcast lecture from the Howard Hughes Medical Institute. Available at www.hhmi.org/biointeractive/neuroscience/ lectures/html.

Hyman, M. and Liponis, M. (2003) *Ultra-Prevention*. New York: Scribner.

Ikeda, T. (1992) "Concentration-effect and Underestimation of Time by Acoustic Stimuli." *Shinrigaku Kenkyu 63*, 3, 157–162.

Iwanaga, M. (1995a) "Harmonic Relationship Between Tempi and Heart Rate." *Perceptual and Motor Skills 81*, 1, 67–71.

Iwanaga, M. (1995b) "Relationship Between Heart Rate and Preference for Tempo of Music." *Perceptual and Motor Skills 81*, 2, 435–440.

Javitt, D.C. and Coyle, J.T. (2004) "Decoding Schizophrenia." *Scientific American 290*, 1, 48–55.

Jeans, J. (1968) *Science and Music*. New York: Dover Publications.

Jourdain, R. (1997) *Music, The Brain, and Ecstasy*. New York: Avon Books.

Kraus, T. and Galloway, H. (1982) "Melodic Intonation Therapy with Language Delayed Apraxic Children." *Journal of Music Therapy XIX*, 2, 102–113.

LeDoux, J. (1998) *The Emotional Brain: The Mysterious Underpinnings of Emotional Life*. New York: Simon & Schuster.

LeDoux, J. (2002) *Synaptic Self: How Our Brains Become Who We Are*. New York: Viking Penguin.

Libet, B. (2002) "The Timing of Mental Events: Libet's Experimental Findings and their Implications." *Consciousness and Cognition 11*, 291–299.

Libet, B. (2003) "Timing of Conscious Experience: Reply to the 2002 Commentaries on Libet's Findings." *Consciousness and Cognition 12*, 321–331.

Llinas, R.R. (2002) *I of the Vortex: From Neurons to Self*. Cambridge, MA: MIT Press.

Loewy, J. (2004) "Integrating Music, Language and the Voice in Music Therapy." *VOICES: A World Forum For Music Therapy 4* 1, 1–25

Magne, C., Schon, D., and Besson, M. (2003) "Prosodic and Melodic Processing in Adults and Children: Behavioral and Electrophysiologic Approaches." In G. Avanzini, C. Faienza, D. Minciacchi, L. Lopez, and M. Majno (eds) *The Neurosciences and Music*. New York: Annals of the NY Academy of Sciences.

Marshall, R. (1989) *The Music of Johann Sebastian Bach: The Sources, the Style, the Significance*. New York: Schirmer Books.

Marshall, R.L. (1991) *Mozart Speaks: Views on Music, Musicians, and the World*. New York: Schirmer Books/Simon & Schuster Macmillan.

McAdams, S. and Bigand, E. (eds) (1993) *Thinking In Sound: The Cognitive Psychology Of Human Audition*. Oxford: Clarendon/Oxford University Press.

Miller, R.A., Thaut, M.H., McIntosh, G.C., and Rice, R.R. (1996) "Components of EMG Symmetry and Variability in Parkinsonian and Healthy Elderly Gait." *Electroencephalography and Clinical Neurophysiology 101*, 1–7.

Milsum, J.H. (1966) *Biological Control Systems Analysis*. New York: McGraw-Hill.

Nordoff, P. and Robbins, C. (1997) *Creative Music Therapy: Individualized Treatment for the Handicapped Child*. New York: The John Day Company.

Ornstein, R. and Thompson, R.F. (1984) *The Amazing Brain*. Boston, MA: Houghton Mifflin.

Overy, K. (2003) "Dyslexia and Music: From Timing Deficits to Musical Intervention." In: G. Avanzini, C. Faienza, D. Minciacchi, L. Lopez, and M. Majno (eds) *The Neurosciences and Music*. New York: Annals of the NY Academy of Sciences.

Pachetti, C., Aglieri, R., Mancini, F., Martignoni, E. and Nappi, G. (1998) "Active Music Therapy and Parkinson's Disease." *Functional Neurology 13*, 57–67.

Panksepp, J. (1995) "The Emotional Source of 'Chills' Induced By Music." *Music Perception 13*, 2, 171–207.

Patrick, G. (1999) "The Effect of Vibroacoustic Music on Symptom Reduction." *IEEE Engineering in Medicine and Biology 18*, 2, 97–100.

Peng, C.-K., Havlin, S., Stanley, H.E., and Goldberger, A.L. (1995) "Quantification of Scaling Exponents and Crossover Phenomena in Nonstationary Heart-Beat Time Series." *Chaos 5*, 82–87.

Peng, C.-K., Mietus, J., Hausdorff, J.M., Havlin, S., Stanley, H.E., and Goldberger, A.L. (1993) "Long-range Anti-correlations and Non-Gaussian Behavior of the Heartbeat." *Physics Review Letters 70*, 1343–1346.

Peretz, I. (2001) "Brain Specialization for Music: New Evidence from Congenital Amusia." In R.J. Zatorre and I. Peretz (eds) *The Biological Foundations of Music*. New York: Annals of the NY Academy of Sciences.

Peretz, I., Champod, A.S., and Hyde, K. (2003) "Varieties of Musical Disorders: The Montreal Battery of Evaluation of Amusia." In: G. Avanzini, C. Faienza, D. Minciacchi, L. Lopez, and M. Majno (eds) New York: Annals of the NY Academy of Sciences.

Povel, D.-J. and Jansen, E. (2002) "Harmonic Factors in the Perception of Tonal Melodies." *Music Perception 20*, 1, 51–85.

Prickett, C.A. (2000) "Music Therapy for Older People: Research Comes of Age Across Two Decades." In: *Effectiveness of Music Therapy Procedures: Documentation of Research and Clinical Practice*, 3rd edn. Silver Spring, MD: American Music Therapy Association.

Prophet, E.C. and Spadaro, P. (2000) *Your Seven Energy Centers*. Corwin Springs, MO: Summit University Press.

Rainnie, D.G., Bergeron, R., Sajdyk, T.J., Patil, M., Gehlert, D.R., and Shekkar, A. (2004) "Corticotrophin Releasing Factor-induced Synaptic Plasticity in the Amygdala Translates Into Emotional Disorders." *Journal of Neuroscience 24*, 14, 3471–3479.

*Roanoke Times* (2001) "Genes Blamed For Tin Ears," 9 March, p.A16.

Roper, N. (2003) "Melodic Intonation Therapy with Young Children with Apraxia." *Bridges: Practice-based Research Syntheses 1*, 8, 1–25.

Schneck, D.J. (1990) *Engineering Principles of Physiologic Function*. New York, New York University Press.

Schneck, D.J. (1992) *Mechanics of Muscle*, 2nd edn. New York: New York University Press.

Schneck, D.J. (1997) "A Paradigm for the Physiology of Human Adaptation." In: D.J. Schneck and J.K. Schneck (eds) *Music in Human Adaptation*. St Louis, MD: MMB Music.

Schneck, D.J. (ed.) (1999) "Music to Our Ears…Brain…Genes…" *IEEE Engineering in Medicine and Biology Magazine (Special Issue on the Role of Music in Human Adaptation, 18*, 2.

Schneck, D.J. (2000a) "Mind/Body: Both or Neither?" *American Laboratory 32*, 14, 6–8.

Schneck, D.J. (2000b) "All God's Creations Got Rhythm!" *American Laboratory 32*, 20, 6–8.

Schneck, D.J. (2001a) "Each of Us is a Minority of One." *American Laboratory 33*, 1, 6–8.

Schneck, D.J. (2001b) "On the Seven Elements of Knowledge." *American Laboratory News Edition 33*, 15, 4.

Schneck, D.J. (2001c) "The Seven Rudimentary Axioms of Reality." *American Laboratory 33*, 24, 6–8.

Schneck, D.J. (2002) "Bad Stress." *American Laboratory 34*, 17, 4.

Schneck, D.J. (2003a) "The Physiology of Relativity" *American Biotechnology Laboratory 21*, 1, 4.

Schneck, D.J. (2003b) "A Biomedical Engineer Views the Human Body." *American Laboratory 35*, 3, 6–8.

Schneck, D.J. (2003c) "A Musician Views the Human Body." *American Laboratory 35*, 5, 6–10.

Schneck, D.J. (2003d) "Englightened Neurosis!" *American Laboratory News Edition 35*, 11, 4.

Schneck, D.J. (2003e) "Energy." *American Laboratory News Edition 35*, 17, 4–6.

Schneck, D.J. (2003f) "How Many Brains Do We Have?: It's Not Enough." *American Laboratory News Edition 35*, 19, 4–6.

Schneck, D.J. and Berger, D.S. (1999) "The Role of Music in Physiologic Accommodation: Its Ability to Elicit Reflexive, Adaptive, and Inscriptive Responses." *IEEE Engineering in Medicine and Biology 18*, 2, 44–53.

Schneck, D.J. and Schneck, J.K. (eds) (1997) *Music in Human Adaptation*. St Louis, MO: MMB Music.

Schneck, J.K. and Schneck, D.J. (1996) "Sensory Integration and Differentiation of Auditory Information as it Relates to Music." Technical Report VPI-E-96-02. Polytechnic Institute & State University, Blacksburg, VA.

Schopenhauer, A. (1995) *The World as Will and Idea.* (First published 1819.) Everyman Philosophy Series, London: Orion.

Seashore, C.E. (1967) *Psychology of Music.* New York: Dover Publications.

Shevrin, H., Ghannam, J.H., and Libet, B. (2002) "A Neural Correlate of Consciousness Related to Repression." *Consciousness and Cognition 11,* 334–341.

Slawson, W. (1985) *Sound Color.* Berkeley, CA: University of California Press.

Sloboda, J.A. (1985) *The Musical Mind: The Cognitive Psychology of Music.* New York: Dover Publications.

Smith, J. (1989) *Senses & Sensibilities.* New York: John Wiley.

Springer, S.P. and Deutsch, G. (1981) *Left Brain, Right Brain.* San Francisco, CA: W.H. Freeman and Co.

Standley, J.M. (2000) "Music Research in Medical Treatment." In: *Effectiveness of Music Therapy Procedures: Documentation of Research and Clinical Practice,* 3rd edn. Silver Spring, MD: American Music Therapy Association.

Standley, J.M. and Prickett, C.A. (eds) (1994) *Research in Music Therapy. A Tradition of Excellence: Outstanding Reprints from the Journal of Music Therapy 1964–1993.* Silver Spring, MD: National Music Therapy Association.

Staum, M.J. (2000) "Music for Physical Rehabilitation: An Analysis of the Literature from 1950–1999 and Applications for Rehabilitation Settings." In: *Effectiveness of Music Therapy Procedures: Documentation of Research and Clinical Practice,* 3rd edn. Silver Spring, MD: American Music Therapy Association.

Stravinsky, I. (1942) *Poetics of Music.* Cambridge, MA: Harvard University Press.

Taylor, R.P., Micolich, A.P., and Jonas, D. (1999) "Fractal Analysis of Pollock's Drip Paintings." *Nature 399,* 3 (June), 422–423.

Thaut, M.H. (1997) "Rhythmic Auditory Stimulation in Rehabilitation of Movement Disorders: A Review of Current Research." In: D.J. Schneck and J.K. Schneck (eds) *Music in Human Adaptation.* St Louis, MO: MMB Music.

Thaut, M.H., Kenyon, G.P., Schauer, M.L., and McIntosh, G.C. (1999) "The Connection Between Rhythmicity and Brain Function." *IEEE Engineering In Medicine and Biology 18,* 2, 101–108.

Thaut, M.H., McIntosh, G.C., and Rice, R.R. (1997a) "Rhythmic Facilitation of Gait Training in Hemiparetic Stroke Rehabilitation." *Journal of Neurological Sciences 151,* 207–212.

Thaut, M.H., McIntosh, G.C., Rice, R.R., Miller, R.A., Rathbun, J. and Brault, J.A. (1996) "Rhythmic Auditory Stimulation in Gait Training of Parkinson's Disease Patients." *Movement Disorders 11,* 193–200.

Thaut, M.H., Miller, R.A., and Schauer, M. (1997b) "Rhythm in Human Motor Control: Adaptive Mechanisms in Movement Synchronization." In: D.J. Schneck and J.K. Schneck (eds) *Music in Human Adaptation.* St Louis, MO: MMB Music.

Tomaino, C.E. (2000) "Working with Images and Recollection with Elder Patients." In: D. Aldridge (ed.) *Music Therapy In Dementia Care.* London: Jessica Kingsley Publishers.

Tortora, G.J. and Grabowski, S.R. (1993) *Principles of Anatomy and Physiology,* 7th edn. New York: HarperCollins College Publishers.

Trehub, S. (2000) "Human Processing Predisposition and Musical Universals." In: N.L. Wallin, B. Merker, and S. Brown (eds) *The Origins of Music.* Cambridge, MA: MIT Press.

Wallin, N.L., Merker, B., and Brown, S. (eds) (2001) *The Origins of Music.* Cambridge, MA: MIT Press.

Warren, R.M. (1999) *Auditory Perception: A New Analysis and Synthesis.* Cambridge: Cambridge University Press.

Williams, D. (1998) *Autism and Sensing: The Unlost Instinct.* London: Jessica Kingsley Publishers.

Woody, C.D. (1982) *Memory, Learning, and Higher Function.* New York: Springer-Verlag.

# Subject Index

music therapy *cont.*
  retraining the fear response
    with 114–16, 145,
    147–52, 156–8, 160,
    183, 189, 252
  and rhythm 189, 231–5, 252
  termination of 150
  and timbre 200–4, 206–7
  *see also* case studies
music therapy clinicians 246,
  247
musilanguage 29

National Institute of Mental
  Health (NIMH) 121–2
National Theater of the Deaf
  143
natural frequency 49–50
natural selection 68, 107
natural sounds 32
nature/nurture relationship 79,
  239, 240–9
  in clinical settings 244–7
necrobiosis 120
negative thinking 104, 106
neocortex 74, 75
neogenesis *see* anatomical
  remodelling
neonates 242–3
neopallium 75
nervous system
  metameric 84
  parasympathetic 76–7
  peripheral 19
  physiological entrainment
    through 118, 119–22
  plasticity of the 24, 25, 105
  sympathetic 76–7, 99, 102
  *see also* central nervous system
neural excitation/inhibition 118,
  119, 120
neural firing 77, 83–4, 129–30
neural networks 24, 84, 86
  biasing 119, 129–33
  generated 105
  processing/coding capacity
    84–5, 86
neurotransmitters 58–9, 77, 78,
  123, 137, 243
Newton, Isaac 177
non-linear behaviour 198
non-verbal clients *see* case studies,
  Laura
norepinephrine 99–100
Normal distribution 55
norms, of the body 91, 92
notes 55–6
nucleoproteins 123
numerators 82–3

objective reality 38–9
obsessive-compulsive behaviour
  234
occipital lobe 75

octaves 164, 193, 196, 208
olfactory bulbs 72
operating window 76, 82
opioids 127
optimization fraction 83
Organ of Corti 167
organization 229–30, 236
organs
  of the body 33, 36
  natural frequency of free
    vibration 49–50
Oriental medicine 133–4
ossicular chain 165–6
otolith organs 139
oval window 166, 167, 168,
  169
overtone frequency spectrum 56,
  165, 190, 192–3, 196,
  199, 203, 207, 208

pace 144–52, 158, 187
  metrical indication of 146
  in music therapy 145–52
  and pattern 155–6, 157
  qualitative indication of 146
pain control 127
paleocortex 73
paleoencephalon 87, 181
paleopallium 75
panic attacks 112
paradigm 19–22
parahippocampal gyrus 73
parasympathetic nervous system
  76–7
Parkinson's disease 146
parolfactory area 73
partial tones *see* harmonics;
  sub-harmonics
pattern 152–7, 158, 187
  and form 225
  and melody 179
  and pace 155–6, 157
  and pulse 153–6, 157
pentatonic scales 172
perception 61
  and the brain 75
  cross-processing 174–5,
    176–8, 187–8
  delayed, conscious 87
  and the frequency of
    vibration of energy 46–9
  Gestalt laws of 62, 80–2, 86,
    154, 162, 171, 174,
    179, 204, 213
  immediate, subconscious 87
  and melody 163, 173–6
  of threat 92, 96, 97, 99–100,
    104, 109, 112–14, 115,
    124, 206, 249
  and transduction 64
  *see also* hearing;
    proprioception; tactile
    system; vestibular
    system; vision

perceptiveness 132
percussion instruments 212
  primitive 29
perfect pitch memory 170–1,
  175, 187
performance anxiety 131
periodicity (recurring cycles) 34,
  47–8, 138–9, 142–3, 162
peripheral nervous system 19
perseveration 151, 234
personality types, music-based
  126, 210, 237, 241
phenotypes 79, 241
phobias 21
phrases 163, 173, 184, 224
physical function, music as
  analogue of 33–5
physical properties, non-constant
  198
physical science 15
physical states 230
physical therapists 146
physics 21, 36–7, 38–60,
  235–6, 247, 248
  energy 39–56, 61
  recurring events 45–8
physiological
  accommodation/adaptation
    25, 78–9, 80, 241
  to fear 103–9
  and learning 108
  and physiological
    entrainment 117, 126
physiological entrainment 16,
  20, 25, 54, 80, 106–7,
  117–37, 138, 204, 240
  of chords 210, 211, 212,
    214
  definition of 117–18
  and fear 115, 116
  of form 222
  mechanisms of 118–19
  to music 241
  and periodicity 48
  of pitch 184, 209
  of prosody 184
  and rhythm 120–1, 145,
    149, 157
  through biasing of
    information-processing
    networks 119, 129–33
  through biochemical catalysis
    118, 127–9
  through the nervous system
    118, 119–22
  through
    stimulation/inhibition of
    genetic material 118,
    122–7
  through transport/utilization
    f energy 119, 133–6
  in vibroacoustic medicine 36
physiological resolution 52

# Author Index